PARANORMAL PHENOMENA

OPPOSING VIEWPOINTS®

Other Books of Related Interest in the Opposing Viewpoints Series:

American Values
America's Future
Constructing a Life Philosophy
Death and Dying
Religion in America
Science & Religion

PARANORMAL PHENOMENA

OPPOSING VIEWPOINTS®

David L. Bender & Bruno Leone, *Series Editors*

Terry O'Neill, *Book Editor*
Stacey L. Tipp, *Assistant Editor*

OPPOSING VIEWPOINTS SERIES ®

Greenhaven Press, Inc.   PO Box 289009   San Diego, CA 92198-0009

133

P223

Library of Congress Cataloging-in-Publication Data

Paranormal phenomena : opposing viewpoints / Terry O'Neill, book editor. Stacey L. Tipp, assistant editor.
    p.   cm. — (Opposing viewpoints series)
    Summary: Presents opposing viewpoints on the existence of paranormal phenomena such as extrasensory perception, unidentified flying objects, and the prediction of the future.
    ISBN 0-89908-487-7 (lib. bdg.). — ISBN 0-89908-462-1 (pbk.)
    1. Parapsychology—Controversial literature.   2. Parapsychology.
[1. Parapsychology.]   I. O'Neill, Terry, 1944-   .   II. Tipp, Stacey L., 1963-   .   III. Series: Opposing viewpoints series (Unnumbered)
BF1042.P27   1990
133—dc20   90-24081

"Congress shall make no law . . . abridging the freedom of speech, or of the press."

First Amendment to the U.S. Constitution

The basic foundation of our democracy is the first amendment guarantee of freedom of expression. The Opposing Viewpoints Series is dedicated to the concept of this basic freedom and the idea that it is more important to practice it than to enshrine it.

Contents

Chapter 4: Can the Future Be Predicted?

Chapter 5: Can Humans Interact with the Spirit World?

Why Consider Opposing Viewpoints?

"It is better to debate a question without settling it than to settle a question without debating it."

Joseph Joubert (1754-1824)

The Importance of Examining Opposing Viewpoints

The purpose of the Opposing Viewpoints Series, and this book in particular, is to present balanced, and often difficult to find, opposing points of view on complex and sensitive issues.

Probably the best way to become informed is to analyze the positions of those who are regarded as experts and well studied on issues. It is important to consider every variety of opinion in an attempt to determine the truth. Opinions from the mainstream of society should be examined. But also important are opinions that are considered radical, reactionary, or minority as well as those stigmatized by some other uncomplimentary label. An important lesson of history is the eventual acceptance of many unpopular and even despised opinions. The ideas of Socrates, Jesus, and Galileo are good examples of this.

Readers will approach this book with their own opinions on the issues debated within it. However, to have a good grasp of one's own viewpoint, it is necessary to understand the arguments of those with whom one disagrees. It can be said that those who do not completely understand their adversary's point of view do not fully understand their own.

A persuasive case for considering opposing viewpoints has been presented by John Stuart Mill in his work *On Liberty*. When examining controversial issues it may be helpful to reflect on this suggestion:

The only way in which a human being can make some approach to knowing the whole of a subject, is by hearing what can be said about it by persons of every variety of opinion, and studying all modes in which it can be looked at by every character of mind. No wise man ever acquired his wisdom in any mode but this.

Analyzing Sources of Information

The Opposing Viewpoints Series includes diverse materials taken from magazines, journals, books, and newspapers, as well as statements and position papers from a wide range of individuals, organizations, and governments. This broad spectrum of sources helps to develop patterns of thinking which are open to the consideration of a variety of opinions.

Pitfalls to Avoid

A pitfall to avoid in considering opposing points of view is that of regarding one's own opinion as being common sense and the most rational stance, and the point of view of others as being only opinion and naturally wrong. It may be that another's opinion is correct and one's own is in error.

Another pitfall to avoid is that of closing one's mind to the opinions of those with whom one disagrees. The best way to approach a dialogue is to make one's primary purpose that of understanding the mind and arguments of the other person and not that of enlightening him or her with one's own solutions. More can be learned by listening than speaking.

It is my hope that after reading this book the reader will have a deeper understanding of the issues debated and will appreciate the complexity of even seemingly simple issues on which good and honest people disagree. This awareness is particularly important in a democratic society such as ours where people enter into public debate to determine the common good. Those with whom one disagrees should not necessarily be regarded as enemies, but perhaps simply as people who suggest different paths to a common goal.

Developing Basic Reading and Thinking Skills

In this book, carefully edited opposing viewpoints are purposely placed back to back to create a running debate; each viewpoint is preceded by a short quotation that best expresses the author's main argument. This format instantly plunges the reader into the midst of a controversial issue and greatly aids that reader in mastering the basic skill of recognizing an author's point of view.

A number of basic skills for critical thinking are practiced in the activities that appear throughout the books in the series. Some of the skills are:

Evaluating Sources of Information. The ability to choose from among alternative sources the most reliable and accurate source in relation to a given subject.

Separating Fact from Opinion. The ability to make the basic distinction between factual statements (those that can be demonstrated or verified empirically) and statements of opinion (those that are beliefs or attitudes that cannot be proved).

Identifying Stereotypes. The ability to identify oversimplified, exaggerated descriptions (favorable or unfavorable) about people and insulting statements about racial, religious, or national groups, based upon misinformation or lack of information.

Recognizing Ethnocentrism. The ability to recognize attitudes or opinions that express the view that one's own race, culture, or group is inherently superior, or those attitudes that judge another culture or group in terms of one's own.

It is important to consider opposing viewpoints and equally important to be able to critically analyze those viewpoints. The activities in this book are designed to help the reader master these thinking skills. Statements are taken from the book's viewpoints and the reader is asked to analyze them. This technique aids the reader in developing skills that not only can be applied to the viewpoints in this book, but also to situations where opinionated spokespersons comment on controversial issues. Although the activities are helpful to the solitary reader, they are most useful when the reader can benefit from the interaction of group discussion.

Using this book and others in the series should help readers develop basic reading and thinking skills. These skills should improve the reader's ability to understand what is read. Readers should be better able to separate fact from opinion, substance from rhetoric, and become better consumers of information in our media-centered culture.

This volume of the Opposing Viewpoints Series does not advocate a particular point of view. Quite the contrary! The very nature of the book leaves it to the reader to formulate the opinions he or she finds most suitable. My purpose as publisher is to see that this is made possible by offering a wide range of viewpoints that are fairly presented.

David L. Bender
Publisher

Introduction

"Americans express a belief in the existence of paranormal, psychic, ghostly, and otherworldly experiences and dimensions to a surprising degree. These beliefs . . . are almost as common among Americans who are deeply religious in a traditional sense as in those who are not."

George H. Gallup Jr. and Frank Newport, *The Skeptical Inquirer*, Winter 1991.

According to a 1990 Gallup survey, 93 percent of all Americans questioned say they believe in some form of paranormal phenomena. These phenomena include extrasensory perception (ESP), reincarnation, ghosts, communication with spirits, psychic healing, the devil, witches, the healing power of crystals, and others. This survey is indicative of a curious fact: In spite of society's superior medical and technological knowledge, most people still believe in worlds that defy rational explanation. This persistence in belief has produced an equally persistent group of scientists and others who do not believe in these phenomena and attempt to rationally explain the occurrences people report. Indeed, the issue of paranormal phenomena mirrors a debate that has gone on for centuries, the belief in reason versus faith.

To be sure, countless reports exist from people who believe they have had eerie paranormal experiences, including several common types. For example, thousands of people have reported the unsettling experience of thinking of someone and then receiving a phone call from that same person. Or many other people report having intuitively felt that a close friend or relative was in trouble, only to have received confirmation that the intuition was correct. On the other end of the spectrum is a fantastic array of experiences that includes people who have been kidnapped by extraterrestrial visitors or have had out of body experiences. Many of these phenomena have become such a part of human experience that people find it difficult to deny that some of these occurrences are more than accidental intuition, hallucination, or quackery.

These experiences have prompted scientists to investigate and apply rigorous tests to prove whether the paranormal exists. Although investigation began in the nineteenth century, it became much more systematic in 1927. In that year, psychologist J.B. Rhine founded the first parapsychological laboratory at Duke University in North Carolina. Rhine attempted to apply controlled laboratory conditions to test people who claimed to possess powers of ESP, telepathy, and other intuitive abilities. Rhine reported finding several people who he believed possessed supernatural powers.

More recently, scientists at Stanford Research Institute in Menlo Park, California, tested Uri Geller, alleged psychic. Geller claims to be able to read minds, bend spoons, fix broken clocks and appliances with mental energy alone, and perform numerous other amazing feats. Although the tests were not incontrovertible, they seemed to show that Geller's abilities were far beyond those of any ordinary person. Again, diehard skeptics insist that Geller was able to defraud the scientists and evade discovery.

To date, no one has come up with undeniable evidence that paranormal phenomena exist. But in the end, the search for proof seems beside the point. As writer Joseph Henry Newman said, "Reason is one thing and faith is another and reason can as little be made a substitute for faith, as faith can be made a substitute for reason." Although Newman spoke of faith in God, the comparison remains apt for any topic of supernatural origin. For a majority of Americans, there are small pockets of faith that reason cannot fill. It is in these pockets that the paranormal resides.

Paranormal Phenomena examines the debate between skeptics and believers. The issues debated are: Do Paranormal Phenomena Exist? Are UFOs Real? Does ESP Exist? Can the Future Be Predicted? Can Humans Interact with the Spirit World? For each of these questions, the reader may find absolute answers elusive. It is ultimately up to each individual to decide whether the impossible is sometimes possible.

Do Paranormal Phenomena Exist?

Chapter Preface

Paranormal phenomena are events or experiences that seem to have no logical explanation. This fact leads many people to conclude that these phenomena do not exist. But some parapsychologists, however, believe they have successfully proven that they do. Gertrude Schmeidler, an experimental psychologist who studied ESP [extrasensory perception] under laboratory conditions at Harvard and The City College of New York, says, "The weight of affirmative evidence [for ESP] . . . is compelling." One of the people she evaluated was psychic Ingo Swann, famed for his remarkable telepathic powers and his ability to affect environmental conditions with his mental powers alone. For example, Swann was able to change the air temperatures inside sealed glass bottles by using his mental powers alone.

However, Schmeidler's documentation and that of other parapsychologists remains controversial. Hard-core skeptics believe that *no* evidence has ever been found that supports paranormal phenomena. One of the best-known skeptics is Canadian stage magician James Randi. He claims that sleight-of-hand and other magic tricks explain many so-called paranormal events. To back up his skepticism, he has established a set of objective criteria and offered a $10,000 prize to anyone who can successfully demonstrate the existence of paranormal phenomena. So far, no one has claimed the prize. Other skeptics include scientists who claim that natural explanations account for all known "paranormal" events. According to these experts, investigations prove that geologic, atmospheric, and, especially, psychological factors cause most so-called paranormal phenomena.

In this chapter, skeptics and believers present their evidence to prove whether paranormal phenomena exist.

> *"There are simple explanations for every paranormal effect."*

Paranormal Phenomena Can Be Explained

David F. Marks

David F. Marks is a psychologist at Middlesex Polytechnic in Enfield, England. He has written numerous articles about the paranormal, always taking a skeptical view. In the following article, written for *Fate* magazine, he describes a number of common paranormal phenomena and offers common-sense explanations for them.

As you read, consider the following questions:

1. Marks indicates that many things that appear to be paranormal are really frauds. List two such examples.
2. The author says that the "subjective validation" factor influences the acceptance of many paranormal phenomena. What does he mean by "subjective validation"?
3. Marks suggests that anybody can learn to do paranormal activities such as cold reading, remote viewing, and Geller effects. Do you think he is right? Try the method he suggests for one of these and see if it works for you.

David F. Marks, "The Case Against the Paranormal," *Fate*, January 1989. Reprinted with permission.

A phenomenon is defined as "paranormal" if it contravenes some fundamental or well-established scientific principle. There are a large number of allegedly paranormal effects, claimed by some to be inexplicable by science but in fact amenable to normal or natural explanations.

Many such phenomena (such as thought photography and metal-bending) rely on hidden physical effects. Others rely on hidden psychological effects such as astrology, graphology, tea-leaf and tarot-card reading, the I Ching, and mediumship.

In this article I explain each of these phenomena as simply and as scientifically possible. While it is impossible in one article to explain every instance of every kind of effect in complete detail, it is a relatively easy task to identify the particular modus operandi once all the relevant facts are brought to light. . . . Instead I review the claims of professional performers, psychics and others who want us to believe that paranormal phenomena can be reliably produced or witnessed, usually by payment of money in exchange for a book or other literature or a performance, a reading or a service. . . .

Geller Effects

Self-proclaimed psychic Uri Geller is trying to make a comeback on the British psychic scene after disappearing without a trace during the early 1980's. His current performances differ little from those so widely acclaimed in the 1970's: key-bending, spoon-breaking, psychic repairs of "broken" watches and clocks, mental telepathy and clairvoyance. Geller refuses to demonstrate his effects in the presence of skeptics and will not even participate in discussions when I or other skeptics such as James Randi are present.

One amusing incident occurred in the 1970's in New Zealand when Geller refused to appear on a television show with the late Richard Kammann and me. Geller, with manager in hot pursuit, fled the studios. As Geller sulked in his hotel room, Kammann and I gave a live demonstration of Geller's whole repertoire on national television. Actually we may have outperformed him because we covered the entire routine in just 20 minutes, whereas Geller normally requires a full two hours.

How facile it would all seem if Geller honestly stated at the start of his act that it is all a scam: "I am a conjurer. Using sleight of hand, I bend spoons and get stopped watches to start again." Frankly I would far rather watch a decent juggler or acrobat because at least there is an element of genuine skill involved.

I won't try the reader's patience by describing the whole Geller Routine. This can be found in *The Psychology of the Psychic* (1980), coauthored by Kammann and me. The current

18

discussion will be restricted to metal-bending and watch-starting.

As we explained in our book, there are many ways of making small objects bend:

(1) Distract everybody, bend the object manually, conceal the bend and then reveal the bend to the now-attentive onlookers. This is Geller's usual method. The bend is made either by tweaking the object with two hands or by levering it in something tough like a belt buckle or the head of another key with a hole in the top.

JOHNSON ONCE MORE FAILS TO GRASP THE CONCEPT OF THE PARANORMAL.

Reprinted with permission of *The Skeptical Inquirer.*

(2) Geller (or an accomplice) prestresses the object by bending it many times until it's nearly at the breaking point. Later it can be used to dazzle unsuspecting audiences as it bends, appears to melt or even snaps in two pieces following the slightest pressure from Uri's wiry fingers.

(3) Often collections of metal objects (for example a bunch of keys or a drawer of cutlery) contain one or more items that are

already bent. Geller tells you he'll bend something and when you examine the whole set of objects carefully, the bent item is found and Uri takes credit.

(4) When an object is already bent, Geller will often say that it will continue to bend. He may move the object slowly to enhance the effect or place it on a flat surface and push down on one end. But many people will believe they can see an object slowly bending purely as a result of Geller's suggestion that it is doing so.

(5) Substitute objects already bent for the ones provided.

Starting "broken" watches is even easier. Geller starts watches by warming, shaking, holding and handling them. Uri (or anybody else for that matter) can get about 50 percent of stopped watches to start ticking by physical holding and handling. These watches are not broken in the first place and merely require warming or shaking or moving to start them again. Probably they did not tick for very long since in most cases they need cleaning and lubricating. But that doesn't matter; most people accept the sound of the ticking as a miracle of psychic power. . . .

Remote Viewing

One reason Geller became famous was his involvement with a series of disastrously-controlled experiments conducted by Harold Puthoff and Russell Targ of SRI [Stanford Research Institute] International in Menlo Park, Calif. Geller was allowed to operate unobserved in a room which had potential visual and audio communication with the area where drawings were chosen and displayed for Geller to reproduce by ESP [Extrasensory Perception]. This experiment was lauded as "cheat-proof" by *The New York Times*.

The same two investigators, physicists by trade, discovered the remarkable phenomenon of remote viewing in which you or I or anybody else can see with the mind's eye any place chosen at random now or at any time in the future. Such a generously paranormal effect defeated even Targ and Puthoff's novel physical theory because remote viewing breaks the inverse square law of energy against distance. The experiment is run when an experimenter drives to a geographical site while the subject remains back with the first experimenter. The subject then "tunes in" on the outbound experimenter and describes his location. Several such sessions are run and then an independent judge tries to match up the descriptions with the sites.

Before we rewrite all physics textbooks, it is well to examine the methodological flaws in the original remote-viewing protocols. You can drive a whole fleet of buses through the methods Targ and Puthoff uses. The transcripts containing the subjects' remote descriptions were full of extraneous but useful information such as dates and references to previous experiments. Hence the judges could easily match the transcripts to the list of places which were provided in the correct original order. Even after parapsychologist Charles Tart of the University of California at Davis categorically declared that he had removed all of the verbal clues, Christopher Scott and I found a surplus of them remaining. . . .

Faith Healing

[Magician and paranormal investigator James] Randi's recently-completed investigation of American faith healers shows the widespread use of fraud and fakery. While there is clearly a strong placebo component, by no means exclusive to alternative therapies, there is an increasing use of high technology in faith healer's practices. Take, for instance, what Randi found when he investigated evangelist Peter Popoff.

Careful Assessment Needed

People do have certain expectations in their experiences and this awareness that people do misperceive and misinterpret ordinary happenings is important. James Randi pointed out that a simple suggestion of paranormal events is enough to cause people to notice and report previously unnoticed "unusual" events. When a certain metal-bending psychic has been on radio or television, reports have come in from people noticing that their silverware was bent. But how many of those people took notice of the bends in their spoons and forks before they were told to do so by the psychic? Careful assessment is needed of all subjective paranormal experiences if we are to help people understand what is going on in their lives, paranormal or not.

Loyd M. Auerbach, *Fate*, June 1988.

Popoff was noted for his ability to "call out" members of his audience in which Popoff selects an individual by name and gives specific details of the patient's illness, doctor and present condition. This information, Randi and Steve Shore discovered, is obtained by Popoff's wife Elizabeth and others who circulate among early arrivals at the auditorium, discuss their medical conditions and other personal details and then determine their seating position within the audience. "Healing cards" are also used to establish the prayer needs, names and addresses of a large number of participants.

At one healing session in San Francisco Civic Center, Alec Jason, posing as a repair man, used an electronic scanning device to zero in on a radio signal at 39.170 megahertz on which Elizabeth Popoff conveyed specific information to a receiver in her husband's ear. Mrs. Popoff used a mobile television studio trailer parked outside the auditorium to transmit the essential information to Peter Popoff's hidden receiver so that he could perform his dramatic calling-out effect. Using TV monitors in the trailer, Mrs. Popoff could even direct her husband to specific individuals for whom highly specific information had been listed prior to the show.

The Popoff episode provides just one example of what appears to be a general trend in the American faith-healing fraternity, the use of high-tech equipment and electronic media to convert the serious business of health care into a charlatan's paradise, a new brand of show business. Legitimatized as a "religion," this lucrative tax haven for the unscrupulous is a cynical mockery of both the state and its more gullible citizens. . . .

Cold Reading

As Ray Hyman described it in the title of a classic paper published in 1977 in *The Zetetic*, "cold reading" is an interview technique for convincing strangers that you know all about them. Such readings are based on three assumptions: (1) that people operate according to a single set of psychological principles; (2) that our problems and concerns relate to a single set of live events: birth, puberty, work, marriage, children, divorce, old age, illness and death; and (3) that in the majority of cases people come to talk about their problems with love, money and health. Some of its more popular forms are tarot-card reading, astrology, crystal-gazing, the I Ching and psychometrics in the Spiritualist and, perhaps to some extent, the psychodiagnostic senses.

Hyman lists 13 rules of the game. These rules are easily learned. I once coached a journalist, Josh Easby, on these rules in a 15-minute telephone call and he subsequently won a public contest against a professional clairvoyant. The rules are:

(1) Be confident.

(2) Use statistics, polls and surveys to make intelligent guesses about your client based on their demographic and socioeconomic characteristics (age, place of birth, occupation).

(3) Profess modesty.

(4) Gain the client's confidence and cooperation.

(5) Use a gimmick such as tarot cards, a crystal ball, a palm, tea leaves or I Ching sticks. These provide technical plausibility while distracting the client from the true modus operandi.

(6) Use a familiar set of stock phrases or spiel. These are vital and are often sufficient purely by themselves. Examples: "I see troubled waters ahead"; "I see a new person in your life, or is it the passing of an existing relationship?"

(7) Keep your wits about you. Home in on whatever the client needs or wants.

(8) Use the "fishing" technique. Phrase statements as questions, wait for the reply, and then feed back the same information in a slightly different form.

(9) Be a good listener.

(10) Be dramatic.

(11) Act as if you know more but aren't telling. This makes you look wise and understanding, two definite pluses for any would-be counselor, psychic or otherwise!

(12) Flatter whenever possible.

(13) Always tell clients what they want to hear. You can find this out by fishing—rule 8.

Asking Questions

One of the most effective ways to deal with extraordinary claims is by learning how to ask the right questions. This enables one to separate the essentials from the nonessentials and get right to the heart of the matter. For example, what is the claim being made? Are there alternative explanations? How can you test the various hypotheses offered? Have you been told the full story? And so on.

Al Seckel, *The Skeptical Inquirer*, Spring 1989.

Experiments have shown that human beings are all too willing to accept a general personality reading as true for themselves even though it is based upon absolutely zero specific information. This is the well-known fallacy of personal or subjective validation.

At its most general the factor of "subjective validation" applies to any situation in which people look for meaning and significance in relating two sets of information. Of course when these information sets are dependent in some way, the validation or matching process can be creative and lead to exciting new discoveries. But when the information sets are independent, all we have is an illusory correspondence which fools us into thinking something is there when it isn't. Many apparently paranormal phenomena are based upon illusions and delusions of a subjective validatory kind for which Hyman's 13 rules provide one compelling framework.

Conclusions

Contrary to the claim that science cannot provide explanations for the paranormal, there are simple explanations for every paranormal effect.

2

"The scientific case for the paranormal is persuasive."

Explanations for the Paranormal Are Inadequate

D. Scott Rogo

D. Scott Rogo (1950-1990) was a prolific writer about the paranormal. In addition to a regular column in *Fate* magazine, he frequently wrote articles for other parapsychology journals and he wrote more than a dozen books on paranormal topics. In the following viewpoint, he responds to David F. Marks's attack on the paranormal. Rogo says that while some paranormal phenomena clearly are explainable, others are not.

As you read, consider the following questions:

1. Rogo suggests that Marks unfairly denigrates research on remote viewing. What two criticisms does Rogo make of Marks's evaluation?
2. What example does Rogo offer to show the validity of cold readings?
3. Which author do you find more convincing—Marks or Rogo? Why?

D. Scott Rogo, "The Case Against the Case Against the Paranormal," *Fate*, January 1989. Reprinted with permission.

When discussing the paranormal with a skeptic, I like to emphasize our common assumptions, not our differences. Both the open-minded skeptic and the legitimate parapsychologist know how difficult paranormal research can be.

We agree that (1) the claims made by self-proclaimed psychics are often bogus; (2) some "psychic" effects—such as Kirlian photography—result from perfectly explainable physical or psychological phenomena; and (3) many experiments carried out in parapsychological laboratories turn out, when examined closely, to suffer from methodological and statistical flaws.

There is, in fact, only a single important difference between the informed skeptic and the serious parapsychologist. While the skeptic maintains that these three factors are sufficient to explain ostensible paranormal phenomena, the parapsychologist holds that beneath the considerable nonsense genuine psi exists. If David F. Marks' arguments were wholly persuasive and beyond refutation, the parapsychologist would have nothing to say in response to them. One reason I accept the reality of the paranormal is that the skeptic often makes an unconvincing case. Marks is no exception.

Few parapsychologists would dispute much of what Marks says here. No mainstream parapsychologist believes in the paranormality of psychic surgery, popular firewalking or other bogus mysteries. But when they target the more legitimate aspects of parapsychological concern, Marks' arrows fall wide of the mark.

Geller Effect Revisited

Skeptics and proponents both have long been exasperated with Uri Geller, the Israeli psychic who attracted wide attention in the 1970's. Even in his heyday Geller was a difficult subject to work with. Sometimes he failed to show up for experiments, freely changed the conditions under which he worked, and generally played cat-and-mouse with would-be experimenters. I once spent an afternoon with Geller testing his alleged ESP [Extrasensory Perception] power and walked out of the radio station unconvinced that I had seen anything paranormal. . . .

Despite the reservations I developed from my own experience, however, I cannot completely dismiss the experiences of my colleagues. . . .

Some Magicians Convinced

It is interesting to note that even some previously-skeptical magicians believe in Geller's powers. Probably the most remarkable account comes from Artur Zorka, a member of the Occult Investigation Committee of the Society for American Magicians. When Zorka met Geller for a television program, he handed him a fork to bend. When Geller grasped the implement, its handle literally exploded and sent pieces flying through the room. There is also the interesting report of Leo Leslie, a Danish magician who has written a book on Geller. He writes that a key, lightly stroked by Geller, bent in his own hand while its nickel coating cracked and curled.

Because of Geller's notoriety, ego and theatrics, skeptics cannot be blamed for their negative feelings. But I must take exception to Marks' charge that during his stint at the Stanford Research Institute (SRI) "Geller was allowed to operate unobserved in a room which had potential visual and audio communication with the area where drawings were chosen and displayed for Geller to reproduce by ESP."

The Burden of Proof

The answer to the question of whether the existence of psi . . . has been established is clearly "yes.". . .

If the burden of proof is on the claimant, then that burden must apply whether the claim is being made on behalf of conventional theory or paranormal theory. Until such claims are backed up scientifically, our subject matter remains anomalous and the mysteries remain mysteries.

John Palmer, *Journal of the American Society for Psychical Research*, April 1987.

I don't know where Marks got his information but in fact the situation was more complicated than his account would lead one to believe. In a series of experiments conducted by Harold Puthoff and Russell Targ in the early 1970's, Geller was sequestered in a sealed booth, where he successfully reproduced (purportedly by telepathy) drawings randomly chosen from a dictionary and placed on an outside wall.

These experiments were challenged by James Randi in his book *Flim-Flam!* (1980) in which he claims Geller could have seen through a hole in the chamber used for cables. Randi also suggests that Geller could have been cued through the hole by a confederate.

To investigate these serious charges, the editors of *Fate* suggested I visit SRI and look into them. So on June 12, 1981, I flew to Menlo Park, Calif., examined the room and spoke with those researchers involved in the experiments—both the believers and the skeptics. I found that the criticisms of these experiments were based on erroneous information. The hole could not have been used to see the targets and was obstructed during the experiments. It was also in a different location from that given by Randi. Nor were the two individuals claimed by Randi to be likely "confederates" present during the critical experiments. . . .

Remote Viewing

Since Targ and Puthoff conducted their research at the prestigious Stanford Research Institute it is not surprising that they received considerable publicity. Much of this publicity concerned their research into a procedure they call remote viewing. . . .

The usual remote-viewing session is conducted by three persons: the experimental subject and two researchers. One of the researchers remains with the subject throughout the session, while the second experimenter drives to a geographic site located nearby. This location is determined by randomly selecting a target site from a pool of predetermined geographically-distinct locations. When the outbound experimenter arrives there, he occupies himself by enjoying the scenery for 15 minutes or so. During this crucial time the experimenter back in the laboratory encourages the subject to "make contact" with the outbound person and describe where he is. Sometimes remarkable coincidences show up between the target location and the subject's report.

But the experiment still isn't finished.

To ensure that these correspondences do not result from coincidence, usually a series of experimental sessions will be held with randomly-selected locations. The transcripts of the subject's reports are subsequently randomized and given to a judge who personally visits the sites or looks at photographs of them. The independent judge then tries to match the individual reports to the corresponding target locations.

Marks correctly states that there were methodological flaws in the early SRI remote-viewing research. Cues such as references to previous sessions were left in the transcripts; these may have helped the judges figure out the order of the sessions. But is it true that the "list of places [target locations] was provided in the correct original order?"

Seeking an answer to that question, I spoke with Arthur Hastings who was the judge in the critical remote-viewing series Marks discusses. Dr. Hastings told me that while the list of sites was given to him in the original order, *he did not know that*. Nor did he form his evaluations from visiting the sites in the order given on the list. He chose the target locations randomly before visiting them. When he reviewed a specific site, he read through the subject's transcripts and tried to choose the best correspondence. He repeated this procedure for each of the locations. In other words, for all practical purposes Hastings randomized both the targets and the subject's responses and still made several correct match-ups. . . .

But the real problem is that Marks unfairly simplifies the research. Critics like him cite the early SRI work, cite its weaknesses and proclaim that remote viewing has been "explained." Never do they give parapsychologists credit for learning from their mistakes. Not counting those papers published specifically from the SRI research between 1973 and 1982, some 27 remote-viewing experiments were reported by researchers from other laboratories. Several of these experiments were conducted when the flaws in the early SRI work were known; yet they still succeeded. Why do the skeptics ignore this better-controlled research? . . .

The second critical issue Marks fails to address is that his methodological criticism deals exclusively with the statistical success of remote-viewing experiments. He never considers the rich contents of the sessions. Remote-viewing experiments have two exciting features which contribute to their success or failure. While the results can be statistically evaluated by mathematically weighing the judge's rankings, sometimes the comparisons between the subject's report and the target sites seem too remarkable to explain normally.

For example, an especially successful series of precognitive remote-viewing sessions were conducted in 1977 by John Bisaha (of Mundelein College in Chicago) and Brenda Dunne. For five consecutive mornings Dunne—in Wisconsin—tried to remote view the location where Bisaha would be visiting in Eastern Europe the next day. One of the targets was a circular restaurant raised on stilts over the Danube River. Dunne's remote perception from a distance of 5000 miles reads:

> I have the feeling that [the agent] is somewhere near water. I seem to have the sensation of a very large expanse of water. There might be boats. Several vertical lines, sort of like poles. They're narrow, not heavy. Maybe lamp posts or flagpoles. Some kind of circular shape. Almost like a merry-go-round or a gazebo. The large round thing. It's round on its side, like a disc. It's like a round thing flat on the ground, but it seems to have height as well. Maybe with poles. Could possibly come to a point on top. Seeing vertical lines again. Seems to be a strong impression, these vertical lines. No idea what they could be. . . . A definite sensation of being outside rather than in. Water again. . . .

While several critics have dealt with the statistical features of remote-viewing research, skeptics such as Marks don't even try to explain these detailed and abundant correspondences. . . .

Faith Healing

Can the power of religious faith heal people? Marks observes, legitimately, that some theatrical evangelists use fakery in their performances. But he limits his remarks to only a single performer.

Science is gradually learning that faith and prayer may possess a psychic component. In the August 1986 issue of *Fate* I reported on the research Dr. Randy Byrd of San Franscisco General Hospital presented that year to the American Heart Association. Dr. Byrd's research demonstrated that recovering cardiac patients fared better when prayed for than a control group (matched by computerized selection). The subjects did not know that they were being prayed for and the people praying were scattered throughout the country. Despite these tight controls the prayed-for patients suffered fewer postoperative infections, problems with edema or required intubation. . . .

So much for research on faith healing. But what about religious healers themselves? . . .

Probably the best look at the scientific case for faith healing was prompted by the ministry of the late Kathryn Kuhlman, the popular (and controversial) Pittsburgh-based evangelist. . . .

Beginning in the late 1960's Allen Spraggett, then the religion editor of the *Toronto Star*, investigated Kuhlman's healing by checking the medical records of the recipients. . . .

The Healing of George Orr

An especially remarkable healing was that of George Orr who was cured of an eye injury on May 4, 1947, while attending one of Kuhlman's meetings in Franklin, Pa. Orr had little vision in his right eye due to an injury he suffered in 1925. He had been working for the Laurence Foundry Company in Grove City, Pa., where his job entailed casting iron. A bit of molten iron splashed into his eye and burned it severely. The injury was examined by Dr. D.C. Imbrie who found the eye obstructed by a scar over the cornea. It was so damaged that Orr could see little except peripherally.

Orr petitioned the state's Department of Labor and Industry for compensation and in 1927 it issued its evaluation supporting the request. The report stated that the worker's injury was "equivalent to the loss of the use of the member for industrial use" and that "the claimant is entitled to complete compensation . . . for the loss of an eye." Dr. Imbrie, who personally testified when the hearing was convened, declared that the injury was permanent because the scar produced by the burn could not be corrected by surgery.

In 1947 Orr and his wife drove to Franklin to watch a Kathryn Kuhlman service. Impressed, they returned to hear her preach a few more times. They drove to Franklin again with friends on May 4. This time Orr prayed for his own healing. Within moments he felt a tingling in his eye which felt as if an electrical current were passing through it. The eye began to tear. Orr couldn't stop the tears which threatened to stain his coat.

Not until he was driving home, however, did he realize that he could see fully through the damaged eye. When he checked in a mirror, he found that the scar had simply disappeared. Dr. Imbrie was called in to reexamine the eye two years later and he was flabbergasted.

Orr's healing is particularly impressive since the reconstruction could not have been due to spontaneous remission. Although he was under no medical treatment, the scar healed instantaneously, completely and permanently. . . .

More Study for Mysterious Phenomena

Parapsychology starts with the recognition that certain phenomena seem to occur that are not readily explainable through existing scientific models. One is thereby forced to assume either that the majority of people throughout human history are in error, or that these phenomena should be studied further in an attempt to understand their nature and cause.

Theodore Rockwell, *Journal of the American Society for Psychical Research*, July 1989.

There is a growing medical literature on the paranormal power of faith. Dr. Rex Gardner, a fellow of the Royal College of Obstetricians and Gynecologists in England, has published a book entitled *Healing Miracles* (1986) which examines a number of inexplicable healings. In each case the healing resulted from petitionary prayer and was documented by a physician.

Cold Readings

Anybody who works with psychics knows they can sometimes skillfully extract information from their clients. The use of the cold reading is just one such example. Another ploy is "fishing" for information, in which the psychic will ask leading questions and revise his original remarks accordingly.

Ever since the 1930's experimental parapsychologists have realized that psychics can pick up information from their clients by evaluating their appearance, demeanor and speech. As a result they developed methods to control these problems. Many different procedures were developed but the most consistently employed use some sort of "ranking" method.

For such an experiment, the experimenter first asks clients to contribute token objects for the psychic to "read" but the clients never sit with the psychic, who gives the readings in the presence only of the experimenter. The experimenter later transcribes the impressions. When the readings are completed, the transcripts are edited and randomized. The clients then read through the records and rank them by trying to guess which reading was meant for them personally. Of course, if the alleged psychic really possesses extrasensory gifts, a client should be able to rank his personal reading first or second.

The transcripts are carefully edited to make sure that no remarks pertinent to the token objects could cue the client. If the token object is a ring, for instance, the researcher could edit such comments as "this ring was a gift from. . . ."

Some psychics have been tested under these conditions and triumphed. Dr. Gertrude Schmeidler of the City College of New York conducted successful experiments using similar procedures with the late Caroline Chapman, a well-known New York psychic, in the 1950's.

A more recent research project using these statistical procedures was published in 1973 by the Psychical Research Foundation. The PRF study focused on the clairvoyance of Lalsingh (Sean) Harribance, a psychic from Trinidad. Between 1960 and 1972 he was something of a psychic-in-residence with the organization.

During their early work with Harribance, the PRF investigators experimented to see if their subject could differentiate between pictures of males and females in sealed envelopes. When these experiments were successful, they decided to evaluate Harribance's "readings" on similar pictures. For a critical series of 10 trials, Harribance—while supervised by the experimenters—gave his psychic impressions of 10 concealed photographs of men. When he finished the readings, the transcripts for the sessions were typed and the entire series given to the clients. Each was asked to read through them and choose the one most relevant to him.

While this experiment was still in progress, 10 more trials were completed using concealed photographs of women. These transcripts, too, were turned over to the clients for similar judging.

Since the psychic was not face-to-face with the sitters, he could not fish for information. Nor would cold-reading generalizations work since the clients didn't know which of the readings were specifically for them. Despite these conditions, however, the clients chose the correct readings (prompted by their photographs) to a statistically significant degree.

Case Against Paranormal Not Proved

Space does not permit a response to every criticism Marks makes. . . . But as I observed earlier, the honest parapsychologist and the intelligent skeptic have much in common. We both have considerable nonsense to sort through as we study the paranormal. It is for this reason that the skeptic and the parapsychologist should work hand-in-hand, each keeping the other's bias in check.

31

I think that the scientific case for the paranormal is persuasive and I think most serious parapsychologists feel the same way. The scientific and experimental literature on the subject is enormous and the skeptics cannot ignore it by selectively focusing on weak research or by relying on strawman exposures of showmen pretending to be psychics.

3

"Knowledge of the laws of physics supports skepticism about reports of UFOs, ESP, astrology, and other such matters."

Science Does Not Support Paranormal Phenomena

Milton Rothman

Milton Rothman, a retired physicist, has a special interest in applying the rules of science to prove that paranormal phenomena are impossible. He has written several books. Among them are *Discovering the Natural Laws* and *A Physicist's Guide to Skepticism*. In the following viewpoint, he claims that people tend to base their belief in paranormal phenomena on several mythical "facts." He explains why those "facts" are false and why paranormal phenomena have no basis in scientific evidence.

As you read, consider the following questions:

1. What five myths does Rothman say belief in paranormal phenomena is based on? Does he make convincing cases against these myths?
2. The author says scientists are different from the skeptics who believe that no knowledge is certain. How do scientists, even skeptical ones, behave differently?
3. Much of Rothman's argument against paranormal phenomena is based on the law of conservation of energy. What is this law and, according to Rothman, why does it make paranormal phenomena impossible?

Milton Rothman, "Myths About Science . . . and Belief in the Paranormal," *The Skeptical Inquirer,* Fall 1989. Reprinted with permission.

Investigations of paranormal phenomena are most often carried out on a case-by-case basis. Investigators go into the field to determine what people actually saw when they say they saw a UFO [Unidentified Flying Object]. The statistics and methods of parapsychology researchers are examined to make sure that no errors were made. Faith healers are carefully observed to see if anybody is actually cured. The prime rule is: Find out what actually happened and expose what tricks, if any, were used to produce the observed effects. And we are urged to avoid a priori judgments and to keep our minds open to the possibility of the occurrence of any kind of an event.

And yet some of us with training in science feel that another approach is legitimate. We should be able to apply to paranormal claims the same methods of deduction that we use in evaluating ordinary physical phenomena. Proper use of previously validated physical principles should enable us to make educated judgments concerning the plausibility of some of the claims to which we are exposed. After all, one of the things we learn in physics is how to decide between the kinds of actions that may happen in nature and those that are not allowed to happen. These decisions are governed by the fundamental principles of physics. . . .

Standard Responses

Invariably, whenever I attempt to explain how knowledge of the laws of physics supports skepticism about reports of UFOs, ESP, astrology, and other such matters, I receive a number of standard responses. These responses demonstrate that much thinking about science has some of the characteristics attributed to mythology. In this article, I would like to show that much of what passes for logical argumentation consists of the repetition of certain clichés that are believed to be true by large numbers of people. These statements are believed to be true because strong psychological forces maintain their presence in human folklore: People want to believe them, and belief in the validity of these ideas provides emotional payoff. Nevertheless, these beliefs have little or no validation in reality. It is for this reason that I call them myths. . . .

1. Nothing Is Known for Sure. . . . The idea that "nothing is known for a certainty" plays a useful political role in the arguments of those espousing one or more paranormal phenomena. If nothing is known for sure, then any one of our present laws of nature may be overturned in the future and replaced by a contrary law. If nothing is known for sure, then it is impossible for scientists to say that a given phenomenon is forbidden by nature. If nothing is known for sure, then future advanced civilizations may be able to do all kinds of amazing things that we now consider impossible. Thus the belief that nothing is known for sure is a prior condition for believing in the other myths to follow. . . .

The philosophical position of skepticism comes down to us from antiquity. It is related to Platonism, which teaches that true reality consists of the thoughts within the mind. It follows that ideas concerning the world outside of our minds are simply constructs manufactured from the raw materials of our individual thoughts. In this kind of universe it is impossible to be certain of anything, not even of our own existence.

Significantly, the growth of modern science has accompanied a move away from Platonism and its replacement by the concept that there does exist a real world outside our bodies and that we all learn about that real world by interpreting signals entering our brains through the channels of our sensory organs. In the realistic philosophy of modern neuroscience there is no separate "mind" but only the workings of the physical nervous system. . . .

Extreme Skepticism

The person who prefaces all arguments with the statement that "we don't know anything for sure" is exhibiting an extreme form of skepticism. His doubt is directed against scientists who claim that psychics cannot foretell the future or that UFOs cannot remain suspended above the earth with no visible means of support. Because the believer in the paranormal wants to believe that nature does allow such phenomena, he often wraps himself in the cloak of an excessively rigorous skepticism directed against scientific knowledge. . . .

The scientist, on the other hand, is a pragmatic skeptic. He believes in the importance of looking at physical evidence, and he believes that there is now enough evidence to cast doubt on most paranormal claims, using scientific deduction from validated physical principles. . . .

2. Nothing Is Impossible. If we start with the premise that nothing is known for sure, then it becomes impossible for anyone to say that a proposed action is impossible, for it requires knowledge to make judgments concerning matters of fact. However, if we agree that at least some of our knowledge is certain, or at least verified to a high degree of certainty, then we are in a position to say that some events are not permitted by nature. This is because nature possesses a specific structure characterized by a number of physical symmetries, discovered during the past century, that govern the behavior of all the particles that comprise matter. Because of these symmetries, certain actions are allowed to take place in nature and certain other actions are not allowed to take place.

An important symmetry principle (time symmetry) is related

to the law of conservation of energy, which has been verified to an extraordinarily high degree of precision. It is this law that allows us to say with confidence that it is impossible to build a device (a perpetual-motion machine) whose operation creates energy out of nothing. It must be emphasized that modern physics gives new meaning to the idea of proving that perpetual-motion machines cannot work. In the past, the method of logical induction required that every possible kind of machine be tested in order to be sure that none of them would work. This would require an indefinite number of tests. Even then you could never be sure, for at any time a different kind of process might come along to allow the creation of energy from nothing. But modern physics finds only four different kinds of energy existing in nature (corresponding to the four forces of particle physics). Thus conservation of energy has only to be tested by showing that in any reaction among any of a relatively small number of particles, interacting by only four kinds of forces, no energy is created or destroyed. Since everything is made of such particles, it follows that conservation of energy is true for all processes in nature. . . .

Guarding Against Deception

A crucial lesson is the necessity of guarding against deception. This includes deception by outright liars and hoaxers, by the deluded, and by writers who range from the merely negligent to the cynically manipulative. And it also includes self-deception, a too-willing acceptance of fanciful claims—even, on occasion, a stubborn refusal to heed clear danger signals, in which the term *gullible* is appropriate. An antidote to deception is to recall the maxim that "extraordinary claims require extraordinary proof," and, for self-deception, to consider the thesis that gullibility is fostered by want and to analyze one's motives accordingly.

Joe Nickell with John F. Fischer, *Secrets of the Supernatural*, 1988.

Conservation of energy applies to more than perpetual-motion machines. It also throws doubt on claims of ESP, precognition, dowsing, and other mainstays of parapsychology. Belief in parapsychology is generally associated with a belief in mind-body dualism—the idea that the mind is separate from the body and of a nonphysical nature so that information can enter the mind by some nonphysical means. However, modern neuroscience treats "mind" as something that emerges from the operation of the physical brain. Nowhere do scientists find evidence of psychic energy, spirit, soul, *elan vital*, or other necessities of mysticism. Therefore all neuroscience starts with a physical model, whose basis is that a number of electrons and ions must be set into motion within the nervous system in order to originate a thought within the brain. Setting electrons and ions into motion requires energy, and this energy must come from somewhere.

When we analyze the situation in detail, we realize that no physical force exists in nature capable of transmitting organized energy (information) from one brain to another without the use of the normal sensory organs. Such a force would have to be capable of working over long distances and be strong enough to move electrons and ions about. The electromagnetic force is the only force in nature with the right properties, but we know that the amount of electromagnetic radiation emitted from the brain is far too small to have the claimed effects. (And radiation from the brain could not explain either direct perception at a distance or precognition.) This evidence makes us highly suspicious of any kind of subjective experience claimed to result from external information stimulating thoughts without passing through the conventional sensory channels. . . .

No Solid Foundation

3. Whatever We Think We Know Now Is Likely to Be Overthrown in the Future. If we allow that "nothing is known for sure," then all our knowledge has a fluid basis. Nothing has a solid foundation or core. Indeed, there is a pseudo-democratic hint from some quarters that all theories are equal because they are merely matters of opinion, which ignores the empirical basis of scientific theory. This attitude leads to the possibility that whatever we think we know now will be shown to be false and replaced by a new theory in the future. It is true that many past theories have been replaced by newer theories: The earth-centered solar system was replaced by the sun-centered model; caloric theory was replaced by kinetic theory; ether was replaced by electromagnetic theory; and so on. The resulting feeling of impermanence is often exploited by believers in the paranormal when they say: "Our theories of the mind will change in the future to allow for ESP," or "Relativity will be replaced by a new theory that will allow us to travel faster than light," or "Evolution will be replaced by creationism.". . .

In the past, some false theories have been replaced by correct theories: replacement of the earth-centered solar system by the sun-centered system, for example. The new paradigm is a correct one and will not change in the future. In general, the evolution of theories is from the less correct to the more correct, as instrumentation and experimental methods improve. . . .

The history of science is much too complex to treat simply as a succession of one theory after another. There are many theories that have not changed since their inception. For example, the concept of energy as quantitative measure of changes going on in a system has never required a fundamental change, although it has been necessary to add new forms of energy as they have been discovered (and subtract some found unnecessary). . . .

For these reasons I believe it is perpetrating a myth to say that "whatever we think we know now is likely to be overthrown in the future." This is merely a debating device used by those who do not want to admit that physics includes some knowledge of a permanent nature.

Unknown Forces

4. Advanced Civilizations of the Future Will Have the Use of Forces Unknown to Us at Present. When I say that telepathy and other forms of ESP cannot work because there is no force in nature capable of transmitting information directly into the human mind without the intervention of the normal sensory organs, one possible response is that there are forces in nature that we know nothing of but which will be discovered in the future. Similarly, if I say that there are no forces in nature capable of propelling a space vehicle from the earth to Alpha Centauri with a travel time of less than a hundred years, a possible response is that advanced civilizations of the future will have the use of forces we cannot conceive of now.

I think the concept of new and unknown forces is a myth, for several reasons. First, forces do not arise from nothing; nor can human beings generate forces at will. Humans never really "control" nature in the deepest sense of the word. All humans can do is to arrange objects so that when these objects do what they have to do as required by the forces of nature, then the result agrees with our desires. There are four of these natural forces:

	Long-Range	Short-Range
Strong	Electromagnetic	Strong nuclear
Weak	Gravitational	Weak nuclear. . . .

What of other possible forces? There is no denying the possibility of other forces existing in nature, and physicists are constantly looking for them. For the past several years we have heard many reports of a new kind of gravitational force that either is repulsive in nature or varies with distance differently than the ordinary gravitational force. But this force is exceedingly weak—so weak that all the experiments to date give contradictory results, making one wonder whether this is another chimerical quest. A force that weak is of no use to us for practical purposes. What we need is a force that is both strong and long-range.

And that leads us to the crucial question: Where is there room in nature for another force that is both strong and long-range? My argument is that if such a force existed it would already have been observed. Remember, forces do not arise out of nothing. They exist as interactions between fundamental particles. But the four known forces are sufficient to explain the behavior of all the fundamental particles that make up normal matter. To get another force you would need a new class of particles. . . .

The Role of Misperception

The unreliability of our individual senses is . . . demonstrated when we examine the recollections of observers of recent incidents. Eyewitness testimony is commonly thought to be the most reliable form of evidence in a criminal investigation. Numerous experiments, however, have repeatedly shown that being present at the scene of a crime, or even watching such an incident, does not necessarily qualify one to describe what actually happened or to recognize the participants later. Indeed, erroneous eyewitness testimony is remarkably frequent. . . . The "facts" that fit the most obvious interpretation are the ones believed, regardless of reality. . . .

An understanding of the physiology of our senses enforces the view that our consciousness is presented with an approximate simulation of reality. In most instances this simulation is good enough. However, in certain environments an erroneous simulation can lead to a sincere belief in the sighting of a UFO, a mythological animal, or a ghost, or the absence of approaching traffic. . . .

Anthony G. Wheeler, *The Skeptical Inquirer*, Summer 1988.

Since the human brain consists of ordinary matter, there is no possibility of explaining the phenomena claimed by parapsychology with the aid of new and unknown forces. . . .

Advanced Civilizations

5. Advanced Civilizations on Other Planets Will Possess Great Forces Unavailable to Us on Earth. The UFO as portrayed by modern mythology is a saucer-shaped object that hangs high in the air unsupported by any visible means. There are no forces known in nature that can hold such a large mass motionless high in the air. Some UFO enthusiasts claim the trick is done by magnetic fields. However, we know a great deal about magnetic fields, and such a feat of levitation cannot be performed by such means. A magnet needs another magnet to push against in order to levitate (and fields strong enough to do the job would be detectable all over the country). Rockets won't supply sufficient force for more than a few minutes. What else is left? The answer always given at this point is: *Advanced civilizations on other planets possess great forces unknown to us on Earth.*

The response to such a statement is essentially the same as that given for myth No. 4. There are only four different forces in existence, and of these only the electromagnetic force has the range and strength to do useful work for humans. And this force is unable to hold a massive vehicle suspended in midair without a visible light and sound show. There is no reason to believe that planets orbiting distant stars have other kinds of forces, because when we analyze the light coming from those distant stars we find that all the stars contain the same kinds of matter and the same kinds of energy as our own solar system. Things are not different in other parts of the universe. In fact, this statement of uniformity is the central premise of modern cosmology. If the entire universe started from one big bang and spread out from that initial mass, then matter everywhere must be the same, for it all comes from the same source. There is no way for other parts of the universe to be made of different kinds of matter with properties radically different from our own.

Epilogue

Myths are rarely countered by facts. Once born, they carry on independent lives. But it is necessary to be aware of them if we are to maintain a realistic view of this universe. Knowledge of the laws of physics—especially the conservation laws—helps us make decisions about the borderline between myth and fact, between fantasy and reality.

"Anomalous phenomena, by their very nature, will not obey the requirements laid down by Science."

Devotion to Science's Rules Obscures the Truth

Lynn Picknett

Lynn Picknett has written and edited several books on the paranormal. She was deputy editor of *The Unexplained*, a British periodical that deals with paranormal topics. She is a member of the Society for Psychical Research and the College of Psychic Studies in London. In the following viewpoint, she argues that adults enslave themselves to certain ideas about the way things are, closing their minds to anything that does not go along with these ideas. Still, she says, people cannot simply ignore the evidence all around them that unexplained things happen. She believes people should open their minds and accept that the paranormal exists.

As you read, consider the following questions:

1. Picknett says there is a "worldwide conspiracy" against the paranormal. What does she mean?
2. Picknett suggests that we allow ourselves to be brainwashed by science. Why does she think this is harmful?
3. Milton Rothman, the author of the opposing viewpoint, believes the universe is governed by rather strict laws; Lynn Picknett believes "chaos rules." Which author do you agree with more? Why?

Excerpted, with permission, from *Flights of Fancy?: One Hundred Years of Paranormal Experiences* by Lynn Picknett. New York: Ballantine Books, 1987.

There is a worldwide conspiracy in which, although we may not realize it, we all participate. Most of us are implicitly members at birth, but true initiation comes only when we reach the age of reason—when we acknowledge, no matter how reluctantly, that Peter Pan only flies with the aid of strings and pulleys, that miracles only happen to people in the bible (and perhaps not even then), that fairies, gnomes, angels and devils are folklore, and that Santa Claus is dead. On the day we are welcomed into the Great Conspiracy we receive a rule book in which is inscribed just one rule: avoid the impossible. Then we are struck blind, deaf and dumb and patted on the head. From this position, we know where reality begins and ends. Dreams alone have the power to take us away from the bondage of this self-enforced freemasonry. We are grown-ups.

Grown-Up Rule: Avoid the Impossible

Frantically, we tell the world how to behave by drawing up a list of rules. The law of gravity, for example, encourages the belief that because most people do not suddenly float up to the ceiling, all levitation is humanly "impossible." But . . . people do float and fly, extravagantly flouting our cherished rules. In retaliation we effectively ground them by declaring them, and their witnesses, liars and dupes.

Our conditioning as fully paid-up members of the Great Conspiracy means that we will do almost anything to obey the rule—*avoid the impossible*. Most of the time we don't even notice anomalous events, but if they are very intrusive we can always force them to fit civilization as we know it, rather like Cinderella's stepsisters and the glass slipper. If we can't blame a levitation or a ghost or spontaneous human combustion on something the Establishment (i.e. the High Command of the Conspiracy) will recognize, then we can always get ourselves certified insane before they do it for us. Like Cinderella's stepsisters who cut off their toes rather than admit the slipper did not fit, we will go to any lengths to fit the round peg of the paranormal into the square hole of the "normal." If we can't then the tendency is to deny it ever existed. (Who wanted to marry the rotten old prince anyway?)

Strange Events

Consider the following examples of anomalous events and test your reactions to them:

In the 1980s a very down-to-earth British journalist was sitting outside a pavement-café in a back street of Paris. Suddenly the last car in the row parked across the street jumped of its own accord with such force that all the others in front shot forward a couple of feet. All the cars were empty and there was no one near.

In 1657, a young lad from Somerset was going about his business when he was abruptly lifted from the ground by an invisible power and levitated until his head touched the ceiling. He was then returned to the ground equally mysteriously. Henry Jones was afflicted in this way for a year; once he was thrown 27 m (30 yd.) over a garden wall, but he was never hurt physically by these attacks. It was, of course, a grave offense to break the ground rules like this, and the neighbors were beginning to look askance, believing him to be bewitched. (If it happened today we wouldn't even allow ourselves that handy explanation to fall back on.) But fortunately, before the authorities asked him to help them with their inquiries, the tormentor, whoever or whatever it was, left him in peace. From then on Henry Jones kept his feet firmly on the ground like anyone else.

In 1904 in Falkirk, Scotland, neighbors found what they had to assume was the body of Mrs. Thomas Cochrane, a well-connected widow, "burned beyond recognition" lying on cushions and pillows that were not even singed. No one had heard her cry out and there was no fire in the grate nor any other source of fire or heat in the room. She had been destroyed by heat estimated in excess of 3000°F, yet it had failed to ignite the surroundings. This is typical of spontaneous human combustion (SHC).

Unexplained Phenomena

As long as there have been human beings, people have claimed experiences with phenomena that, according to the prevailing religious or scientific orthodoxy, were not supposed to exist.

Jerome Clark, *Omni*, February 1987.

In the mid-nineteenth century a Spiritualist medium, Daniel Dunglas Home, plunged his lily-white hands into the fire, lifting out red-hot coals in a borrowed handkerchief. Neither his hands nor the handkerchief showed the slightest signs of exposure to heat. He then conferred his incombustibility on the onlookers; when he handed them the live coals, they too suffered no damage and felt no heat.

At about the same time an Eastender, young Florrie Cook, regularly fell into a trance in her cabinet (a curtained-off recess) and shortly afterwards a woman in white emerged to walk among the sitters (those who attended the seances). She even perched flirtatiously on their laps and chatted inconsequentially to them. She claimed to be the physical materialization of a long-dead pirate's daughter, Katie King. Despite the fact that she looked *almost* exactly like her medium, many witnesses believed that she was indeed modern proof of the resurrection of the body—among them the eminent scientist William (later Sir William) Crookes.

Suspend Disbelief

To recognize the impossible you must suspend your disbelief which everyone is riddled with, as your reactions to the stories mentioned above no doubt reveal. Jumping cars? How many cognacs had the witness consumed? Or perhaps the driver had accidentally left something switched on, or something . . . anyway, cars do not behave in this way. At least one car did. Levitating boys? Well, it was in the wilds of Somerset back in 1600-and-God-knows-when. Enough said.

Spontaneous human combustion (SHC) is very, very nasty as anyone who has read Dickens's *Bleak House* knows. But surely, we cry hopefully, that's just fiction? Unfortunately, Dickens based Krook's death on reports of real-life cases; it happened then and it happens now, despite coroner's elaborate attempts to explain away the horror: perhaps Mrs. Cochrane was taken from her house and foully murdered by person or persons unknown, her body burnt and returned to her pillows where she was found? There is no evidence that this is what happened in this instance, nor in any of the dozens of other known cases of SHC. Uncomfortable though it is, the fact remains that people burst into flames apparently from within, while their clothes and surroundings escape undamaged. It could happen to you.

At the other extreme, human incombustibility as exhibited so flamboyantly by D.D. Home (and others, before and since) is absolutely impossible. We all know what happens if we play with fire. But then we have never tried it in the company of Mr. Home.

And as for Florrie Cook and Katie King, the whole thing is a fraud and an insult to our intelligence. Miss Cook was clearly a confidence trickster (and very likely no better than she should be); moreover she is said to have confessed. QED.

Explaining Away Our Freedom to Think

Our first list of representative mysteries and miracles have been explained away, or at least enough doubt has been sown to make further investigation appear to be a forlorn exercise. Perhaps it's easier to relinquish our freedom and give ourselves back to the warmth and comradeship of The Conspiracy . . . ?

Be absolutely clear on this point: making friends with the impossible is not for the fainthearted or, and this may seem a paradoxical statement, for the gullible. After all, only the easily swayed will disbelieve the testimony, of not only generation after generation, but even the evidence of their own eyes. As for the fainthearted, the High Command, be they priests, scientists, or today's priest-scientists, have been known to take dissidents to one side with painful effect. Ordeal unto death by crucifixion, the rack, the stake, and trial by the media have been the fate of those who describe the real world as they have actually experienced it, rather than the world that operates according to the rules they know. Become a friend of the impossible and you automatically figure on someone's hit list. You have been warned.

A Strange World

Something strange is going on.

We live in a world whose realities are defined by science, which tells us how things work. And yet there are some things which don't seem to work that way at all. Our science tells us that these things are impossible and don't exist, yet they stubbornly refuse to go away. There are relatively few of them and they are often elusive and hard to control, but they are there for anyone to see. They exist.

Lyall Watson, *Beyond Supernature*, 1988.

Even if you are finally proved innocent of fraud and the phenomenon you have witnessed is accepted (very possibly disguised as a newly discovered "natural law") by the scientific brotherhood, don't expect them to apologize for their former skepticism. The frontiers of the "possible" are always being redefined—that's "progress"—but it's small comfort to those who were martyred for being ahead of their time.

Painful Road of Discovery

The slow and painful tale of scientific discovery reads like a grim fairy story: Once upon a time, not so long ago, scientists sneered at the peasants who came running to them (this was in France actually, but it could have been anywhere). Great stones had hurtled out of the sky and crashed into the earth. Come, said the peasants to the scientists, and we will show you. But the scientists would not go to see for themselves, so the peasants brought some pieces of the stones to them. Pray do not bother us with your superstitions, said the scientists, they are merely rocks that have been struck by lightning. How can stones fall out of the sky when there are no stones in the sky? they scoffed. But meteorites kept falling just the same.

Early European explorers of the dark continent sent reports back to learned journals of their encounters with huge, hairy manlike monsters. What nonsense, said the professors in their gentlemen's clubs, it must be the effect of the heat (poor old

Carruthers). But gorillas continued to exist nevertheless.

In our arrogance we believe we must give events permission to happen or creatures permission to exist. As the Book of Genesis says, "In the beginning was the word. . . ." The existence of the Loch Ness monster was deemed a subject not even fit for debate until Sir Peter Scott gave the elusive creature a name: *Nessitera rhombopteryx.* Unfortunately, this mouthful was later discovered to be an anagram. Rearrange the letters and you get: "Monster hoax by Sir Peter S". . . .

With or without our puny acknowledgement, and outside of our control, the impossible has a field day. Unbolt the rivets of reason, remove the blindfold of dead knowledge, and see for yourself.

In 1986 millions of Wimbledon's tennis fans witnessed the short, sharp rebellion of a humble tennis ball against the tyranny of the Great Conspiracy. Live on television the rogue ball skimmed *through* the mesh of the net, exhibiting with true chutzpah which scientists and parapsychologists call "matter through matter transference." Even BBC's [British Broadcasting Corporation] urbane commentator Dan Maskell was moved to muse that this was "really quite remarkable," and viewers were treated to an action replay of what was, in effect, more a milestone in television and, indeed, human history than Neil Armstrong's giant leap for mankind.

But the more outrageous the impossibility, the shorter our memories of it; play continued and the event did not even figure in the inevitable end-of-Wimbledon compilation of clips showing players falling over and umpires eating their sandwiches in the rain. Like many anomalous events it was spontaneous and over in a split second. Blink and you missed it, even given a brief action replay. Millions witnessed the event but how many remember it? It is part of our human condition, or rather human conditioning, that even viewers who remember it happening refuse to see its significance. A shrug and a yawn, a wave of apathy, actually mask our terror at the unleashing of the true, wild world we suspect hovers outside our five senses, like demons howling at the edge of the magic circle in which we live. If we allow ourselves to believe that our beloved, safe rules can be broken then perhaps they will, once and for all, fail us—with far more serious repercussions than a sudden rash of delinquent tennis balls. Chaos would rule.

Chaos Does Rule

Chaos, in fact, does rule, but only the brave dare acknowledge the fact. Making friends with the impossible means taking a firm stand; refusing to be brainwashed by the gullible materialists who have taken away our childhood. They are a motley crew but they tend to consist mainly of scientists who jealously guard their rule-making monopoly; conjurers who would pay good money to learn the tricks of the impossible but if they can't then they become its implacable enemy; journalists, who see the impossible in terms of the great Sex Scandal—Peter Pan is really a girl (Shock! Horror!); and to a large extent, parapsychologists. This last category used to be called psychical researchers, but today it is mandatory to be an "-ology" to win the respect of the scientific Strong Arm Boys and the grants at universities. As Bill Murray's parapsychologist says in *Ghostbusters*: "Back off man, I'm a scientist . . ."

Sound Evidence

As a child I had been fascinated by spiritualism, ghosts and magic, and had devoured all the books in the 'occult' section of our local library, from poltergeists to voodoo. But around the age of eleven my mother presented me with a chemistry set and an uncle produced a book on astronomy, and I fell under the spell of the potent magic of science. Suddenly the 'occult' seemed absurd and slightly disgusting. . . .

As I began to study the subject systematically this attitude soon changed. I was struck first of all by the impressive consistency of reports of telepathy, 'second sight' and precognition. If they were really lies or delusions they ought to possess as much variety as a shelf-full of novels: in fact, they all sounded remarkably similar. The same was true of reports of magic and contact with 'spirits': you would expect to find very little in common between the beliefs of an African witch-doctor, an Eskimo shaman and a Siberian medicine-man. In fact they are practically interchangeable. Invented ghost stories—by writers like Dickens or M.R. James—are full of a most weird diversity of occurrences; real ghost stories all sound alike. It was soon obvious to me that I was not studying a subject full of imaginative inventions or impostures, but a fairly narrow range of facts, just as in astronomy or cybernetics. As a result I soon became convinced that the evidence for poltergeists, premonitions and second sight is as sound as the evidence for atoms and electrons.

Colin Wilson, *Beyond the Occult*, 1988.

With a few notable exceptions, parapsychologists are "moles" for the Great Conspiracy; they grovel to the Establishment and will never in a million years accept the impossible (unless they discover it for themselves). But more significantly, anomalous phenomena, by their very nature, will not obey the requirements laid down by Science. The paranormal (which is the impossible slowed down so we can perceive it) tends to behave like a particularly temperamental prima donna, who must be flattered and coaxed into giving her greatest performance—but she will only do it for her fans. Too often, parapsychologists turn the star into a ruined Judy Garland and try to croak her way over that rainbow while the audience throws bread rolls at her. Or, with scientific fervor they seek to strip, weigh and measure her—and what self-respecting star would allow that? As one friend of the impossible remarked, "All this experimentation is like trying to make two strangers fall in love in a laboratory."

Anything Can Happen

To believe that anything can, and probably will, happen is to be free. And because the nature of the phenomena is whimsical we, too, as its friends, can be blissfully inconsistent in our favoritism: we may applaud D.D. Home and despise Florence Cook, look askance at fairies and ponder deeply about spontaneous human combustion, fire extinguisher to hand. Proof and disproof is from Alice-land anyway, whatever the men in white coats say. The paranormal puts on the motley, not rubber gloves.

If you make friends with the impossible it will make friends with you. The Cosmic Joker may have a wicked sense of humor, but he gets lonely laughing at his own jokes. We have stood in the corner too long—let's go out and play.

Distinguishing Between Fact and Opinion

This activity is designed to help develop the basic critical thinking skill of distinguishing between fact and opinion. Consider the following statement: "Several thousand people claim to have encountered UFOs." This is a factual statement because it contains information that can be verified by checking books on UFOs. But the statement "Claims of UFO encounters are the products of truly disturbed minds" is an opinion. Many people— especially those who report having encountered UFOs—believe such encounters are factual.

When investigating controversial issues it is important that one be able to distinguish between statements of fact and statements of opinion. It is also important to recognize that not all statements of fact are true. They may appear to be true, but some are based on inaccurate or false information. For this activity, however, we are concerned with understanding the difference between those statements that appear to be factual and those that appear to be based primarily on opinion.

Most of the following statements are taken from the viewpoints in this chapter. Consider each statement carefully. *Mark O for any statement you believe is an opinion or interpretation of facts. Mark F for any statement you believe is a fact. Mark I for any statement you believe is impossible to judge.*

If you are doing this activity as a member of a class or group, compare your answers with those of other class or group members. Be able to defend your answers. You may discover that others come to different conclusions than you do. Listening to the reasons others present for their answers may give you valuable insights into distinguishing between fact and opinion.

> *O = opinion*
> *F = fact*
> *I = impossible to judge*

49

1. We should be able to apply to paranormal claims the same methods of deduction that we use in evaluating ordinary physical phenomena.

2. Literature exists describing how physics and mathematics may be used to judge the validity of paranormal claims.

3. In the series of experiments at the Stanford Research Institute, physicists examined the paranormal abilities of Uri Geller.

4. It is often difficult to predict what is going to happen in a given situation.

5. People have been known to burst into flames apparently from within, while their clothes and surroundings escape undamaged.

6. In our arrogance we believe we must give events permission to happen or creatures permission to exist.

7. To believe that anything can, and probably will, happen is to be free.

8. A phenomenon is defined as paranormal if it contravenes some fundamental or well-established scientific principle.

9. You can drive a whole fleet of buses through the holes in the methods some scientists use.

10. There are simple explanations for every paranormal effect.

11. Experiments have shown that people will accept a general personality description from a "psychic" even though it is based upon absolutely no specific information.

12. A series of precognitive remote-viewing sessions were conducted in 1977 by John Bisaha and Brenda Dunne.

13. Anyone who works with psychics knows they can sometimes skillfully extract information from their clients.

14. The scientific case for the paranormal is persuasive.

15. The skeptic and the parapsychologist should work hand-in-hand, each keeping the other's bias in check.

16. The concept of new and unknown forces is a myth.

17. Science is gradually learning that faith and prayer may possess a psychic component.

18. Dr. Rex Gardner, a fellow at the Royal College of Obstetricians and Gynecologists, has published a book entitled *Healing Miracles*.

Periodical Bibliography

The following articles have been selected to supplement the diverse views presented in this chapter.

Loyd Auerbach	"Psi and the Art of Magic," *Fate*, June 1988. Available from PO Box 64383, St. Paul, MN, 55164-0383.
Experientia	"Investigating the Paranormal." Special section, April 15, 1988. Available from Birkhauser Verlag, PO Box 133, CH-4010, Basel, Switzerland.
George H. Gallup Jr., and Frank Newport	"Belief in Paranormal Phenomena Among Adult Americans," *The Skeptical Inquirer*, Winter 1991.
C.E. Lindgren	"The Future of Parapsychology," *Fate*, December 1990.
David F. Marks	"Investigating the Paranormal," *Nature*, March 13, 1986.
Lloyd Morain	"How Pseudo-Scientists Get Away with It," *The Humanist*, March/April 1988.
John Palmer	"Have We Established Psi?" *The Journal of the American Society for Psychical Research*, April 1987.
Theodore Rockwell	"Psi Is Not a Mere Anomaly," *The Journal of the American Society for Psychical Research*, July 1989.
Carl Sagan	"Night Walkers and Mystery Mongers: Sense and Nonsense at the Edge of Science," *The Skeptical Inquirer*, Spring 1986.
Al Seckel	"Rather than Just Debunking, Encourage People to Think," *The Skeptical Inquirer*, Spring 1989.
Phillip Stevens Jr.	"The Appeal of the Occult: Some Thoughts on History, Religion, and Science," *The Skeptical Inquirer*, Summer 1988.
Ian Stevenson	"Was the Attempt to Identify Parapsychology as a Separate Field of Science Misguided?" *The Journal of the American Society for Psychical Research*, October 1988.

2 CHAPTER

Are UFOs Real?

PARANORMAL
PHENOMENA

Chapter Preface

Reports of UFOs—unidentified flying objects of possible extraterrestrial origin—can be found in historical documents dating back at least to Biblical times. Some experts, for example, believe the fiery chariot described by the prophet Ezekiel was actually an extraterrestrial visitation. In addition, some students of ancient cultures believe that certain artifacts, such as the immense, centuries-old earth drawings in Nazca, Peru, prove that aliens visited earth many centuries ago. In recent history, "waves" of UFO sightings have been reported every decade or so since the late nineteenth century and individual sightings occur almost daily.

It was not until 1947, however, that the modern era of UFOs began. In that year, one particularly convincing sighting sparked the interest of scientists and military experts. On June 24, private pilot Kenneth Arnold reported seeing a group of saucer-like UFOs as he was flying over the Cascade Mountains in Washington. Because Arnold was a respected pilot and numerous other reports corroborated his story, it could not be ignored as the fantasy of a crackpot. As a result, Arnold's report was one of the incidents that prompted the United States Air Force to begin more than twenty years of exhaustive investigation of thousands of UFO sightings reported by civilians and military personnel. Then, in 1969, the Air Force officially ended its UFO investigations, stating that no conclusive evidence of extraterrestrial visitation had been found.

Many people thought that the Air Force's conclusions should have settled the question. However, reports of sightings continue, as well as accounts of encounters with extraterrestrial beings. Thousands of people claim to have seen UFOs and to have been abducted for study by their occupants. A number of private and government organizations continue to study this puzzling phenomenon.

The authors of the following viewpoints debate whether evidence has been found to prove the existence of UFOs.

"What I saw in the sky . . . was a gigantic blackness."

UFOs Are Real

Whitley Strieber

Several years ago, Whitley Strieber, author of popular horror novels, underwent a series of frightening and mysterious experiences that he believes were encounters with extraterrestrial visitors. Strieber underwent medical and psychological evaluation and counseling but could find no explanation for his experiences. Convinced that he had indeed observed and been abducted by aliens, Strieber described his ordeal in *Communion*, a book that remained on *The New York Times* best-seller list for several months. The following viewpoint is an excerpt from his succeeding book, *Transformation*. In it he describes a horrifying night during which he believes his young son was abducted by extraterrestrials.

As you read, consider the following questions:

1. What physical evidence of UFOs does Strieber present in this viewpoint?
2. On the morning following this experience, what did Strieber's son do that convinced Strieber the boy had truly been abducted by aliens?
3. Strieber says his son "protected himself" by choosing to call the experience a dream. What does Strieber mean?

Adapted from "The Lost Boy," chapter one of *Transformation* by Whitley Strieber, © 1988 Wilson & Neff, Inc. Reprinted by permission of Beech Tree Books, an imprint of William Morrow and Company, Inc. (Subheadings and inserted quotations have been added by Greenhaven Press.)

The night of April 2, 1986, was cool and damp in the corner of upstate New York where we have our cabin. My son was on spring break and he, my wife, Anne, and I were spending an uneasy week there. It had been bought as a place of peace and relaxation, but had turned out to be something very different.

Beginning in October of the previous year, we'd had a series of devastating nighttime encounters with what appeared to be aliens. I had been the direct victim of most of these encounters, and they had all but shattered me.

Strange Disturbances

But they had also fascinated me. Were we really in touch with nonhuman beings of some sort? That certainly appeared to be the case. I'd undergone an exhaustive series of medical and psychological tests that had proved me healthy and sane. I was not the victim of any disease that might cause hallucinations. What's more, there had been a few witnesses. On the night of October 4, 1985, two friends, Annie Gottlieb and Jacques Sandulescu, had been disturbed by some extremely strange lights, sounds, and sensations while I was under virtual attack from the visitors. In March 1986 a friend of my son's had seen a small flying disk move past our living-room window while we were eating dinner. She was a seven-year-old girl and totally unaware of the UFO [unidentified flying object] phenomenon. That night I had a spectacular direct encounter with the visitors. . . .

In the middle of the night I was disturbed by what felt like somebody giving me a sharp jab to my left shoulder. . . .

I got out of bed, thinking that I would go down and check on my son, and perhaps walk outside for a few minutes. The air was quite chilly, so I put on some rubber-soled slippers and a thick terry-cloth robe.

The Bed Was Empty

I walked downstairs into the most appalling experience of my life. . . .

The bed was a stark, white emptiness. I looked under it, beside it. A flash of hope went through me as I rushed into the bathroom. But he wasn't there either.

I knew with a parent's awful certainty that he wasn't in the house. Still, I thought maybe he had been sleepwalking. I searched the basement. I was just sure that he was here somewhere, he had to be. . . .

A few minutes later I'd searched every closet and room. I had to face the fact that my seven-year-old was not in the house at three-twenty in the morning. There was no possibility that this was a hallucination. My little boy was gone, really gone. Incredibly and inexplicably the burglar alarm was off. I thought to wake Anne and call the sheriff.

I was going upstairs to get her when I seized on a last, faint hope and decided to look outside. . . .

The "Bizarro" cartoon by Dan Piraro is reprinted by permission of Chronicle Features, San Francisco, CA.

I hadn't grabbed a flashlight and it was very dark. I went to the end of the porch, thinking to walk near the road where the trees were thinner and there was more light. That way I could see, and I'd get to [my son's] tent without risking a fall.

I jumped down off the end of the porch and started toward

the road. Above me there was quite a broad expanse of sky, and as I hurried along I noticed something moving there.

I stopped and looked up, confused by this suggestion of motion where there shouldn't be any. What I saw was absolutely stunning. A cold shock went through my body and my heart started running in my chest. In that instant I was swept from the real world and back into the fearsome strangeness that had been assaulting us.

What I saw in the sky, apparently no more than a few hundred feet above treetop level, was a gigantic blackness. It covered easily a third of the firmament, blotting out the stars. It was simply immense, a featureless void. It showed no lights, it didn't glow—it was a black place in the sky. It could as easily have been a hole as real as a disk hanging silently in the air. The movement I had detected was the prick of stars winking in and out as the border of the thing moved.

I thought it was a cloud. Its wide, curving edge was very sheer, but surely that could be accounted for by some wind phenomenon. The cloud moved as I moved, so exactly in synchronization with me that it seemed oddly connected to me. It was as if this entire, huge object were linked to my motions. Of course the moon will do that behind the trees. But I was seeing the object not against nearer trees but against the more distant stars. Thus the movement either was actual or was violating a law of perspective.

I didn't much care which it was; I was going to turn and walk away from it, then into the woods toward the tent.

Suddenly I heard a voice, clear in the silence: "Can you go back upstairs by yourself or do you want us to help you?"

It wasn't overly loud, but it shattered the quiet. I stopped, frightened, not sure where it had come from. On the far side of the road I saw three dark shapes hanging above the brush. They were blocky and small, as if covered by black or dark-blue sheets.

That voice had been so final, so absolutely authoritative, and so implacable. Suddenly I realized what was happening: That was a gigantic unknown object up there, and my son must be in it. I had interrupted the visitors in the middle of one of their abductions.

Deep Fear and Sorrow

A fearful shuddering passed through me from head to toe. My whole body shook. I was losing control. A band of pain went around my chest; I could hear the blood pounding in my head. I'd never felt anything like it. I thought I was having a heart attack or some kind of seizure. I writhed. It was as if something deep within me were literally trying to escape from my skin.

I was filled with an inexpressible sadness. I wanted just to stand there and scream. I stumbled a few more steps toward the object.

Then I stopped, noticing that the stars were coming out all around it. It seemed to be shrinking.

This observation relieved me. Maybe I was, after all, dealing with a waking dream. Of course, that's what it was. It must be that: a horrible, insane waking dream. Then the object—which had now disappeared completely—suddenly reappeared as a flat, yellow disk about half the size of a dime. Its glow took on a faint pink tint and it darted off to the north, streaking like a meteor.

Evidence Cannot Be Squelched

Approximately one-half of the people in the United States believe in UFOs and one out of eleven thinks they have seen them.

Not only do people believe in the existence of UFOs, many accept that thousands among us have been abducted by extraterrestrials. And as more books and reports are published, the evidence can no longer be squelched.

Edith Fiore, *Encounters*, 1989.

I understood that it hadn't been shrinking at all. It had been going up very quickly and in absolute silence.

I have never felt so helpless or so lonely as I did at that moment. I knew what I had suffered in the past at the hands of these bizarre visitors. Images of my little boy going through the same things tormented me.

They repeated their question and I think that they may have floated a little closer to me. I was furious and totally impotent. I did not think that I would ever see my son again. And how in God's name would I explain what had happened to him to his mother or to the sheriff, or to anybody?. . .

I went back to the house. I remember how it looked, dark and foreboding, a little bit as if it belonged to another world. The faint glow of Andrew's night-light illuminated the windows of his room. The house was still and silent.

The Familiar Is Strange

This familiar place now seemed strange and otherworldly. What had just happened was so weird that it had shattered my assumptions about the world around me. My own living room was an alien chamber full of bizarre artifacts. I looked around, as if from the other side of the world—and all I saw was my familiar chair, the table and lamp beside it, the TV and videotape recorder, the magazine stand, the small bookshelf beside the stairs.

Was this real? And what about what had just taken place outside—was that also real?

I do not think that I can express how lost I was at that moment, or how angry and bitter and cheated I felt. How did conventional science explain that big, black thing in the sky? *That thing wasn't supposed to be real.* Then where in hell was my child?. . .

Remembering what they had wanted me to do, I marched upstairs like a soldier. I was perishing inside. I went over to the bed and sat down on it.

Evidence Exists

The evidence that there are objects which have been seen in our atmosphere, and even on terra firma, that cannot be accounted for either as man-made objects or as any physical force or effect known to our scientists seems to me to be overwhelming. I have read two or three dozen respectable books, and many more less so, and I have listened to addresses by a dozen or more eminent speakers, in which a very large number of sightings have been vouched for by persons whose credentials seem to me unimpeachable. It is striking that so many have been trained observers, such as police officers and airline or military pilots. Their observations have in many instances . . . been supported either by technical means such as radar or, even more convincingly, by visible evidence of the condition of the observers or—and this is common to many events—interference with electrical apparatus of one sort or another.

Lord Hill-Norton, foreword to *Above Top Secret* by Timothy Good, 1988.

I sensed that they were in the bedroom with me, but that didn't seem to matter. I might as well have been paralyzed for all the control I had over myself. This was a subtle thing, though. On the surface I felt normal. It was just that I was walking across a room, going to bed, when alarms were screaming in my mind that something had happened to my child. It was as if somebody else were controlling my body. And yet, I did not feel as though I were struggling.

I threw off my robe and slippers, lay down in bed, and felt the most wonderful sensation of warmth spread over my body. Helplessly, I was swept off into a dreamless, black sleep.

Morning Comes

When I woke up it was light outside. I opened my eyes. Birds were singing, and I could see the hazy green of new growth on the trees near the windows.

At first I had the feeling that one gets upon waking from a

nightmare and realizing that all is well. The morning seemed fresh and good and full of promise.

But that lasted for only a few seconds. The night came flooding back, and with it the memories. I felt sure I was about to go downstairs to an empty house.

I couldn't move a muscle. Beside me Anne was breathing softly. I felt so terrible for bringing her and our son back to this house at the edge of hell.

A small sound came from downstairs. At first I couldn't believe my ears, then I heard the *pad pad pad* of my son's footsteps. He was coming to our bed, just like he had every morning since he could escape from his crib!

Was this true? Was it possible?

He burst through the door with his stuffed dog Puppy under his arm and a wide grin on his face.

I couldn't talk, I couldn't move. The tears were pouring down my face. But he didn't notice that. He dove into the bed and snuggled down between us and he was warm and real and I hugged him hard.

Over the next few hours my old arrogance reasserted itself. It had to. I could not otherwise live with the total power of the visitors.

They could do anything they wanted to me and my family. That was so unbearable that I just tuned it out. . . .

By the time breakfast was over, I had decided that the events of the night before weren't even worth reporting. They'd been nothing more than a nightmare brought on by the state of disquiet I was in.

Reality Is God's Dream

It was a warm day and Anne and I took folding chairs out onto the deck that afternoon. We both began reading novels and enjoying the sun. Andrew was playing nearby with his toy trucks. . . .

My boy made a sound like a train whistle, a long, high tone that seemed to reach right to the center of my heart.

He grew tired of his game and came to me.

"Whatcha reading?"

"A book about America in the nineteenth century called *Dream West.*"

"*Dream West?*"

"Yes."

"Y'know, I've been thinking. Reality is God's dream."

I looked at him. I was a little surprised, not so much at the statement but at the quiet force in his voice. Reality is God's dream?

"What happens if God wakes up?"

He stared at me for a moment with an almost quizzical expression on his face—then burst out laughing.

The afternoon passed uneventfully. We drove into town for some groceries.

Later Andrew said, "The unconscious mind is like the universe out beyond the quasars. It's a place we want to go to find out what's there."

There came into my mind as the shadows of the day grew long the thought that my little boy could not have said that. I was embarrassed at myself for underestimating him: He *did* say it.

The Safety of a Dream

We were out on the deck together just after sunset. Andrew looked toward the woods. "Y'know, I had a funny dream last night. I dreamed I was floating in the woods and this huge eye was looking down at me. It was funny. It was like it was real but it was a dream." He looked at the shadows, some of them already deep. "Wasn't it a dream, Dad?"

"What do you want to think?"

"I want to think—a dream."

"That sounds good to me, then." Like so many of us, he had chosen to protect himself from the reality of the visitors by calling them a dream. So be it.

"When the human nervous system is stimulated beyond its normal capacity . . . for long periods of time . . . it eventually begins to operate in paradoxical ways. Typically . . . hysteria results."

UFOs Are Hallucinations

Bill Ellis

Bill Ellis teaches English and American Studies at Pennsylvania State University at Hazleton. He is interested in supernatural folklore and has written the entry on "Abductions" for the *Encyclopedia of American Popular Beliefs and Superstitions*. In the following viewpoint, he proposes that experiences like those described by Whitley Strieber in the previous viewpoint can be explained by the influence of certain cultural myths. He specifically discusses Strieber's own experiences as recounted in his first abduction book *Communion*.

As you read, consider the following questions:

1. What similarities does the author see between Strieber's alien experiences and religious conversion?
2. What physical causes does Ellis suggest may be partially responsible for experiences like Strieber's?
3. What cautions does Ellis recommend for rationalists and skeptics who are confronted with accounts like Strieber's?

Bill Ellis, "The Varieties of Alien Experience," *The Skeptical Inquirer*, Spring 1988. Reprinted with permission.

Scholars who study the folklore of past and present cultures may have some useful perspectives to offer about the many recent reports of abduction by aliens. At the conclusion of his review of Whitley Strieber's *Communion*, Ernest H. Taves suggests that either Strieber is mentally ill or he is consciously perpetrating a hoax, "playing a joke on his readers.". . . Robert A. Baker suggests a far simpler explanation: that Strieber is a fantasy-prone personality sincerely describing what he believes he remembers. From the perspective of psychology, Baker suggests several recognized and well-understood mechanisms for such "memories," including hypnogogic hallucination, confabulation, and inadvertent cueing by the hypnotist.

Folklore Alternatives

Folklorists familiar with accounts of supranormal experiences can, however, suggest two additional mechanisms at work: one may explain Strieber's experience; the other certainly accounts for his actions since his "abduction."

1. On October 4 and December 26, 1985, Strieber may have actually experienced an event, common to many other cultures and individuals, in which he felt paralyzed and then believed he was levitated and subjected to indignities by nonhuman agents.

2. Whether Strieber experienced this event or not, he did undergo, during the period from January to March 1986, an experience identical to that of religious conversion.

Collections of legends and folktales, both European and otherwise, contain a variety of "real life" accounts that contain close parallels to elements of modern abduction stories. Most of these are anonymous, migratory tales that have no weight as evidence. Some, however, contain alleged firsthand experiences. Strieber himself notes these parallels and cites them as support for the "reality" of his abduction. The more carefully recorded cases, however, make it clear that these earlier abductions, like Strieber's, were subjective in nature. Anne Jeffries (ca. 1626-1698), an illiterate country girl from Cornwall, was one such celebrated abductee. In 1645 she apparently suffered a convulsion and was found, semi-conscious, lying on the floor. As she recovered, she began to recall in detail how she was accosted by a group of six little men. Paralyzed, she felt them swarm over her, kissing her, until she felt a sharp pricking sensation. Blinded, she found herself flying through the air to a palace filled with people. There, one of the men (now her size) seduced her, and suddenly an angry crowd burst in on them and she was again blinded and levitated. She then found herself lying on the floor surrounded by her friends.

Significantly, the accounts note that the experience left her ill for some time, and only after she regained her health did she "recall" this experience. Still, like Strieber, Jeffries claimed that this encounter was followed by further contacts with the "fairies," and she was taken seriously enough by the local authorities in 1646 to be arrested for witchcraft and imprisoned.

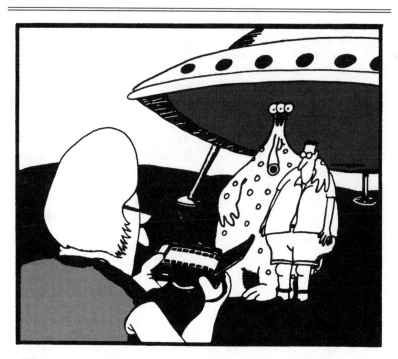

"Yes, yes, already, Warren! . . . There *is* film in the camera!"

THE FAR SIDE cartoon by Gary Larson is reprinted by permission of Chronicle Features, San Francisco, CA.

A more recent incident, with some connections to Strieber's alleged experience, was reported by theologian Henry James Sr. One afternoon in May 1844, relaxing in his chair, James suddenly felt the presence of some invisible, ineffably evil being squatting in the room with him. Rationally, he recognized that his emotion "was a perfect insane and abject terror, without ostensible cause"; still he found himself completely paralyzed while (as in Strieber's October 4 experience) his mind was flooded with images of "doubt, anxiety, and despair." The senior James eventually found release in the fringe religion of Swedenborgianism, while his sons dealt with the impact of this experience in their own ways. William James provided one of the first rational anatomies of paranormal encounters in *The Varieties of*

Religious Experience; Henry James Jr., dealt with the lingering threat of such events in his fiction, ranging from *The Turn of the Screw* to *"The Jolly Corner,"* both of which contain suggestive parallels to *Communion.*

"Old Hag" Theory

Some light has been thrown on such experiences by folklorist David Hufford. In Newfoundland, he found, the term "Old Hag" referred to a fairly common phenomenon in which a person who is (as Strieber was on October 4 and December 26) relaxed but apparently awake suddenly finds himself paralyzed and in the presence of some nonhuman entity. Often the sensation is accompanied by terrifying hallucinations—of shuffling sounds, of humanoid figures with prominent eyes, even (rarely) of strange, musty smells. Often the figure even sits on the victim's chest, causing a choking sensation.

Like Baker, Hufford at first assumed that the consistencies present in victims' accounts of the Old Hag could be explained by previous exposure to oral traditions—the "cultural source hypothesis." It is interesting, though, that when he moved his base of research to the United States, Hufford found the experience just as common here as in Newfoundland—affecting perhaps more than 15 percent of the population. Despite the absence of a folk tradition naming and explaining it, many of the specific details of the Old Hag hallucination recurred in victims' experiences, leaving them profoundly confused and reluctant to talk for fear of ridicule. Hence the phenomenon remains largely unstudied by psychologists and practically unknown (as a general phenomenon) to the general public.

Surveying the psychological and psychiatric literature relating to the experience, Hufford found no evidence that the Old Hag was linked to neurological or psychotic illnesses. During this event, evidently, the brain functions as if asleep, producing the characteristic paralysis and apnea; hence it is similar to the hypnogogic hallucination. The peculiar stability of the hallucinations' content across cultural boundaries and in the absence of traditions concerning it, however, remains unexplained. Hufford suggests that the most likely explanation is that the Old Hag might be the side-effect of a documented but poorly understood derangement of the sleep pattern, akin to narcolepsy.

Sleep and Indoctrination

Strieber's October 4 visitation, along with the similar experiences of paralysis and physical manipulation reported by many abductees, might be explained by some form of abnormal sleep pattern, producing a distinctive set of hallucinatory events. Future studies need to focus carefully on the phenomenology of such events, which may reveal genuine correspondences among "abduction" events. In this regard, the main value of Strieber's book to folklorists is that much of it was committed to writing soon after the experiences themselves. The interpretations accepted after the fact by the victim (or imposed on him by others) are of less value, as they tend to force the details of the experience into a culturally acceptable mold.

Myths and Fantasies

With such memories [of alien abductions]—whether you recover them by hypnosis or by direct, fully conscious interchange between the person who claims to have had the experience and the person who is interviewing him or her—what you're probably dealing with is a pervasive modern myth that has been much propagandized, circulated, and diffused through the telling and the retelling and the re-retelling of the story. The more it's told, the more all kinds of people on the border are prone to pick up the myth and share it with others. I don't mean on the border of nuttiness. I mean on the border of confusion about their own lives, their own past, and maybe with some present emotional crisis or merely some unbearable loneliness. In that state, they could be lying. More typically they are probably attempting to grope their way out of their own confused identity toward some order and meaning by having this "recall," which grows upon itself and becomes a spun fantasy.

Milton Rosenberg, *The Skeptical Inquirer*, Spring 1988.

On the other hand, it is not necessary to assume that a neurological experience could provoke detailed memories of abduction. Strieber may have confabulated either or both experiences; we cannot tell for sure. Nevertheless, there is no question that early in 1986 Strieber underwent a quasi-religious conversion, assisted (probably innocently) by Budd Hopkins [an alien abduction researcher] and his analyst, Robert Klein.

The classic process of indoctrination is described by William Sargant: When the human nervous system is stimulated beyond its normal capacity ("transmarginally") for long periods of time —either deliberately by agents wanting to indoctrinate a person or unintentionally by the person undergoing a lengthy period of psychological stress—it eventually begins to operate in paradoxical ways. Typically, the individual begins to over-respond to weak stimuli; ultimately, his or her previous thought and behavior patterns begin to change and a state of hysteria results, during which the individual is highly susceptible to new concepts and philosophies. It is unrealistic, Sargant warns, to expect a person to resist the process of conversion once it has begun. Even recognition that one is being indoctrinated, he notes, may not delay breakdown.

This process has been institutionalized in the religious rites of many cultures and the pattern frequently occurs in the narratives of "born-again" Christians. Strieber's account of events, evidently based on a journal kept before and during his hypnotic sessions, is structurally identical to such narratives. In January we find him in psychological disarray, alienated from his wife, unable to read or write, and suffering from a variety of physical symptoms. At this point, Strieber tells us, images began to float into his mind. In a state of extreme suggestibility, then, Strieber began reading and talking to friends about UFOs, [Unidentified Flying Objects] a process climaxing with his discovery of an account of an abduction experience that contained some minor correspondences with the images he was "recalling."

Psychological Crisis

This point of contact evidently led to a psychological crisis a few days later:

> I was sitting at my desk when things just seemed to cave in on me. Wave after wave of sorrow passed over me. I looked at the window with hunger. I wanted to jump. I wanted to die. I just could not bear this memory, and I could not get rid of it.

At this precise moment, Strieber contacted Hopkins, who gave him assurances that his memories were indeed similar to those of others. Strieber wept in relief and "went from wanting to hide it all to wanting to understand it." Then Hopkins introduced the idea of looking for a previous encounter, and Strieber—for the first time—began to look at the October 4 events as possibly paranormal. Given this task, Strieber left this interview "a happy man."

Sargant's research leaves little doubt that Strieber was, when he contacted Hopkins, transmarginally excited. Loss of sleep combined with obsessive, uncontrollable thought patterns "overloaded" his brain and left him susceptible to the slightest idea that would give his anxieties a licit avenue. Further, the extreme significance put on small details—the slim correspondences that suddenly seem concrete proof of the visitations' reality—exhibits the paradoxical phase of this process. In Strieber's words, "There did seem to be a lot of confusion . . . and perhaps even an emotional response on my part greatly out of proportion to what seemed a minor disturbance."

Guided Memories

It is not surprising that the hint provided by Hopkins led to the intense moment during Strieber's first hypnosis session in which he suddenly "remembered" the little man by his bed and responded with 20 seconds of prolonged screams. This reaction, common to many other hypnotized "abductees," represents the moment of abreaction, in which the convert's pent-up emotions are released in a controlled way through emotionally reliving the event that the indoctrinator (in this case, Hopkins) has suggested actually caused the anxieties.

Delusions from the Unconscious

I now have zero faith in the premise that UFOs represent anything special in external reality other than misperceptions colored by cultural influences. . . .

I have no doubt that these [visions of alien abduction] are delusions that spring from the unconscious mind. Strieber suspected as much; but what would *you* rather believe if you were in his shoes: that your mind was playing tricks or that you were a "chosen one" intermittently beamed up to a higher realm of being?

Ronald D. Story, *The Skeptical Inquirer*, Spring 1990.

This process has been used therapeutically since World War II to treat stubborn cases of battle shock and trauma. Significantly, Sargant reports, it was found that it was not necessary to make the patient recall real-life incidents. Rather, "it would often be enough to create in him a state of excitement analogous to that which had caused his neurotic condition and keep it up until he collapsed; he would then start to improve. Thus *imagination would have to be used in inventing artificial situations, or distorting actual events. . . .*"

Recognizing this pattern in *Communion* explains why Strieber acts less like a playful hoaxer than a religious convert. Indeed, judging from psychological tests, the conversion experience largely restored his mental health, dispelling his self-destructive tendencies and restoring his writing abilities. Further, Strieber was left with the status of a "chosen one" and a mission whose quasi-religious nature is explicit in the book's title.

From a folklorist's perspective, the two alternatives are not mutually exclusive; indeed, a confusing neurological attack may require a conversion experience to dispel the anxiety produced. Henry James Sr., we note, took the first steps toward regaining his mental health when he learned from a certain Mrs. Chichester that the encounter he had had with evil was known among Swedenborgians as "vastation." And, Hufford reports, one surgeon unnerved by an Old Hag experience was literally reduced to tears when he found it described in psychological literature as "idiopathic SP." Strieber may, then, have fallen into the abductees' camp exactly for the reasons he describes: to find convenient cultural language for a psychological event that otherwise would have to be labeled "fraud" or "madness." If Strieber sincerely believes that he is not consciously fabricating his experience, and if he is not mentally ill, then the hard-line rationalist position, as stated by Taves, gives him no alternative but to proceed on the assumption that the aliens are real. We actually leave him no other psychologically sound option.

The pity is, though, that concepts like "vastation" or "Old Hag" derive from cultural systems with complex psychological checks and balances. To accept the Newfoundland conception of Old Hag, for instance, one must also accept the reality of witchcraft. But the tradition also comes prepared with countercharms—sleeping with a sharp knife, for instance—known to be effective against repeat attacks. Such a practice, like any fetish, would materially reduce the anxieties of the victim (though perhaps not those of his bedmate). The concept "alien abduction," by contrast, leaves the victim unprotected against future visits, which no open knives, strings of garlic, burglar alarms, or concentrated skeptical thought patterns can repel. So accepting the concept may immediately reduce anxieties, but at the cost of inviting recurrent attacks.

Regaining Control

The progress of Strieber's "visitations" after his conversion shows him gaining some degree of psychological control over his visitors—making the visionary face move as he pleases or, in the last scene, actually inviting them to return so that he can show his lack of fear. But it is unclear whether his missionary role will communicate the same control to other troubled souls who may have experienced—or who may find relief in "remembering"—similar events. If the Triad Group that Strieber has formed to collect and analyze abduction accounts actually turns over to qualified professionals a corpus of similar experiences, some good may come from Strieber's missionary work. Competent psychologists may be able to examine the phenomenology of the events described and determine more exactly what mechanisms lie behind them. This in turn may suggest more specific and appropriate psychological treatment for the victims. Time will tell.

In the meantime, the rationalist community needs to be cautious not to commit itself too quickly to a presumption of fraud. Even Baker, as sympathetic as he is to abductees, still suggests that books based on their accounts should be labeled "science fiction," a move that has the effect of calling their stories conscious fictions. Perhaps rationalists (and bookstores) ought to abandon the simple dualism of classifying narratives into "fiction" and "nonfiction" and follow folklorists in their more complex scheme: "tale" (conscious fantasy), "history" (unquestionable fact), and—in the middle—"legend" (alleged but disputable fact). The need of Strieber and other abductees to hedge their accounts with proofs of their veracity is itself proof of the debatable status of their narratives, just as oral accounts of ghosts, manlike apes, and other anomalous phenomena are spiked with details, corroborations, and even disclaimers, to the point of losing the forward motion of the story.

Sargant notes that a sense of humor is one of the surest blocks to conversion, and mirth is doubtless our first line of defense against works like *Communion* that convey a patently missionary message. But humor, like an oversharpened razor carelessly used, may turn on its user. We need to admit that sane, intelligent people may sincerely perceive, or come to believe, that they have been attacked or abducted by paranormal agents. In the case of persons who (like Strieber and, before him, the Hills) seem to be objectively disturbed by memories of abduction, the proper response is not amusement but concern—not over the risk of UFO invaders, but over the treatment of such victims.

We should insist that they receive appropriate professional evaluation and treatment. Otherwise such victims will continue, as we all must, to adjust to life at a high level of uncertainty. At present this means they will seek out those who will listen to their experiences without assuming they are either lying or mentally ill. Unfortunately this leads them to the UFOlogists, whose sympathy inevitably must be less for the suffering individuals than for the value their testimony may have for supporting the extraterrestrial hypothesis.

Whether this price is a fair one for maintaining our own fiction that "intelligent" people do not experience apparently paranormal events, I leave the skeptical community to decide.

"Perhaps we were witnessing a long-term study of humans by an alien race."

Aliens Have Abducted Human Beings

Pamela Weintraub

The following viewpoint is excerpted from an article Pamela Weintraub wrote for *Omni* magazine. In it she describes the experiences of several people who claim to have been abducted by visitors from space. She also discusses the impact such events have on the abductees' lives.

As you read, consider the following questions:

1. Under hypnosis, Steve Kilburn revealed a detailed story of abduction by extraterrestrials. According to the author, what did Kilburn's experience suggest to artist-turned-UFO researcher Budd Hopkins?
2. According to Weintraub, when psychologists studied "abductees," what kind of people did they find?
3. According to this viewpoint, how do alien abductions affect the lives of those who experience them?

Browsing through B. Dalton's in Syracuse, New York, Bruce was alarmed by an eerie display of books. Emblazoned on the covers, staring out at him in multiples from the showcase grid, was a haunting face: grayish skin, pointed chin, receding lips, and massive, dewdrop eyes. The color of molten basalt, the eyes held him mesmerized until he broke their discomfiting gaze. He grabbed the book—Whitley Strieber's best seller *Communion*, about the author's encounters with alienlike "visitors"—off the shelf. "I just looked at it," Bruce says, "then I turned to the manager and said, 'The eyes are wrong.' "

Instantly embarrassed, Bruce left without purchasing the book. *How do I know if the eyes are right or wrong?* he chastised himself. *I didn't draw the picture.*

But a nagging sensation—one so horrific he'd pushed it from his mind for years—told him he might have drawn a picture like the one on the cover of *Communion* himself. As he left the bookstore that day, and for a long time afterward, Bruce says, "memories flooded in like water rushing through a hole in a dike."

Experiencing a UFO

Early one evening during the summer of 1978, it seems, Bruce had been driving home from a relative's house with his wife, Marion, and adopted son, Steven. Scanning the sky, he noticed what seemed like a low-flying plane headed in for a landing. "There was this loud whooshing sound," Bruce recalls. "I thought it was a plane in trouble, trying to land and buzzing me to clear the road. So I sped up, trying to pull away."

But though Bruce remembers pushing the accelerator down full force, the car didn't move at all. In fact, he says, the rubber on the tires began to burn, and the whole vehicle started to overheat. "I figured," Bruce recalls, "that the best thing to do was to shut the car down."

A second later, Marion looked out the window and let out a bloodcurdling scream. Bruce locked the doors, rolled up the windows, and threw a blanket over Steven, instructing him not to move. Then, looking behind him, he saw some figures approaching. "What registers in my mind," he says, "are two very formal military figures. Their uniforms were homogeneous— beige from the neck up and black from the neck down.

By this time, Bruce recalls, Marion's behavior had become bizarre. "She's under the impression that the door is unlocked instead of locked. So she keeps trying to lock it, but she's doing just the opposite. And she believes the window is down instead of up. So she's rolling it down, *thinking* that she's rolling it up. There's this struggle between us to keep the door locked. She's getting very mean, almost like a cornered dog. And then she lets out another scream. I spin around, and oh, my God, I'm staring into these humongous eyes. I'm transfixed. All of a sudden I hear a door slam behind me, and Marion is gone. She's just walking along with this guy, sort of on a stroll toward, well, for lack of a better word, a ship."

"I'm getting tired of being mistaken for a weather balloon!"

According to Bruce, he leaped out the door to try to get Marion back when three more figures surrounded him. "My sense of self-preservation," Bruce says, "was suddenly very strong. I was curious, but I didn't want to risk going on that ship, so I did something I'm not proud of. I tried to see if I could send Steven, who would tell me what he saw. Should he not return, then I would have evidence I could take to the authorities. So I pulled the seat forward and leaned in to get Steven, and that's when I was jabbed. Right in the rear. I felt like I'd been poked with a hatpin."

From that point on, Bruce says, everything was cloudy. He was, he's sure, dragged down the road a bit. But the next thing he knew, he was back in his car with Marion and Steven, driving home. The family returned two hours later than expected. As far as the "experience" was concerned, nothing was said.

Bruce's chilling story (and the accompanying block of missing time for which he could not account) makes him one of the growing number of people who claim to be UFO abductees. The abductees say, among other things, that large-eyed, gray-skinned, four-foot-tall aliens are swooping down from the skies to take them away. These ghoulish visitors put their victims in a trance and literally float them out of car or bedroom windows onto spherical ships. The medical examinations that reportedly occur aboard alien vehicles are painful and extreme: Biopsies (later appearing on the skin as long, straight cuts or simply as scoops) are performed on arms and legs. Transponder implants that enable aliens to track their subjects like caribou are inserted in the eyes, nose, ears, and even the brain. And most disturbing of all, painful surgical procedures remove human eggs and sperm. The result, many abductees contend, is a race of human-alien hybrids gestated in artificial wombs, raised in alien nurseries, and sent, ultimately, into the unknown reaches of space. The hybrids' suspected purpose: to provide a genetic shot in the arm and new evolutionary vigor for the ailing alien race.

Hundreds Report Abductions

Hearing such stories, one has the natural instinct to give the so-called abductee a wayward glance and run. But these days that's hard to do. Hundreds of people worldwide, in countries from Canada to Brazil, now claim the abduction experience. What's more, the strange details they conjure up—from the appearance of the visitors to the surgical procedures they perform to the symbols on the alien ship—are often uncannily similar. And the half dozen respected psychiatrists and psychologists who have studied this odd group find no evidence of psychopathology. The abductees have suffered a severe, unspeakable trauma, yes. Most are overly cautious, many neurotic. But according to a spate of standard personality and intelligence tests, the question of whether the abductees are *crazy* can be unequivocally answered with a no.

Explanations put forth by experts in a variety of fields are numerous: repressed rape or child abuse, ancient racial memories stored in the genes, mass hysteria, culturally induced dreams, transcendental right-brain states, and more. Some have said that the abductees form the core of a powerful new religion, one sure to supplant Christianity and subvert the progress of science. Others, including more than a few of the abductees, insist the reports are literal and the experiences real. . . .

The dispute would be settled, of course, if UFOlogists could come up with some aliens. But much to their chagrin, the E.T.'s [extraterrestrials] appeared, full-blown, in the stories of a group of charlatans known as the contactees. In the standard contactee story, the Earthling was sitting in his yard when gorgeous, Nordic-looking aliens swooped down from the sky. These benevolent E.T.'s eagerly told the contactee about the secrets of propulsion and the mysteries of their home planet—invariably an Eden with no taxes, no divorce, and no war. One contactee said he went to the moon and dined with the lunar king. Another said he went to Jupiter and brought back a native dog that, oddly enough, looked like a Saint Bernard. Whatever the specifics, the contactee was always given a mission: to try to stop atomic testing, end all wars, and promote peace on Earth. Such a mandate, of course, meant forming organizations, writing books, hitting the lecture circuit, and producing record albums of music from Pluto—all for a hefty profit. Hundreds of deluded people ended up converting to UFO religions and cults, but as the tall tales and questionable activities of the contactees continued, the field of UFOlogy itself fell into disrepute.

The Ten Most Common Signs of Abductions by Extraterrestrials

- Inability to account for periods of time
- Persistent nightmares and/or dreams of UFOs and/or aliens
- Sleep disorders
- Waking up with unusual bodily sensations
- Appearance of mysterious marks on the body
- Feeling monitored, watched, and/or communicated with
- Repeated sightings of UFOs
- Vague recollections of a close encounter
- Unexplained healing of ailments or afflictions
- Reacting with fear of and/or anxiety about UFOs and/or ETs

Edith Fiore, *Encounters*, 1989.

In the aftermath of this hysteria there emerged one contact story different from the rest: the saga of Betty and Barney Hill. Barney was a black post-office worker and an official in the New Hampshire NAACP [National Association for the Advancement of Colored People]. Betty was a white social worker. Coming back from a vacation in Canada, they reportedly saw what would be called a typical UFO. Then Barney inexplicably turned left onto a side road. That was all the Hills remembered until two hours later, when they found themselves 35 miles farther down the road, without any idea how they had gotten there.

They began to have bad dreams and finally went to see psychiatrist Benjamin Simon, who used hypnotic regression to bring them back to the incident. Under hypnosis the Hills said that extraterrestrials had impelled them to leave the car and walk to the craft, where they were separated and given examinations. Betty said they stuck a needle in her navel and then took skin and nail samples. Barney claimed they took a sample of his sperm.

Like most other skeptics of the day, Budd Hopkins, a young artist splitting his time between Cape Cod and New York City, didn't think much of this story. But one day in 1964, while driving to an afternoon party in Provincetown, he saw an elliptical, pewter-colored object hovering over the dunes. After three minutes, it seemed to Hopkins, the object simply zoomed off, disappearing in the clouds.

At the party Hopkins discussed his experience, only to find that other guests had had similar sightings as well. That summer Hopkins bought a couple of UFO books. And every now and then he brought the subject up at a party.

But his interest in UFOs didn't intensify until 1975, when George O'Barski, owner of the liquor store across from Hopkins's Manhattan town house, had a sighting of his own. "I walked in to get a bottle of Soave for dinner," Hopkins recalls, "and I found George pacing back and forth behind the counter, obviously disturbed. 'A man can be driving home, minding his own business,' O'Barski fumed, 'and something can come down out of the sky and scare him half to death.'"

The story he then told Hopkins was incredible, to say the least. O'Barski lived in North Bergen, New Jersey, and, as was his habit, he'd been driving his car through North Hudson Park on the way to an all-night diner in Fort Lee after work. As he passed through the park, O'Barski said, he saw a roundish, 30-foot-long ship circumscribed by windows. Then he watched in disbelief as a narrow panel opened to release a ladder. Down the ladder climbed some ten humanlike figures, each three and a half to four feet tall and wearing a one-piece, light-colored garment. The figures carried spoonlike instruments and containers, O'Barski claimed, and proceeded to collect samples of the earth. Inside of four minutes the strange individuals and their craft were gone.

Hopkins investigated the story, found five corroborating witnesses (not to the occupants, just to the apparent craft), and published his findings in *The Village Voice*. The *Voice* story was reprinted in *Cosmopolitan*, and Hopkins's avocation—as a UFO-logist—was off to a start.

Hypnotism and Missing Time

Even back then Hopkins was aware of the issue of missing time. O'Barski, who claimed his sighting lasted four minutes, had returned home a couple of hours after he would have on any normal night. But it wasn't until 1976 that Hopkins considered a preposterous notion: What if UFO witnesses were losing track of hours, even days, because aliens were abducting them, then forcing them to forget?

That idea walked into Hopkins's life in the form of Steve Kilburn (not his real name), a tennis instructor he'd met through one of the investigators helping with the O'Barski case. One day, after an informal UFO gathering that Kilburn happened to attend, he approached Hopkins nervously. "There's probably nothing to it," he confided, perhaps because Hopkins seemed more accessible than others at the meeting, "but something may have happened to me when I was in college. I can't remember anything specific, but something has always bothered me about a certain stretch of road I used to pass through whenever I left my girlfriend's house in Maryland." Kilburn recalled no strange lights in the sky, and he only *suspected* a gap of missing time. Nonetheless, he told Hopkins, "I'd like to try hypnosis just to see if there's anything at all to my feeling."

Unbelievable Possibility

Many scientists in fact maintain an active interest in SETI—the search for extraterrestrial intelligence. And yet almost none of these scientists have taken the time to look into the UFO phenomenon as it inarguably exists: a phenomenon consisting of tens of thousands of reports of apparent craft sightings, landings, photo and radar evidence and accounts of the temporary abduction and examination of human beings. . . .

There is an all-too-human reason for this lack of curiosity. . . . The possibility that extraterrestrial intelligence may already be visiting our planet, as the UFO evidence implies, and treating the human species as laboratory specimens for some elusive and perhaps unfathomable purpose—that is a truly disturbing idea. We all know, of course, a basic scientific truth: It can't happen here.

Budd Hopkins, *Intruders*, 1987.

Encouraged by the O'Barski episode, Hopkins agreed to help. He recruited New York psychologist Aphrodite Clamar, referred to him by psychiatrist Robert J. Lifton, Hopkins's friend and an expert in the psychology of survivors. Known for her deft use of hypnotism in psychotherapy, Clamar is as down-to-earth as her name is exotic (her family is Greek). Combining a strong skepticism of UFOs with the unique ability to suspend judgment, no matter how extraordinary a client's claim, Clamar put Kilburn into a deep trance. To abate his fear, she provided him with a protective image: "a warm, solid house to stay in, safe from everything threatening, but from which you will be able to watch any events that might unfold outside."

From the depths of hypnosis Kilburn explained that while driving home on the night in question, he'd grown increasingly drowsy, until he felt his car turn violently, "like a huge magnet just sucked it over to the right." Looking up into the sky, he noticed two strange lights. To ease his fear he pulled the car over and stepped out. Walking down the road a bit, he said, he met with four or five tiny individuals, including one who seemed to be the boss. Their faces were dull, chalky white, "like putty," he told Clamar; and their walnut-shaped eyes, devoid of pupils, were huge and liquid black. One was bending down, digging in the earth.

Kilburn also recalled a clamp, "almost like an arm," affixed to his right shoulder. At this point, he told Clamar, he was totally paralyzed, and the creatures used the instrument to turn him around. The next thing Kilburn knew, he was walking up a ramp. Sitting on a table in a curved, misty-white room, beneath an elaborate diagnostic instrument hanging from the ceiling, he felt the excruciating pain of a needle running along his spine. He was examined over the length of his body: hips, stomach, arms, legs, and thighs. "I feel like a frog," he told Clamar at one point in the session. . . .

Repressed Experiences

Kilburn's story shook Hopkins to his roots. "It was nothing I wanted to accept," Hopkins says. "Yet it seemed totally real." What's more, it seemed to fly in the face of the traditional abduction scenario established by Betty and Barney Hill. Instead of remembering portions of the UFO experience consciously, as the Hills had, Kilburn had totally suppressed his experience. "This opened up the possibility that the experience, whatever it was, had been suppressed in others," Hopkins explains, "and that abduction was widespread.". . .

By 1981 Hopkins and Clamar had worked with 11 abductees. As a professional psychologist, Clamar didn't particularly believe that bona fide aliens were coming to Earth. She was impressed, however, by her clients' "frightening experiences, which both mystified and disturbed them. I did not find any drug users among the subjects, nor any alcoholism, nor any strange habits or exotic perversions," she says. "Most were satisfied with their choice of careers and relatively successful. In a sense," she adds, "they were run-of-the-mill people. I could find no common thread that tied them together—other than their UFO experiences—and no common pathology, indeed, no discernible pathology at all."

Clamar didn't know what to make of the group; nor did she *want* to impose an interpretation on the incredible reports. But, she suggested to Hopkins, it would be advisable to subject some abductees to an independent battery of psychological tests.

"Here was a group of people who had consistently bad press, who were described as crazy, paranoid, and marginal," Clamar says. "Yet the people I hypnotized did not appear to fit these stereotypes. This, however, was only my impression, not a fact that I could support with hard data. I wanted a way to quantify the abduction experience and its effect."

So Clamar and Hopkins went ahead and recruited New York psychologist Elizabeth Slater, who tested nine group members for, among other things, creative potential. She was not told that they were in any way involved with UFOs. Slater administered a Rorschach test, in which subjects are asked to interpret ink-blots; the Bender Gestalt test, in which they reproduce geometric figures; the Wechsler adult intelligence test; the thematic apperception test in which testees described a series of pictures; and the Minnesota multiphasic personality inventory, which profiles individuals and evaluates their tendency to lie.

After completing her study Slater reported that except for one person—a schizophrenic—the group showed no particular psychopathology. "These people didn't seem alike in any way except for their tendency to be overly sensitive, guarded, and vigilant," she says. "They were careful but not paranoid, and they shared a greater than average intelligence and a richness of inner life.

"When I found out these people claimed to be abductees," Slater adds, "I was flabbergasted. I tend to be a skeptical person, but I find their stories hard to dismiss. I worked on an inpatient unit for two years, and I'd never heard such stories. People reported the CIA [Central Intelligence Agency] was bugging their phones, they heard the voice of the Devil, or they had a desire to kill themselves or their spouses. But alien abduction is something that I had just never heard. I won't say I believe these people were abducted, but I do believe they aren't crazy. I have no explanation for this group. Psychologists, moreover, can't demonstrate facts. They can only try to understand what people experience and perceive."

Psychological Profiles

To get to the bottom of the claims, Hopkins and Clamar also sent ten abductees to Donald Klein, director of research at the New York State Psychiatric Institute. Klein had offered to do psychohistories—psychological profiles taking the subjects' entire lives into account—to see whether he could find anything to account for their stories and claims. Working with staff psychiatrist Abigail Feuer, Klein found that all ten abductees, including author Whitley Strieber, were sane. The researchers found a high degree of anxiety in all the subjects, to be sure. One of the ten had somewhat of an alcohol problem. But nobody emerged as a sexually abused child or the victim of an alcoholic parent. No patterns, no trauma, no insanity, and no psychological explanation emerged. In other words, the institute team found nothing that in any way would suggest a cause.

While psychologists claimed merely that the abductees were sane, Hopkins decided to take a stand. Perhaps we were witnessing a long-term study of humans by an alien race, he suggested, who "could be fitting our children with monitoring devices and extracting them decades later." The purpose he did not know.

"Most UFO reports . . . if carefully investigated, become IFOs—that is, Identified Flying Objects."

Alien Abductions Can Be Explained

Paul Kurtz

Noted philosopher and skeptic Paul Kurtz is the author of numerous books, several of them on paranormal topics. He is also editor of the humanist magazine *Free Inquiry.* In the following viewpoint, Kurtz discusses two prominent cases of purported abductions of humans by extraterrestrials and suggests that natural events, fantasy, the power of suggestion, and hoaxes are likely explanations.

As you read, consider the following questions:

1. According to the author, what are some of the common causes that turn UFOs into IFOs.
2. List the main alternative explanation Kurtz offers in each of the UFO abductions described in this viewpoint.
3. Why does Kurtz believe people continue to believe in UFO "myths"?

Excerpted, with permission, from *The Transcendental Temptation: A Critique of Religion and the Paranormal* by Paul Kurtz. Buffalo, NY: Prometheus Books, 1986.

꜀ꓱodern UFOlogy began on June 24, 1947, when Kenneth Arnold reported that he saw a formation of nine disclike objects over Mt. Rainier, in the state of Washington. Arnold said that each disc resembled a "saucer skipping over water." His claims were given worldwide attention, and subsequently "flying saucer" sightings have been reported by tens of thousands throughout the world. Believers run into the millions. In some years, UFO [Unidentified Flying Objects] reports became epidemic, and public interest increased enormously. These reports have come from most countries in the world, and from all strata of society. Are extraterrestrial beings and spacecraft visiting and observing life on the planet earth?

The accounts of UFOs have varied, but there seems to be a common syndrome: strange objects in the sky, cylindrical or saucer-shaped, glowing or flickering lights, making beeping noises, darting about at incredible speeds, taking off at odd angles, suddenly standing still, or disappearing. There have been many reports of human encounters with humanoid creatures who came out of these saucers, and even incredible accounts of having been abducted, examined, taken to other galaxies and then returned to earth.

Evaluating Claims

What is genuine in these accounts, and what is sheer fantasy? If we are committed to the empirical method, must we not take the testimony of eyewitnesses seriously? These reports were not rare or isolated in number, but have been numerous. There are at least two salient considerations: (1) Did the events occur as reported? (2) How should we interpret what people claimed to have seen? Can natural explanations be given?

UFOlogy divides into two major camps: (1) UFO believers who are convinced that at least some of the UFOs are extraterrestrial in origin, and that knowledge of them is being systematically withheld from the public by national governments (but for what purpose is unclear). (2) Skeptics who have examined the evidence and have offered prosaic natural interpretations of the phenomena. Most UFO reports, they say, if carefully investigated, become IFOs—that is, Identified Flying Objects, objects in the sky that are commonly misperceived or misinterpreted. Most of the accounts can be explained as bright stars, the moon, or planets that stand out in the sky (Venus, Mars, Jupiter), meteors, weather and other balloons, helicopters, passenger or military planes, missile launches, reentering manmade rockets and satellites, searchlights, flares, fixed ground lights, and other visual anomalies—even birds, bolt lightning, kites, or unusual cloud formations. In some cases, sightings have been a prank or hoax. Not all UFOs have been identified, primarily because there is no evidence corroborating the claims of the initial eye-witnesses. Thus an air of mystery attends those cases that still have not been fully explained to everyone's satisfaction.

Reprinted with permission of *The Skeptical Inquirer.*

Let us examine some of the classic cases. I will focus on [two] of the most highly discussed instances of abduction, by witnesses who claim to have had direct encounters with extraterrestrials.

Betty and Barney Hill

J. Allen Hynek, noted UFO investigator and astronomer, has labeled abduction cases "close encounters of the third kind." No doubt the most celebrated case and also the most thoroughly documented abduction on record is that of Betty and Barney Hill, residents of Whitfield, New Hampshire. According to their testimony, they were driving in northern New Hampshire on their way home from a vacation in Montreal on the evening of September 19, 1961. Sometime between 10:00 P.M. and midnight, their attention was captured by an erratically moving light in the sky, which seemed to be following their car. The sky was clear and the moon was shining brightly, low in the southwest. Betty said that she had seen a star or planet below the moon, but soon afterwards, she reported, she saw a second object in the sky, which was a bigger and brighter "star" above the first object. This, she said, was a UFO. Barney at first believed it to be an ordinary object, perhaps an airplane or satellite, but Betty claimed it was a flying saucer and insisted that Barney stop the car and look at it. "It's amazing," she exclaimed.

Barney got out of the car, looked at the object with binoculars, and thought he saw a double row of lighted windows and aliens within, sneering at him and turning their backs to pull levers. The leader of the aliens appeared to be a "Nazi," he said. Terrified, he jumped back into the car and they hastily drove off. Betty reported that Barney was in a "hysterical condition," fearing that they were going to be captured. The aerial craft, they alleged, continued to follow their car. It was at this point that their journey was supposedly interrupted. According to the story, they heard a short series of beeping sounds coming from the rear of the car, which caused the car to vibrate. They said that they lapsed into drowsiness. When they regained consciousness, they found that two hours had elapsed and that they were some thirty-five miles south of where the beeping sounds had begun.

Intense Questioning

The Hills were subjected to intense questioning by dedicated UFO proponents, who met with them within weeks following the alleged encounter. They were plagued by nervous disorders and frightening dreams and nightmares about being taken aboard an extraterrestrial spacecraft. After two years, Barney was so disturbed that he was forced to seek the help of a psychiatrist, Dr. Benjamin Simon of Boston. Under hypnosis, Barney and Betty Hill attempted to account for the "two lost hours." They told of being taken aboard the spacecraft and of being examined by the strange creatures. Moreover, Betty Hill claimed to have seen a "star map," which described the star system from which the UFO came. Fifteen stars on this map were allegedly matched by Marjorie Fish, an elementary school teacher, to stars in the sky, and this is often cited by UFO believers as independent confirmation that the Hills' story is true. Betty's tale is concluded when she and Barney were returned to the car some two hours later.

What is to be made of this famous case? Robert Sheaffer, a

UFO skeptic, reports that if we consult weather reports and astronomical charts of that day, we can piece together certain facts: the moon was shining, the first planet they saw was Saturn, and the other bright object was probably Jupiter, which had reached the position they described. If one is riding along in a car, it appears that the planet is moving when the car does. "If a genuine UFO had been present, there would have been three objects near the moon that night: Jupiter, Saturn, and the UFO. Yet they reported seeing only two."

Were their imaginations responsible for the rest of their story? It is interesting that Dr. Simon, who put the Hills under hypnosis two years after the event, held that the entire event "was a fantasy . . . in other words, it was a dream. The abduction did not happen." According to Dr. Simon, Betty had described many specific details of the abduction, whereas Barney seemed to remember almost nothing. Dr. Simon indicated that the abduction incident was *not* a common, shared experience, and it is suggested that Barney had derived his knowledge of the alleged abduction from hearing Betty recount her dreams. Dr. Simon told Philip Klass he did not believe the Hills had been abducted, but rather that the story was a fantasy they had come to believe and retold under hypnosis.

What about the star map Betty saw? Sheaffer points out that the map could match many areas of the sky, that there are many star patterns which would fit Betty's sketch. Some UFO believers maintain that radar sightings at that time corroborate the story. Pease Air Force Base in Portsmouth, New Hampshire, several miles away, reported an unidentified object on its radar at 2:14 A.M., but there was no corroboration by the Airport Surveillance Radar. Sheaffer maintains that radars are sensitive to many targets, including even birds and insects. Moreover, the radar anomaly occurred later, many miles away. Thus, there is actually no independent corroboration of the Hills' "eyewitness testimony" of the encounter.

UFO Landings

Indeed, subsequent developments in the Hill case strain our credulity further. Betty Hill, in 1977, began talking about a "UFO landing spot" in southern New Hampshire, which she would visit three times a week to observe UFOs. Even UFO devotees have avowed that she is able to see UFOs when no one with her can. On one occasion, reports John Oswald, field investigator for a UFO group (who accepts abduction stories), Mrs. Hill was unable to "distinguish between a landed UFO and a street light." This raises the interesting question of whether UFO abduction reports are like mystical or revelatory experiences, uncorroborated but built up out of firmly held psychological convictions. . . .

A second highly publicized event occurred on October 11,

1973, in Pascagoula, Mississippi. Two shipyard workers, Charles Hickson, 42, and Calvin Parker, 19, claimed to have been kidnapped by a UFO while fishing on the Pascagoula River. They maintained that they heard a buzzing or zipping sound, and saw a round flying saucer hovering over the ground. The vehicle was flashing blue lights. Hickson's accounts of the event were contradictory. On one occasion he said that the vehicle was eight to ten feet wide, and on another he described it as twenty to thirty feet long. According to his account, three humanoids emerged from the UFO and floated toward Hickson and Parker. They were described as about five feet tall, with grey crumpled skin, elephantlike, egg-shaped heads, no necks, and clawlike arms. Two of the creatures took hold of Hickson and floated him aboard the UFO, where he was taken into a brightly lit chamber. A third creature grabbed Parker, who fainted, and also floated him into the craft. The humanoids examined Hickson with an object that resembled an eye but was not attached to anything. He felt completely paralyzed when they did so. About twenty minutes later they floated Hickson outside, where he rejoined the greatly disturbed Parker, who had regained consciousness. The UFO then shot straight up and disappeared. Parker, having passed out, was unable to supply any details of the event. After several hours, the two men got up enough courage to relate their tale to the sheriff, and this miraculous incident rapidly became public news.

Flimsy Tales

Most psychologists agree that such tales [of alien abduction] spring not from the alien world of extraterrestrials but from the dark interior world of the human psyche.

Psychologists and other researchers generally agree that abduction evidence produced by UFOologists is flimsy at best and fraudulent at worst, most accurately described as science-fiction cultism.

Elizabeth Bird, *Psychology Today*, April 1989.

What are we to make of this incredible story? Was it verifiable? Should it be accepted as a genuine encounter? The UFO buffs—a group of committed believers—seem to have almost a quasi-religious desire to accept the E.T. [extraterrestrial] hypothesis. Hickson and Parker were interviewed by two well-known UFO experts, Professor James A. Harder and Dr. J. Allen Hynek. Harder concluded that "there was definitely something here that was not terrestrial. . . . Where they came from and why they were here is a matter of conjecture, but the fact that they are here is true, beyond a reasonable doubt." And Hynek cautiously maintained, "There is no question in my mind that these two men have had a very terrifying experience. Additional credibility was given to Hickson's testimony when it was revealed that he had taken a lie-detector test. Meanwhile, the case aroused a great deal of interest, especially in the Mississippi area, where there were a number of similar reports of UFOs.

A Clever Hoax?

Fortunately this case, like the previous case, has been examined by skeptics, who can provide alternative explanations. Klass maintains that the evidence points to the strong possibility of its being a cleverly contrived hoax. According to Klass, the lie-detector test was given to Hickson by an inexperienced operator. Efforts to get Hickson to take another test or to test Parker were unsuccessful. Klass discovered that Hickson had filed for bankruptcy a few months earlier. He speculated that Hickson hoped that his story would lead to film or TV offers, motives that one can only infer and not confirm.

What are we to make of these abduction cases? Are they hoaxes? Were the accounts of the abductees simply hallucinations, or was there a combination of motives? Some commentators have found similarities between abduction stories, near-death experiences, and drug-induced hallucinations. The common threads running through these stories are similar: the seeing of a bright light, a buzzing sound, a sense of floating out of one's body, moving through a tunnel or corridor, encountering a being or beings bathed in light, undergoing examination, and then returning to real life. This leads one to speculate whether the transcendental temptation is also an important factor in the UFO phenomenon—not only for the 200 or more reported abductions but also in the general population's willingness to believe in the phenomenon. UFOlogy, at least for some, seems to function as a quasi-religious phenomenon.

Millions of people claim to have seen strange things in the sky that they cannot explain by natural means, and which they attribute to an extraterrestrial, out-of-this-world source. Unable to give a causal explanation, they read in a magical account, reminiscent of spiritual, psychic, paranormal, supernatural, or other miraculous events. Is a similar, subtle, psychological process at work, with only the content of the beliefs differing but the origin and function the same?. . .

A Worldwide Phenomenon

What is the evidence in support of the UFO–E.T. hypothesis? I have referred to two of the most famous abduction cases, but actually the number of sightings of UFOs is enormous. In the United States, something like 9 percent of the population, millions of people, claim to have seen a UFO (according to a Gallup poll of 1978). Fifty-six percent of the population say that they believe in UFOs. This is repeated worldwide, so that we are dealing with phenomena of mass proportions. Generally, the "sightings" are of strange lights or objects in the sky behaving in bizarre ways, hovering and darting about at unexpected angles. This is the age of air travel, so people are accustomed to look skyward and see balloons, helicopters, propeller and jet airplanes, rockets, and missiles—all phenomena that would have seemed strange in earlier centuries. But they are also puzzled by other things they think are anomalous and inexplicable.

In 1952, the U.S. Air Force launched a special inquiry, Project Blue Book, to investigate such phenomena. It dealt with approximately 13,000 cases of alleged sightings. After an extended study, the Air Force concluded there was no evidence for the supposition that the phenomena were extraterrestrial. It maintained that it was able to explain approximately 94 percent of the sightings as due to natural causes. The overwhelming majority of cases were based on simple misperceptions and misinterpretations, even by highly trained airline pilots, engineers, and scientists. A lengthy study conducted at the University of Colorado, known as the Condon Report, recommended in 1969 that no further study be made by the Air Force, even though some cases remained "unexplained." UFO believers often point to that fact as significant, but this does not necessarily confirm the extraterrestrial hypothesis, but simply indicates that there is not sufficient data to determine what was present or to corroborate the testimony of eyewitnesses. Not every murder has been solved by police departments, but we are not entitled to suppose that a paranormal agent committed unsolved murders. The burden of proof rests with the advocates of the extraterrestrial hypothesis. And they have not produced sufficient evidence.

Most UFOs Become IFOs

In another important study, Allan Hendry, associated with the Center for UFO Studies, reviewed over 1,300 UFO reports that occurred in a fourteen-month period (August 1976 to November 1977) in the United States. He interviewed, largely by telephone, witnesses who had reported UFO sightings. He concluded that prosaic explanations could account for the great majority of such reports. Hendry found that the reports were global in nature, came from all parts of the United States, and were made by a cross-section of individuals representing all ages, occupations, and educational backgrounds. Reports were of various kinds: those that were "close" (that is, a UFO which was said to appear within 500 feet of the witness), those that influenced the environment (and allegedly left some physical trace), and those that involved meeting occupants or entities. In the 1,307 cases that Hendry investigated, 1,158 were readily translated by him into IFOs (88.6%), 36 cases were excluded as not providing appropriate data (2.8%), and only 113 cases (8.6%) remained as unidentified phenomena. Hendry confesses at the end of his case-by-case study that he was "*still* no closer to the nature of this complex beast" than when he started. He says that much or most of the data is anecdotal testimony of excited witnesses. "*Never* does the evidence suddenly allow a burst of approval for even one UFO, that is, for the extraterrestrial explanation.

What Hendry has uncovered is surely significant. For it is clear that after decades of searching, we still do not have one incontrovertible case that stands up under careful scrutiny. We have no decisive proof, no hard corroborating evidence, that UFOs are extraterrestrial. Perhaps by continuing to investigate such sightings, we will some day discover sufficiently hard and rigorous evidence to corroborate the claim unambiguously. But until we do, an alternative explanation is available, namely, that the UFO phenomenon tells us something about the psychological and sociological behavior of the human species, of the fascination with the unknown, and the hunger for belief in the existence of realities beyond.

Mythology of the Space Age

Here we find the reappearance of a common thread. UFOlogy is the mythology of the space age. Rather than angels dancing on the heads of pins, we now have spacecraft and extraterrestrials. It is the product of the creative imagination. It serves a poetic and existential function. It seeks to give man deeper roots and bearings in the universe. It is an expression of our hunger for mystery, our demand for something more, our hope for transcendental meaning. The gods of Mt. Olympus have been transformed into space voyagers, transporting us by our dreams to other realms. The transcendental temptation has again overcome us. And so we see what we want. We fashion a universe to our liking.

"Psychology provides naturalistic and satisfying explanations for [alien abduction experiences]."

Alien Abductions Can Be Explained Psychologically

Robert A. Baker

Robert A. Baker, professor of psychology at the University of Kentucky in Lexington, writes frequently about the UFO experience. He believes that most "alien abductions" can be explained as a result of psychological factors. In the following viewpoint, he discusses several possible reasons for the experiences many people describe.

As you read, consider the following questions:

1. List the five explanations the author gives for UFO abduction accounts.
2. Does Baker think that people who believe they have been abducted by extraterrestrials should be believed?
3. Why does Baker feel that encouragement of belief in UFO "fantasies" is harmful?

Robert A. Baker, "The Aliens Among Us: Hypnotic Regression Revisited," *The Skeptical Inquirer*, Winter 1987-1988. Reprinted with permission.

For the average person walking down the aisle of a modern bookstore or passing through the checkout lane at the nearest supermarket, it would be easy to conclude that aliens from outer space not only are here but also have joined the Baptist church, have put their kids in school, and belong to the Rotary Club. This conclusion is demanded by the recent rash of nonfiction books about UFO [Unidentified Flying Object] contacts, encounters of the third kind, and human abductions by little gray men from outer space or some other parallel universe. Typical of these tomes are *Communion*, by Whitley Strieber; *Intruders*, by Budd Hopkins; and *Light Years: An Investigation into the Extraterrestrial Experience of Eduard Meier*, by Gary Kinder. According to these and other UFO pundits, abductions by "little gray aliens" are so prevalent they will soon become commonplace and generally accepted as a fact of life by a now skeptical public and press.

My friends and colleagues and I, however, are beginning to believe that we have Alien B.O. or something worse, because none of us has been contacted, interviewed, briefed, threatened, kidnapped, or physically examined by any of the little folk. We, sadly enough, have not even had our car stalled by one of their spaceships. It stalls on occasion, but the problem lies in Detroit rather than with the aliens. Could all this alien activity going on around us be overlooked by responsible authorities? . . .

Most people seem unaware of the fact that there is an already well established branch of psychology, anomalistic psychology, that deals specifically with the kind of experiences had by Strieber, Meier, and the other UFO abductees. This psychology provides naturalistic and satisfying explanations for the entire range of such behaviors. Let us examine these explanations a little more closely and in a little more detail.

Hypnosis and Hypnotic Regression

In France in the 1770s, when Mesmerism was in its heyday, the king appointed two commissions to investigate Mesmer's activities. The commissions included such eminent men as Benjamin Franklin, Lavoisier, and Jean-Sylvain Bailly, the French astronomer. After months of study the report of the commissioners concluded that it was *imagination*, not magnetism, that accounted for the swooning, trancelike rigidity of Mesmer's subjects. Surprisingly enough, this conclusion is still closer to the truth about hypnosis than most of the modern definitions found in today's textbooks.

So-called authorities still disagree about "hypnosis." But whether it is or is not a "state," there is common and widespread agreement among all the major disputants that "hypnosis" is a situation in which people set aside critical judgment (without abandoning it entirely) and engage in make-believe and fantasy; that is, they use their imagination. As stated earlier, there are great individual differences in the ability to fantasize, and in recent years many authorities have made it a *requirement* for any successful "hypnotic" performance. [Psychologist] Josephine Hilgard refers to hypnosis as "imaginative involvement," T.R. Sarbin and W.C. Coe term it "believed-in imaginings," N.P. Spanos and T.X. Barber call it "involvement in suggestion-related imaginings," and J.P. Sutcliffe has gone so far as to characterize the hypnotizable individual as someone who is "deluded in a descriptive, nonpejorative sense" and he sees the hypnotic situation as an arena in which people who are skilled at make-believe and fantasy are provided with the opportunity and the means to do what they enjoy doing and what they are able to do especially well. . . .

Confabulation

Confabulation, or the tendency of ordinary, sane individuals to confuse fact with fiction and to report fantasized events as actual occurrences, has surfaced in just about every situation in which a person has attempted to remember very specific details from the past. A classical and amusing example occurs in the movie *Gigi*, in the scene where Maurice Chevalier and Hermione Gingold compare memories of their courtship in the song "I Remember It Well." We remember things not the way they really were but the way we would have liked them to have been.

The work of Elizabeth Loftus and others over the past decade has demonstrated that the human memory works not like a tape recorder but more like the village storyteller—i.e., it is both creative and recreative. We can and we do easily forget. We blur, shape, erase, and change details of the events in our past. Many people walk around daily with heads full of "fake memories." Moreover, the unreliability of eyewitness testimony is not only legendary but well documented. When all of this is further complicated and compounded by the impact of suggestions provided by the hypnotist plus the social-demand characteristics of the typical hypnotic situation, little wonder that the resulting recall on the part of the regressee bears no resemblance to the truth. *In fact, the regressee often does not know what the truth is.*

Confabulation shows up without fail in nearly every context in which hypnosis is employed, including the forensic area. Thus it is not surprising that most states have no legal precedents on the use of hypnotic testimony. Furthermore, many state courts have begun to limit testimony from hypnotized witnesses or to follow the guidelines laid down by the American Medical Association in 1985 to assure that witnesses' memories are not contaminated by the hypnosis itself. For not only do we translate beliefs into memories when we are wide awake, but in the case of hypnotized witnesses with few specific memories the hypnotist may unwittingly suggest memories and create a witness with a number of crucial and vivid recollections of events that never happened, i.e., pseudo-memories. . . .

Reprinted with permission of *The Skeptical Inquirer.*

There have also been a number of clinical and experimental demonstrations of the creation of pseudo-memories that have subsequently come to be believed as veridical. Ernest R. Hilgard implanted a false memory of an experience connected with a bank robbery that never occurred. His subject found the experience so vivid that he was able to select from a series of photographs a picture of the man he thought had committed the robbery. At another time, Hilgard deliberately assigned two concurrent—though spatially different—life experiences to the same person and regressed him at separate times to *that date*. The individual subsequently gave very accurate accounts of both experiences, so that anyone believing in reincarnation who reviewed the two accounts would conclude the man *really had* lived the two assigned lives.

In a number of other experiments designed to measure eyewitness reliability, Elizabeth Loftus found that details supplied by others invariably contaminated the memory of the eyewitness. People's hair changed color, stop signs became yield signs, yellow convertibles turned to red sedans, the left side of the street became the right-hand side, and so on. The results of these studies led her to conclude, "It may well be that the legal notion of an independent recollection is a psychological impossibility." As for hypnosis, she says: "There's no way even the most sophisticated hypnotist can tell the difference between a memory that is real and one that's created. If a person is hypnotized and highly suggestible and false information is implanted in his mind, it may get embedded even more strongly. One psychologist tried to use a polygraph to distinguish between real and phony memory, but it didn't work. Once someone has constructed a memory, he comes to believe it himself."

Cueing: Inadvertent and Advertent

Without a doubt, inadvertent cueing also plays a major role in UFO-abduction fantasies. The hypnotist unintentionally gives away to the person being regressed exactly what response is wanted. This was most clearly shown in an experimental study of hypnotic age regression by R. M. True in 1949. He found that 92 percent of his subjects, regressed to the day of their tenth birthday, could accurately recall the day of the week on which it fell. He also found the same thing for 84 percent of his subjects for their fourth birthday. Other investigators, however, were unable to duplicate True's findings. When True was questioned by Martin Orne about his experiment . . . True, Orne discovered, had inadvertently cued his subjects by following the unusual technique of asking them, "Is it Monday? Is it Tuesday? Is it Wednesday?" etc., and he monitored their responses by using a perpetual desk calendar in full view of all his subjects. Further evidence of the prevalence and importance of such cueing came from a study by D.N. O'Connell, R.E. Shor, and M.T. Orne. They found that in an existing group of four-year-olds not a single one knew what day of the week it was. The reincarnation literature is also replete with examples of such inadvertent cueing. Ian Wilson, for example, has shown that hypnotically elicited reports of being reincarnated vary as a direct function of the hypnotist's belief about reincarnation. Finally, Jean-Roch Laurence, Robert Nadon, Heather Nogrady, and Campbell Perry have shown that pseudo-memories were elicited also by inadvertent cueing in the use of hypnosis by the police.

As for advertent, or *deliberate*, cueing, one of my own studies offers a clear example. Sixty undergraduates divided into three groups of twenty each were hypnotized and age regressed to previous lifetimes. Before each hypnosis session, however, suggestions very favorable to and supportive of past-life and reincarnation beliefs were given to one group; neutral and noncommittal statements about past lives were given to the second group; and skeptical and derogatory statements about past lives were given to the third group. The results clearly showed the effects of these cues and suggestions. Subjects in the first group showed the most past-life regressions and the most past-life productions, subjects in the third group showed the least. Regression subjects take cues as to how they are to respond from the person doing the regressions and asking the questions. If the hypnotist is a believer in UFO abductions the odds are heavily in favor of him eliciting UFO-abductee stories from his volunteers.

Fantasy-Prone Personalities and Psychological Needs

"Assuming that all you have said thus far *is* true," the skeptical observer might ask, "why would hundreds of ordinary, mild-mannered, unassuming citizens suddenly go off the deep end and turn up with cases of amnesia and then, when under hypnosis, all report nearly identical experiences?" First, the abductees are not as numerous as we are led to believe; and, second, even though Strieber and Hopkins go to great lengths to emphasize the diversity of the people who report these events, they are much more alike than these taxonomists declare. In an afterword to Hopkins's *Missing Time*, a psychologist named Aphrodite Clamar raises exactly this question and then adds, "All of these people seem quite ordinary in the psychological sense— *although they have not been subjected to the kind of psychological testing that might provide a deeper understanding of their personalities*". And herein lies the problem. If these abductees were given this sort of intensive diagnostic testing it is highly likely that many similarities would emerge—particularly an unusual personality pattern that Sheryl C. Wilson and T.X. Barber have categorized as "fantasy-prone." In an important but much neglected article, they report in some detail their discovery of a group of excellent hypnotic subjects with unusual fantasy abilities. In their words:

> Although this study provided a broader understanding of the kind of life experiences that may underlie the ability to be an excellent hypnotic subject, it has also led to a serendipitous finding that has wide implication for all of psychology—it has shown that there exists a small group of individuals (possibly 4% of the population) who fantasize a large part of the time, who typically "see," "hear," "smell," and "touch" and fully experience what they fantasize; and who can be labeled *fantasy-prone personalities*.

Wilson and Barber also stress that such individuals experience a reduction in orientation to time, place, and person that is characteristic of hypnosis or trance during their daily lives whenever they are deeply involved in a fantasy. They also have experiences during their daily ongoing lives that resemble the classical hypnotic phenomena. In other words, the behavior we would normally call "hypnotic" is exhibited by these fantasy-prone types (FPs) all the time. . . .

Fantasy-prone individuals also show up as mediums, psychics, and religious visionaries. They are also the ones who have many realistic "out of body" experiences and prototypic "near-death" experiences.

In spite of the fact that many such extreme types show FP characteristics, the overwhelming majority of FPs fall within the broad range of normal functioning. . . .

Hypnotic Evidence

The new UFOlogy is based on largely uncorroborated events, often revealed in hypnotic sessions. The paucity of evidence is unnerving: a scar, a lost hour, some bright lights in the sky, and—oops!—someone claims to have been abducted by aliens from outer space. Usually the subject has no memory of the abduction until it is revealed in all its stark terror under hypnosis.

Paul Kurtz, *The Skeptical Inquirer*, Fall 1987.

In general, FPs are "normal" people who function as well as others and who are as well adjusted, competent, and satisfied or dissatisfied as everyone else. . . .

It is perfectly clear, therefore, why most of the UFO abductees, when given cursory examinations by psychiatrists and psychologists, would turn out to be ordinary, normal citizens as sane as themselves. It is also evident why the elaborate fantasies woven in fine cloth from the now universally familiar UFO-abduction fable—a fable known to every man, woman, and child newspaper reader or moviegoer in the nation—would have so much in common, so much consistency in the telling. Any one of us, if asked to pretend that he had been kidnapped by aliens from outer space or another dimension, would make up a story that would vary little, either in its details or in the supposed motives of the abductors, from the stories told by any and all of the kidnap victims reported by Hopkins. As for the close encounters of the third kind and conversations with the little gray aliens described in *Communion* and *Intruders*, again, our imaginative tales would be remarkably similar in plot, dialogue, description, and characterization. The means of transportation would be saucer-shaped; the aliens would be small, humanoid, two-eyed, and gray, white, or green. The purpose of their visits would be: (1) to save our planet; (2) to find a better home for themselves: (3) to end nuclear war and the threat we pose to the peaceful life in the rest of the galaxy; (4) to bring us knowledge and enlightenment: and (5) to increase their knowledge and understanding of other forms of intelligent life. In fact, the fantasy-prone abductees' stories would be much more credible if some of them, at least, reported the aliens as eight-foot-tall, red-striped octapeds riding bicycles and intent upon eating us for dessert. . . .

Hypnogogic and Hypnopompic Hallucinations

Another common yet little publicized and rarely discussed phenomenon is that of hypnogogic (when falling asleep) and hypnopompic (when waking up) hallucinations. These phenomena, often referred to as "waking dreams," find the individual suddenly awake, but paralyzed, unable to move, and most often encountering a "ghost." The typical report goes somewhat as follows. "I went to bed and went to sleep and then sometime near morning something woke me up. I opened my eyes and found myself wide awake but unable to move. There, standing at the foot of my bed was my mother, wearing her favorite dress—the one we buried her in. She stood there looking at me and smiling and then she said: 'Don't worry about me, Doris, I'm at peace at last. I just want you and the children to be happy.'" Well, what happened next? "Nothing, she slowly faded away." What did you do then? "Nothing, I just closed my eyes and went back to sleep."

There are always a number of characteristic clues that indicate a hypnogogic or hypnopompic hallucination. First, it always occurs before or after falling asleep. Second, one is paralyzed or has difficulty in moving; or, contrarily, one may float out of one's body and have an out-of-body experience. Third, the hallucination is unusually bizarre; i.e., one sees ghosts, aliens, monsters, and such. Fourth, after the hallucination is over the hallucinator typically goes back to sleep. And, fifth, the hallucinator is unalterably convinced of the "reality" of the entire experience.

In Strieber's *Communion* is a classic, textbook description of a hypnopompic hallucination, complete with the awakening from a sound sleep, the strong sense of reality and of being awake, the paralysis (due to the fact that the body's neural circuits keep our muscles relaxed and help preserve our sleep), and the encounter with strange beings. Following the encounter, instead of jumping out of bed and going in search of the strangers he has seen, Strieber typically goes back to sleep. He even reports that the burglar alarm was still working—proof again that the intruders were mental rather than physical. Strieber also reports an occasion when he awakes and believes that the roof of his house is on fire and that the aliens are threatening his family. Yet his only response to this was to go peacefully back to sleep. Again, clear evidence of a hypnopompic dream. Strieber, of course, is convinced of the reality of these experiences. This too is expected. If he was not convinced of their reality, then the experience would not be hypnopompic or hallucinatory.

The point cannot be more strongly made that ordinary, perfectly sane and rational people have these hallucinatory experiences and that such individuals are in no way mentally disturbed or psychotic. But neither are such experiences to be taken as incontrovertible proof of some sort of objective or consensual reality. They may be subjectively real, but objectively they are nothing more than dreams or delusions. . . .

Dangers of Fantasy

Many readers might feel compelled to ask: "Well, what is so bad about people having fantasies anyway? What harm do they do? You certainly cannot deny they are entertaining. And, as far as the psychiatrists' clients are concerned, whether the fantasies are true or false is of little matter—it's the clients' perceptions of reality that matter and it is this that you have to treat." True, if the client believes it is so, then you have to deal with that belief. The only problem with this lies in its potential for harm. On the national scene today too many lives have been negatively affected and even ruined by well-meaning but tragically misdirected reformers who believe the fantasies of children, the alienated, and the fantasy-prone personality types and have charged innocent people with rape, child molestation, assault, and other sorts of abusive crimes. Nearly every experienced clinician has encountered such claims and then much later has discovered to his chagrin that none of these fantasized events ever happened. Law-enforcement officials are also quite familiar with the products of response expectancies and overactive imaginations in the form of FPs who confess to murders that never happened or to murders that did happen but with which they have no connection. Another problem with the UFO abductee literature is that it is false, misleading, rabble-rousing, sensationalistic, and opportunistically money-grubbing. It takes advantage of people's hopes and fears and diverts them from the literature of science. Our journeys to the stars will be made on spaceships created by determined, hardworking scientists and engineers applying the principles of science, not aboard flying saucers piloted by little gray aliens from some other dimension.

"Reports that are remarkably consistent worldwide seem more likely to be based on real events than subjective fantasies."

Psychological Explanations Are Inadequate

Jerome Clark

Jerome Clark frequently writes about UFOs. In addition to his regular column, "UFO Reporter," in *Fate* magazine, he has written several books on the topic. In the following viewpoint, Clark asserts that psychological explanations for UFO abduction tales do not account for the large number of similar experiences reported worldwide, and they do not account for the content of many of the abductees' stories.

As you read, consider the following questions:

1. Why, according to Clark, are incompetent hypnosis sessions not adequate explanation for the abduction experience?
2. According to Clark, what did the 1977 experiments by Drs. Lawson and McCall show about hypnosis as the source of abduction stories?

Jerome Clark, "UFO Reporter: The UFO Abduction Enigma," *Fate*, July 1989. Reprinted with permission.

Mention "UFO [Unidentified Flying Object] abductions" to any debunker and he is sure to explain patiently to you that such tales are the product of "confabulation." By that he means this:

Virtually all reports of kidnapping by aliens emerge under hypnotic probing, typically by UFO believers and other unsavory types. Fanatical and incompetent, determined to prove the reality of extraterrestrial visitation, they make the elementary error of asking their hypnotized subjects leading questions. Persons in an hypnotic state are unusually suggestible; desiring to please the hypnotist they will respond in a way that they believe provides the answers their questioner wants to hear. Thus they construct—usually innocently—fantasies about encounters with humanoid beings, following cues picked up from the hypnotist. "UFO abductions" have as little basis in reality as stories of "past lives" recounted under hypnosis.

As it happens, this explanation—like much that passes for UFO debunking—is nonsense, but it has at least a surface plausibility. There is no question that hypnosis is a risky complicated procedure full of pitfalls for the unwary. There is, moreover, no doubt that people do fantasize under hypnosis, and there are incompetent hypnotists who through carelessness or desire for affirmation of cherished beliefs direct their subjects to tell them what they want to hear. If this were all there was to the abduction phenomenon, we could all breathe a sigh of relief and go on to something less unsettling and more productive.

Hypnotism Not the Villain

There is, unfortunately, more to it than that—a great deal more, it appears—and virtually no one, ufologist or psychologist, familiar in any serious way with the evidence (whether through first-hand investigation or in-depth analysis) agrees that confabulation is the answer to the mystery. Confabulation is the favorite explanation of the armchair theorist who knows little about the subject.

One major problem with the confabulation hypothesis is that abduction stories do not exist in a vacuum. Unlike many "past-life" narratives, they do not begin and end on the hypnotist's couch. People do not even approach UFO investigators unless they have had odd experiences, portions of which are unaccounted for in their memories. Typically such an experience involves the sighting of a strange flying object at close range—and, in some cases, of the object's occupants.

Immediately following this observation witnesses often have a sense of "missing time," and the next thing they know everything is as it was before the UFO appeared. In a number of cases investigators have been able to substantiate the witnesses' late arrival and their bafflement concerning an unaccounted-for hour or two. In other words, the "missing time" is not an illusion caused by simple absent-mindedness on the witnesses' part, as another glib explanation has it.

'IF THAT WASN'T MY IMAGINATION, I'D BE SCARED STIFF!"

In short, abductees do report consciously recalled UFO encounters and they do fall victim to a period of amnesia. The confabulation hypothesis conveniently fails to address this vital aspect of the abduction phenomenon. Even if one doubts the reality of extraterrestrial kidnappings, one has to acknowledge that a genuine mystery exists here. Confabulation does not explain the sighting and the missing time—both of which occurred far from the hypnotist's couch.

Okay, the skeptic concedes. All that may be so. Still the abduction "memories" elicited by hypnosis remain suspect. "Surely," the skeptic tells you, "*these* are confabulation."

No, they are not, according to a recent study by a leading expert on the abduction phenomenon.

Thomas E. Bullard is a folklorist whose 1982 Ph.D. dissertation at Indiana University was entitled *Mysteries in the Eye of the Beholder: UFOs and Their Correlates as a Folkloric Theme Past and Present.* Dr. Bullard received a grant from the Fund for UFO Research [FUFOR] to conduct an exhaustive comparative analysis of all known abduction accounts and to determine what (if any) patterns could be found in the data. If the patterns were nonexistent or trivial, there would be no reason to consider "abductions" anything other than random fantasies. Earlier writers and investigators had maintained that patterns occur, but none had addressed the question in so rigorous and systematic a way as Bullard would. The results of his inquiries were published in 1987 in the two-volume *UFO Abductions: The Measure of a Mystery.*

UFO Abductions is the most important work ever written on this contentious issue. Certainly it is the only purely objective, non-axegrinding treatment, the one book to which anyone who seeks an utterly honest weighing of the pros and cons can go. In the course of a complex, sophisticated and multifaceted survey which examines just about every conceivable aspect of its subject, Bullard finds a number of robust patterns, including some so subtle that they had escaped the notice even of ufologists. These patterns hold true over time and geography, regardless of who the witnesses or investigators are. Bullard says the cause of abductions remains unknown, but he demonstrates beyond dispute that an *abduction phenomenon* exists.

Worldwide Consistency

The implications are clear enough for the confabulation hypothesis: reports that are remarkably consistent worldwide seem more likely to be based on real events than subjective fantasies—especially when these reports agree in very specific, and not just general, detail.

Moreover, Bullard writes in a major new study, "Any attempt to dismiss abductions as a side-effect of hypnosis runs up against a serious obstacle from the start—not all abduction testimony emerges under hypnosis." Writing in the *Journal of UFO Studies* (Vol. 1, new series) Bullard expands on his FUFOR study and notes that of "104 [abduction] cases qualified as high in both reliability and information content," no fewer than 30 were consciously recalled.

In his 38-page paper (titled "Hypnosis and UFO Abductions: A Troubled Relationship") Bullard reasons that if hypnotic confabulation creates imaginary abductions, the accounts told under hypnosis should be measurably different from the ones related by individuals with full conscious recall. In fact, they are not; the accounts are virtually identical in all important respects.

Hypnotism Works

Hypnotic age regression is an extremely effective therapuetic technique. It gets to the cause of symptoms and problems of all sorts and results in immediate and lasting cures. I have come to believe that a great majority of symptoms are due to repressed trauma. . . .

During the fifteen years that I have been using hypnotic age regression, I have found many of my patients "remembering" what appeared to have been contacts with and abductions by extraterrestrials in spacecraft. Once the repressed traumas had been brought to light, any symptoms or problems caused by them were immediately eliminated. Generally the patients were surprised, even shocked, to find that they had had close encounters.

Edith Fiore, *Encounters*, 1989.

Bullard takes his argument further by comparing reports elicited by four hypnotists (Drs. Clamar, Harder, McCall and Sprinkle), each with a different perspective on the phenomenon, to see if—as one prominent critic has suggested—"the beings a witness describes reflect the personality of the hypnotist investigating the case." Bullard finds no evidence to support this claim. The same range of patterns emerges, consistent with the abduction phenomenon in general. "Rather than a full scale shaping force as postulated by the skeptics," he says, "hypnotists appear less the leaders than the led."

Experiments Support Abductions

Further evidence of the irrelevance of confabulation comes from a series of experiments conducted in 1977 by Drs. Alvin Lawson and William McCall. Volunteers were placed under hypnosis and encouraged—with leading questions, it should be noted—to imagine UFO abductions. The idea was to see if imagined encounters contained the same features as allegedly real ones.

Although a few similarities emerged, on the whole, Bullard observes, there were "many and serious" differences. For example, whereas humanoids figure in 70 percent of the "real" cases, they were described in only 10 percent of the imaginary ones. (Most of the imaginary UFO beings have never been reported in "real" cases and encompass a significantly wider variety of shapes and behaviors.) Other major discrepancies include the appearances of the UFOs and the contents of their interiors.

The Skeptical Argument

Bullard concludes, "Weighed and found wanting time and again, hypnosis cannot shoulder nearly as much responsibility for abductions as the skeptics have proposed. None of their appeals to confabulation, influence by the hypnotist, and experiments with non-abductees stand up under a comparative examination. In light of these findings, the burden of proof now drops on the skeptics. They can no longer repeat their old claims as meaningful answers. For any future rebuttals the skeptics must look deeper into the phenomenon itself rather than simply deduce the hazards of hypnotic testimony from scientific studies of hypnosis, or read theoretical interpretations into abduction reports from a safe distance. The skeptical argument needs rebuilding from the ground up."

Bullard says that whether "objective or subjective . . . experience seems the only adequate explanation for many traits of real abduction stories."

The true nature of that "experience" remains a question waiting for an answer. But even if we still do not know for certain what "UFO abductions" are, at least we know, thanks to Bullard, something about what they are not.

Understanding Words in Context

Readers sometimes come upon words they do not recognize. And frequently, because a word's meaning is unknown to a reader, he or she will not fully understand the passage being read. Obviously, a reader can look up an unfamiliar word in a dictionary; but before doing this, a perceptive reader can often determine the word's meaning by carefully examining the context in which the word appears. That is, the reader may find clues to the meaning of the word in the surrounding text and its underlying ideas and attitudes.

Following are excerpts from the viewpoints in this chapter. In each excerpt, one word is printed in italicized capital letters. Try to determine the meaning of that word by reading the excerpt. Under each excerpt you will find four definitions. Choose the one that is closest to your understanding of the italicized word.

Finally, use a dictionary to see how well you have understood the words in context. It may be helpful to discuss with others the clues that helped you decide each word's meaning.

1. What I saw was a gigantic blackness. It easily covered a third of the *FIRMAMENT*, and completely blotted out the sun.

   FIRMAMENT means:

   a) earth   c) treetops
   b) sky   d) daytime

2. James was at a loss for words as some invisible, *INEFFABLY* evil being suddenly drew close to him.

   INEFFABLY means:

   a) weakly   c) indescribably
   b) visibly   d) affectionately

3. The eyes were the color of molten basalt and they held him
   MESMERIZED until he was finally able to break out of the
   trance in which they had placed him.
   MESMERIZED means:

   a) at arms length   c) under water
   b) hypnotized   d) a short time

4. UFOlogists had hoped they would be the first to find aliens.
   Much to their *CHAGRIN*, however, some very suspect people
   claimed that they had found aliens before the UFOlogists.
   CHAGRIN means:

   a) relief   c) pleasure
   b) regret   d) excitement

5. We still do not have the *INCONTROVERTIBLE* evidence
   needed to silence our critics and end the debate which rages
   over the existence of UFOs.
   INCONTROVERTIBLE means:

   a) legal   c) police
   b) hearsay   d) unquestionable

6. Those unimaginative skeptics who deny the reality of UFO
   sightings tend to look for everyday explanations and offer
   PROSAIC interpretations of the phenomena.
   PROSAIC means:

   a) dull   c) fantastic
   b) flowery   d) creative

7. Without a doubt, *INADVERTENT* cueing also plays a major
   role in UFO-abduction fantasies. Without knowing it, the
   hypnotist gives away to the person being hypnotized exactly
   what response is desired.
   INADVERTENT means:

   a) ineffective   c) unintended
   b) fraudulent   d) unfriendly

8. While people are accustomed to seeing planes, helicopters,
   and balloons in the sky, they are still puzzled by the concept
   of UFOs, which to them remain *ANOMALOUS* and inexplicable.
   ANOMALOUS means:

   a) abnormal   c) ordinary
   b) understandable   d) enormous

Periodical Bibliography

The following articles have been selected to supplement the diverse views presented in this chapter.

Frank Apsi-Ridolfo	"The Primal Fear: Are We Alone?" *Astronomy*, December 1987.
Elizabeth Bird	"Invasion of the Mind Snatchers," *Psychology Today*, April 1989.
Gregg Easterbrook	"Are We Alone?" *The Atlantic Monthly*, August 1988.
Martyn J. Fogg	"Extraterrestrial Intelligence and the Interdict Hypothesis," *Analog*, November 1988.
Donald Goldsmith	"SETI: The Search Heats Up," *Sky & Telescope*, February 1988.
Philip J. Klass	"Communion and Intruders: UFO-Abduction Groups Form," *The Skeptical Inquirer*, Winter 1990.
Philip J. Klass	"New Evidence of MJ-12 Hoax," *The Skeptical Inquirer*, Winter 1990.
Paul Kurtz	"Is There Intelligent Life on Earth?" *The Skeptical Inquirer*, Fall 1987.
Life	"Is Anyone Out There?" July 1989.
Joy Peach	"I Believe in UFOs," *Fate*, April 1990.
Robert Scheaffer	"Psychic Vibrations," *The Skeptical Inquirer*, Winter 1991.
Seth Shostak	"Where Are the Extraterrestrials Hiding?" *Saturday Evening Post*, September 1987.
Pamela Weintraub	"True Confessions," *Omni*, December 1988.

The following periodicals are devoted to reports of UFOs or frequently publish articles on the topic. Unless otherwise noted, all are pro-UFO.

Fate	3510 Western Ave., Highland Park, IL 60035.
Flying Saucer Review	PO Box 12, Snodland, Kent ME6 5JA, England.
International UFO Reporter	J. Allen Hynek Center for UFO Studies, 1955 John's Dr., Glenview, IL 60025.
The MUFON Journal	103 Oldtowne Rd., Sequin, TX 78155.
The Skeptical Inquirer	3025 Palo Alto Dr., NE, Albuquerque, NM 87111 (has a skeptical slant).

3 CHAPTER

Does ESP
Exist?

Chapter Preface

Extrasensory perception or ESP has fascinated the human race for centuries. However, it is only in the last one hundred years that researchers have attempted to study ESP in the laboratory, using the research methods and sophisticated techniques of modern science.

The quality and meaning of this psychic research and the results it has produced are the subject of intense debate. Many people, including members of the Parapsychological Association, believe that the high quality and considerable quantity of ESP research has produced incontestable proof of its existence. On the other hand, skeptics argue that psychic research, with its flawed methods and fraudulent practices, has produced no reliable evidence for the existence of ESP. Skeptics even have their own publication, *The Skeptical Inquirer,* (the official journal of the Committee for the Scientific Investigation of Claims of the Paranormal), which is devoted to debunking paranormal research and claims of psychic experiences.

Despite this division of opinion, both believers and skeptics agree that if ESP was proven to actually exist, and its properties were understood and harnessed by humankind, the consequences would be nothing less than revolutionary. For instance, precognition, the ability to perceive future events, could be used to potentially avoid or prevent disasters. Indeed, a Central Premonitions Registry was established in New York to investigate premonitions from people relating visions of future disaster. The following chapter examines ESP and the reactions it has provoked in both believers and skeptics.

"Parapsychologists closely scrutinize each other's work and have been their own best critics. The experimental data has continued to improve throughout the years."

ESP Is Genuine

Jeffrey Mishlove

Jeffrey Mishlove was the first student at an accredited university in the United States to earn a Ph.D. in parapsychology. He received this degree from the University of California at Berkeley. A long-time teacher and researcher of psychic phenomena, Mishlove believes in the existence of ESP. In the following viewpoint, he examines the concept of ESP and its different components. He also defends the legitimacy of the research which supports the existence of ESP. Mishlove also hosts the television program "Thinking Allowed," which airs on the Public Broadcasting Service.

As you read, consider the following questions:

1. How, according to the author, did psychic researchers improve their techniques in response to outside criticisms of their scientific methods?
2. What, according to Mishlove, have psychic researchers learned about the nature of ESP?
3. Have you ever had one of the psychic experiences (telepathy, clairvoyance, precognition) described by the author?

Excerpted, with permission, from *The Roots of Consciousness: Psychic Liberation Through History, Science, and Experience* by Jeffrey Mishlove. New York: Random House, 1975.

Although many of you . . . will have no personal doubt that extra-sensory perception is real, the effort to establish ESP as a scientific fact has been a continuous struggle. Many subjects whose demonstrations had originally convinced researchers from the SPR [Society for Psychical Research] were later detected using bogus means to dupe these eminent scientists. Fascinated by their few successes, researchers continued undaunted in the midst of failures, criticism, and detected frauds.

Between 1880 and 1940, 145 empirical ESP studies were published which used 77,796 subjects who made 4,918,186 single trial guesses. These experiments were mostly conducted by psychologists and other scientists. In 106 such studies, the authors arrived at results which exceeded chance expectations.

The Work of J.B. Rhine

Perhaps the most publicized early experiments were those published by Dr. J. B. Rhine in 1934 in a monograph entitled *Extra-Sensory Perception*, which summarized results from his experiments at Duke University beginning in 1927. Although this work was published by the relatively obscure Boston Society for Psychic Research, it was picked up in the popular press and had a large impact throughout the world. While earlier research had been fruitful, they were generally neither as systematic nor as persistent as Dr. Rhine's studies.

These experiments used shuffled decks of Zener cards with five sets of five different symbols on them—a cross, a circle, a wavy line, a square and a star. This method reduced the problem of chance-expectation to a matter of exact calculations. Furthermore the cards were designed to be as emotionally neutral as possible to eliminate possible response biases caused by idiosyncratic preferences. However other studies have shown that emotionally laden targets can also work without impairing statistical analysis.

Rhine describes his early work with one of his more successful subjects, Hubert E. Pearce, a graduate divinity student:

> The working conditions were these: observer and subject sat opposite each other at a table, on which lay about a dozen packs of the Zener cards and a record book. One of the packs would be handed to Pearce and he was allowed to shuffle it. (He felt it gave more real "contact.") Then it was laid down and it was cut by the observer. Following this Pearce would, as a rule, pick up the pack, lift off the top card, keeping both the pack and the removed card face down, and after calling it, he would lay the card on the table, still face down. The observer would record the call. Either after five calls or after twenty-five calls—and we used both conditions generally about equally—the called cards would be turned over and checked off against the calls recorded in the book. The ob-

server saw each card and checked each one personally, though the subject was asked to help in checking by laying off the cards as checked. There is no legerdemain by which an alert observer can be repeatedly deceived at this simple task in his own laboratory. (And, of course, we are not even dealing with amateur magicians.) For the next run another pack of cards would be taken up.

The critical reader will find several faults with this experiment. First, as long as the subject is able to see or touch the backs or sides of the cards, there exists a channel of sensory leakage through which the subject might receive information about the face of the cards. Several critics reported that this was why they were able to obtain good scoring results. Secondly, there was no adequate safeguards against legerdemain. For example, what would prevent the subject from making small markings on the cards with his fingernails in order to identify the cards later on? It almost seems as if the optimism of the experimenter that this would not happen could mitigate against sufficiently careful observation. Furthermore, is it really possible for one experimenter to maintain sufficient concentration to insure that the subject does not cheat? Experience of other researchers has sadly shown that this is quite doubtful. Perhaps Rhine did utilize other safeguards. If so he could be fairly criticized for not adequately reporting his experimental conditions, although other experiments in his monograph were admittedly better controlled. Finally, there is no mention of any efforts to guard against recording errors on the part of the experimenter. One can hardly expect the cooperation of the subject, who may have a personal interest in the outcome, to be an adequate control against experimenter mistakes.

Correcting the Problems

As Rhine's positive results gained more attention, arguments of this sort began to proliferate in the popular and scientific literature. It is much to Rhine's credit that he encouraged such criticism and modified his experiments accordingly. In 1940, Rhine, J. G. Pratt and their associates published a work, titled *Extra-Sensory Perception After Sixty Years,* which described the ways in which the ESP experiments had met the thirty-five different counter-hypotheses which had been published in the scientific and popular press.

The areas of criticism which Rhine and Pratt focused on in 1940 included the following: hypotheses related to improper statistical analysis of the results; hypotheses related to biased selection of experiments reported; hypotheses dealing with errors in the experimental records; hypotheses involving sensory leakage; hypotheses charging experimenter incompetence; and finally hypotheses of a general speculative character. In each case, Rhine and Pratt pointed to experimental evidence to counter the hypotheses.

Many prominent mathematicians in the field of probability who have made a detailed investigation have approved his techniques. In fact, in 1937 the American Institute of Statistical Mathematics issued a statement that Rhine's statistical procedures were not in the least faulty. In most experiments, both significant and chance results were reported and averaged into the data.

High scores due to inaccurate recording of results had been reduced to an insignificant level by double-blind techniques in which both subject and experimenter notations were made without knowledge of the scores against which they were to be matched. Errors were further reduced by having two or more experimenters oversee the matching of scores. Furthermore, original experimental data had been saved and double checked for mistakes many times by investigators. Tampering with these original records was prevented by having several copies independently preserved.

Sensory cues were impossible in many tests of clairvoyance because the experimenter himself and all witnesses did not know the correct targets. In other tests, the cards were sealed in opaque envelopes, or an opaque screen prevented the subject from seeing the cards. Often the experimenter and the subject were in completely different rooms.

No Flaws

Those who charged the experimenters with incompetence failed to find any flaws in several experiments. In cases of inadequate reporting, Rhine indicates that further data was always supplied upon request. In several cases, experimenter fraud would have had to involve the active collusion on the part of several teams of two or more experimenters. Critics who claim that the results come only from the laboratories of those with a predisposition to believe in ESP were also ignoring at least six successful studies gathered from skeptical observers.

Other criticisms generally claimed that ESP could not exist because of certain philosophical assumptions about the nature of the universe or scientifically uninformed assumptions of what ESP would be like if it did exist. These assumptions are scarcely sufficient cause to dismiss the carefully observed experimental data.

Of the 145 experiments which had been reported in the sixty year period from 1880 to 1940, Rhine and Pratt were able to demonstrate that six different experimental studies of extrasensory perception were not amenable to explanation by any of the counter-hypotheses offered by critics of parapsychology.

One of the more carefully controlled studies is the Pearce-

Pratt series, which was carried out in 1933 with Dr. J. G. Pratt as agent and Hubert Pearce as subject. In these experiments, the agent and his subject were separated in different buildings over 100 yards apart. Pratt displaced the cards one by one from an ESP pack at an agreed time without turning them over. After going through the pack, Pratt then turned the cards over and recorded them. The guesses were recorded independently by Pearce. In order to eliminate the possibility of cheating, the precaution was taken that both placed their records in a sealed package which was handed to Rhine before the two lists were compared. Copies of these original records are still available for inspection. The total number of guesses was 1,850 of which one would expect one-fifth, or 370, to be correct by chance. The actual number of hits was 558. The probability that these results could have occurred by chance is much less than one in a hundred million.

ESP Is a Fact

It was a strictly orthodox, statistical approach, applied to an unorthodox subject, which gradually wore down academic resistance—and incredulity—in the course of the 45 years since J.B. Rhine established the first Laboratory for Parapsychology at Duke University, North Carolina. Since then, a great number of similar laboratories have been established all over the world—including Soviet Russia and other Communist countries—in which scientists work under the same rigorously controlled test-conditions as researchers in other fields, using sophisticated computers and electronic apparatus to eliminate as far as possible human error in evaluating the results. And the results show that ESP—extransensory perception—is a fact, whether we like it or not. In 1969 the American Association for the Advancement of Science approved the application of the Parapsychological Association to become an affiliate of that august body. That decision conferred on parapsychology the ultimate seal of respectability.

Arthur Koestler, *The Heels of Achilles*, 1974.

The combined probability of those experiments which met all objections critics raised proved absolutely astronomical. If one had conducted ESP experiments every minute throughout the entire history of the earth back to the days when it was a cloud of gas the probability of having encountered such high ESP results by chance, during that entire time would still be virtually negligible, less than one chance in billions.

After the publication of *ESP After Sixty Years*, both the quality and quantity of criticism of ESP research declined. This is not to say, however, that parapsychology met with general acceptance in the United States or in other countries. The work of the para-psychologists was simply ignored by many universities and the major scientific publications. The public guardians were not then ready for ESP.

ESP: A Miracle?

Finally in August, 1955, *Science* carried an editorial on ESP research by Dr. G. R. Price, a chemist from the University of Minnesota, which stated that scientists had to choose between accepting the reality of ESP or rejecting the evidence. Price had carefully studied the data and he frankly admitted that the best experiments could only be faulted by assuming deliberate fraud, or an abnormal mental condition, on the part of the scientists. Price felt that ESP, judged in the light of the accepted principles of modern science, would have to be classed as a miracle. . . . Rather than accept a miracle, he suggested accepting the position of the eighteenth-century philosopher, David Hume, who said that those who report miracles should be dismissed as liars.

Similar criticisms were published by Professor C. M. Hansel. Regarding the Pearce-Pratt experiment, he suggests that after Pratt had left him, Pearce departed from the University Library, followed Pratt to his office and looked through the fanlight of Pratt's door thus observing the target cards being recorded by Pratt. While it is true that Hansel exposed the defect in the experimental design of having left Pearce alone in the library, the structure of Pratt's office would have made it impossible for Pearce to see the cards even if he had taken the great risk of staring through the fanlight of Dr. Pratt's door. In subsequent experiments parapsychologists have eliminated such defects.

Official Recognition

Official recognition of the experimental competency of para-psychologists did not come until December of 1969 when the American Academy for the Advancement of Science granted affiliate status to the researchers in the Parapsychological Association. Recent years have shown authoritative scientific voices displaying a new willingness to deal with the evidence for ESP. In the "letters" column of *Science* for January 28, 1972, there appeared a brief note from Dr. Price titled "Apology to Rhine and Soal," in which Price expressed his conviction that his original article was highly unfair to both Soal (a British mathematician and parapsychologist who also reported outstanding results) and Rhine.

Other criticisms relating to repeatability, fraud, statistical inferences, experimental design and interpretation of data have continued. In fact, the parapsychologists closely scrutinize each other's work and have been their own best critics. The experimental data has continued to improve throughout the years.

While many scientists still argue against the existence of ESP, the majority accept its reality or likelihood. Many scientific journals have carried articles on ESP experiments. . . .

Types of ESP

ESP is generally divided into telepathy, ability to communicate with another mind extra-sensorily; clairvoyance, ability to perceive situations at a distance directly, without the mediation of another mind; and precognition, which is ESP across time into the future. There is still some controversy as to whether telepathy actually exists, or whether it is simply another form of clairvoyance. However, precognition, a most unusual ability in terms of our conventional notions of time and free will, is a rather well-established ESP phenomena. In fact precognition tests afford some of the best evidence for ESP, since sensory leakage from a target which has not yet been determined is impossible. For example, in early studies with Hubert Pearce, the subject was able to guess what the order of cards in a pack *would be* after it was shuffled at the same high rate of scoring (up to 50% above chance levels) as in clairvoyance tests.

A Parapsychologist's View

We naturally like to think of ourselves as somehow more imaginative, more finely attuned to nature's mysteries than other scientists and we look upon the skeptic as, by contrast, a dull dog, hidebound in his narrow and outdated materialism. Such an attitude, I submit, is a hangover from religion and has no place in science . . . If merit is anywhere involved it lies in following the implications of the evidence even when these run directly counter to one's fondest beliefs and expectations.

John Beloff, *Research in Parapsychology 1972*, 1973.

While many people tend to reject ESP because it seems to contradict the classical laws of science, precognition is even harder to swallow for exactly the opposite reason—it seems to imply a completely mechanical, predetermined universe. Ironically, it is this determinism which violates the sensibilities of twentieth-century science. In fact, precognition is very difficult to prove; although its alternatives are not exactly palatable.

For example in the precognitive card guessing studies, one might say that the subject psychokinetically [i.e., using mind over matter] caused the order of the cards to conform to his guesses. Or perhaps, more reasonably, the experimenter, using his clairvoyance subconsciously, determined the subject's guesses and shuffled the cards accordingly. Good precognitive experiments must rule out the possibility of contamination by other forms of psychic interaction. The methodological difficulty in distinguishing different types of extra-sensory transmission and reception had led researchers to use the more general term *psi*.

There is a good deal of evidence to warrant that precognition actually does occur—with all of its ramifications regarding time and free will. For instance, after a mine disaster in Wales, in which 144 people perished, researchers collected reports from individuals who claimed to have had premonitions of the event. Seventy-six reports were received. In twenty-four cases, the percipient had actually talked to another person about the premonition before the catastrophe. Twenty-five of the experiences were in dreams. . . .

There are now many questions about ESP which researchers are attempting to answer through scientific experimentation and observation, but even the early researchers were able to establish a few solid facts about the process. For example, no reliable relationship could be found between ESP scoring in the laboratory and such factors as sex, age, blindness, mental or physical illness, mediumship, or intelligence. Subjects seemed to score better in novel test situations and often when rewards or competition were involved. On the other hand, lengthy and formalized testing in which the subject was given no information regarding his scoring generally resulted in a decline of the subject's ESP ability. . . . No physical factors such as space and time have been found to have a limiting effect on ESP scoring. It was also quickly discovered that ESP is a rather erratic and unstable ability. While a subject may be able to direct his ESP to a particular target, very few tested subjects have ever shown the ability to activate their psychic abilities at will. . . .

Editor's note: This excerpt was taken from the 1975 edition of The Roots of Consciousness. *A revised edition will be published by Ballantine Books in the spring of 1992. The new edition contains newer, more sophisticated research and is recommended to the reader interested in the latest findings in parapsychology. For more information on the "Thinking Allowed" program, write to "Thinking Allowed" 2560 9th St., Suite 123, Berkeley, CA 94710.*

"If you have in the past fallen for the hucksters of psi . . . take hope. The smartest folks in the world are no smarter than you are when it comes to belief in the ridiculous."

ESP Is Nonsense

James Randi

James Randi, otherwise known as "The Amazing Randi," is a world famous magician and escape artist. For many years, he has been active as an investigator of paranormal phenomena, offering a large (and, so far, unclaimed) monetary reward to anyone able to perform a paranormal feat under rigorously controlled conditions. In the following viewpoint, Randi argues that ESP is nonsense, and attempts to expose the flawed methods and fraud which he believes are typical of much ESP research.

As you read, consider the following questions:

1. What evidence does the author provide for his attack on ESP research?
2. Why does Randi believe that scientists in more conventional fields have failed the public with regard to ESP?
3. How, according to the author, was the work of Dr. Soal discredited?

Reprinted from *Flim-Flam!: Psychics, ESP, Unicorns, and Other Delusions* by James Randi, with permission of Prometheus Books, Buffalo, NY.

Belief in the paranormal is not restricted to persons of lesser intellect. One would think that only children believe in Santa Claus, that witches are the delusions of rural bumpkins, and that astrology is the delight of the senile. Not so. Well-read, educated, intelligent people around the world desert common sense and learning to pursue such matters. What surprised me in the extreme was to find that an organization comprised of the intelligentsia seems overly committed to this brand of nonsense! The group is known as Mensa, and membership is limited to those who possess IQs [Intelligence Quotient] in the upper 2 percent of the population.

I am not much deceived by the outward trappings of such an organization. Possession of a "high IQ" often has little to do with one's ability to function as a rational human being. It merely means that some admittedly imperfect tests indicate one has a better-than-average potential for good thinking. Like a scalpel that is never put to use by a skilled hand in a good cause, brainpower is often not put to work.

One unhappy Mensa member has kept me notified of trends in the group. The lead article in the April 1978 *Mensa Bulletin* was entitled "Psi-Q Connection" and asked the pregnant question, "Is there a psychic component to IQ?" The author, Richard A. Strong, is Coordinator of the Psychic Science Special Interest Group and editor of its newsletter. His article wondered if high IQ scores could be due to ESP rather than intelligence—a disturbing thought indeed for Mensa, which may be composed of ordinary folks who cheat and pick up their smarts from others, a sort of cerebral shoplifting!

Some "M's" claim healing powers; many claim to see auras. One Dan Conroy was said to be learning the "sidhis" of Transcendental Meditation so that he could levitate his intelligent body in the air. If he is as successful as the other 39,999 people taught by TM's Maharishi Mahesh Yogi, he's still grounded. . . .

So, if you have in the past fallen for the hucksters of psi, and if you are embarrassed by it all, take hope. The smartest folks in the world are no smarter than you are when it comes to belief in the ridiculous.

Deceiving the Public

The public has been badly served by scientists who lean upon their considerable reputations in other fields to give weight to their declarations on the subject of parapsychology. I have noted that possession of a driver's license permits one to drive an automobile only if the privilege is not abused; perhaps Ph.D.s should similarly be withdrawable in science.

The Computer Age came to parapsychology long ago. Back in the early 1960s, the technology was applied to ESP testing by the

United States Air Force Research Laboratories. A specially designed computer setup dubbed VERITAC was used to test thirty-seven subjects with 55,000 randomly generated numbers to determine once and for all whether psi powers existed. Psychologist C.E.M. Hansel, in closing his book *ESP: A Scientific Evaluation*, remarked, about the then-just-started series of tests, "If twelve months' research on VERITAC can establish the existence of ESP, the past research will not have been in vain. If ESP is not established, much further effort could be spared and the energies of many young scientists could be directed to more worthwhile research." When VERITAC tests, supervised by an electronics engineer, a psychologist, a mathematician, and a physicist, were completed, they proved—once again—that subjects do not have the ability to guess or to influence events any better than chance would have it. The team of scientists involved carefully pointed out a fact that in the decade to follow became blatantly evident: Parapsychologists tend to throw out "nonsignificant" data and report the "positive" material.

The "energies of many young scientists" that Hansel hoped could be directed more usefully are still being squandered on the pursuit of nonsense. VERITAC was thrown out as "nonsignificant.". . .

And just how mysterious is the "levitation" she describes? Really, if science has no explanation, I fear for that discipline. Any high school student could tell that a person is easily lifted when the individual's weight is divided equally among four others, all lifting together on cue and having enormous advantages of position to obtain great leverage. . . .

Bent Paper Clips

The May 1978 issue of the British publication *Psychic News* headlined a great "breakthrough" in paranormal research when Brian Inglis, author of a great deal of other nonsense along the same line, penned "An Historic Bending Experience." It soon became clear just what had really been bent. Drawing on an account in the September 1977 issue of the *Journal of the Society for Psychical Research (JSPR)*, Inglis gave his carefully omissive version of an experiment conducted by John Hasted, Professor of Physics at Birkbeck College, London. It was *supposed* to be a report of a major advance in parapsychology but a number of qualifying truths were cunningly dropped among the codswallop: "Psychics do not as a rule perform well in laboratories, or indeed in exacting test conditions of any kind" and "parascience has been pursuing two elusive quarries, quantifiability and repeatability." So much for the "breakthrough."

Hasted had performed many experiments to prove that children have powers enabling them to bend together masses of paper clips inside glass globes. The December 1976 *JSPR* issue described such tests, admitting that it was found necessary to leave holes in the globes and stating that the "scrunch" of paper clips obtained "cannot be produced physically inside a glass globe containing a small hole, but it can be produced paranormally by child subjects under these circumstances." Then, in a follow-up letter to the *JSPR* in June 1977, Hasted admitted that two experimenters . . . were able to show that "scrunches" were easily made by perfectly ordinary means in glass globes with an orifice as small as 2.5 millimeters. Exit the experiment.

Static Electricity and Little Boys

Another test consisted of hanging ordinary latchkeys from electrical leads terminating in embedded strain gauges to test for bending by paranormal influence. Inglis said these tests were conducted in the homes of the psychics, at their leisure. Children were the subjects, "tests were deliberately kept as informal as possible . . . and the subject was encouraged to do his own thing (making aircraft models) to pass the time."

Rather detailed accounts given by Hasted of the conditions of some experiments led me to suspect that the sharp "spike" tracings he got on his chart recorder connected to the electronic circuitry might be due to static electricity, not paranormal influence. He said the subject squirmed about and held his hands out to the dangling key occasionally, whereupon a result was recorded on the chart. But the very sharp spike is typical of a static discharge registration, so I sent off the circuit diagrams, which were kindly supplied by Professor Hasted, to Dr. Paul Horowitz of Harvard University for comments.

Dr. Horowitz replied, "You are, of course, right in your interpretation. . . . If that 'experiment' convinces anyone of anything, then they typify the utmost in gullibility.". . .

Brian Inglis commented on the Hasted experiments, saying that the skeptics could now fall back on the "last resort argument, collusion." Collusion? Who needs collusion when the experimenter follows weak methodology and the kid is allowed to do things his way? "Hasted has evolved an experiment which physicists can replicate anywhere," Inglis continues, "given the co-operation of a psychic, with whatever protocol they consider necessary." According to this reporter (he was charmed by the Swann magnetometer report too), the Millennium has arrived. But don't slip into the white robes just yet, folks.

As a conjurer, I must comment on Inglis's closing points. He says that conjurers look upon laboratories as "positive havens for deception." Hardly. Only laboratories run by incompetents would offer a conjurer conditions to his liking. Finally, Inglis writes, "Hasted's work will give stage magicians something to practice in the long winter evenings." Wrong. We conjurers (and other rational people) are too busy trying to figure out how men like Hasted and Inglis are still believed as spokesmen for para-science when the record is so damning. Hasted himself has said, "Validation without high credibility of the validators is inadequate. The credibility of a validator is his own responsibility." Very true. . . .

Reprinted with permission of *The Skeptical Inquirer*.

Hasted's work on this subject is *typical* of the entire field. He is a respected and supposedly competent researcher, revered by the believing public as one of the outstanding scientists at work today in parapsychology. The problem is that the public never gets to know the truth about the misleading experiments and discoveries that are reported by parapsychologists.

Briefly, I will touch upon some of the reports that demonstrate the sloppy thinking and procedures often employed by these people. Again, I will borrow Professor John Hasted's reasoning powers to illustrate the case. In December 1977 I wrote to the *JSPR* expressing my amazement that scientists were having such a hard time designing a simple test to determine the validity of ESP. I referred to the tests of spoon-bender Julie Knowles and others, provoking a reply from Hasted. I will enumerate and comment on a few of the points he used in rebuttal.

Referring to my intentions, he said that I was claiming I could "disprove the existence of a phenomenon without even beginning to understand what it is." Wrong. I have never claimed to be able to prove a negative—an impossibility. The burden of proof is on Hasted, who must prove there *is* a phenomenon, not on me to show there is none. The "historic experience" described above is not sufficient. Hasted also charges that "Mr. Randi . . . *demands* that metal be bent in sealed perspex [acrylic plastic] tubes." Wrong again. I have never demanded any such thing. It is the wide-eyed nincompoops (nincompoop: a corruption of the Latin *non compos*—"not of sound mind") who investigate spoon-bending children, who claim the kids can do this. Hasted himself claimed, at the Royal Institution, that his kids could do it! All I'm asking is that they do it for me—and receive my $10,000 and an apology. . . .

Julie Knowles was a young English girl who worked with John Hasted as a spoon-bender. According to Hasted she was a good worker, very strong and dependable. His description made her seem like just the one to walk away with my $10,000. Upon my arrival in England on other business, I received urgent phone calls and letters from Mrs. Hasted, begging me to come to Bath to watch tests of Julie in the lab there. I set aside time to do this and showed up in Bath in the company of colleagues to witness this wonder. We sat Julie in the lab and retreated behind a one-way mirror so as not to disturb her. Her mother, looking very fierce, stayed in a remote office, refusing to come anywhere near me except to collect the check. The girl sat there for two hours holding a spoon, the upper bowl of which was blackened with carbon to prevent her touching it without leaving evidence both on her hands and on the spoon that she had done so. Hasted sat nearby, saying constantly that he was seeing the spoon bend and nodding and smiling encouragingly. He had signed an agreement saying that our protocol was satisfactory, and he expected success. I knew damn well that as soon as Julie was discovered not to have any psychic powers working, he would rationalize like mad. I was right.

Rationalizing Failure

Hasted later complained that the protocol was complicated (it was not), that I had said Julie was "highly touted" (she was, by both Hasted and his wife), and that I had failed to test the unbent spoon for such changes as "nominal strain, residual stress, dislocation loop density, microhardness, grain structure, electrical resistance, specimen dimensions, etc." He ignores the fact that, unlike certain poor experimenters, we who designed the protocol for testing Julie Knowles *specified in advance* that we were testing for gross bending of a simple teaspoon, a feat the girl was said to be able to do. We did not intend to search for obscure peripheral effects and decide after the fact that *any* discovery was significant. When Hasted goes to the races he is not allowed to collect at the betting window if a horse he bet on to win comes in sixth and sideways. He simply does not recognize an adequate and proper experiment when he sees one! . . .

An Airtight Case?

Despite the many falling heads in the parapsychology hierarchy, until recently it was difficult for this skeptic to handle the problem presented by the work done in the 1940s by Dr. S. G. Soal in England. Soal reported that he had discovered a powerful psychic, Basil Shackleton, and the half-million tests that were run on him seemed to prove conclusively that he had genuine ESP powers. It appeared to be an airtight case. . . .

Soal used a table of logarithms to compile a list of numbers from 1 to 5 in random order. He chose the eighth digit from every hundredth logarithm, subtracting 5 when it was between 6 and zero—not by any means a perfect system, but relatively good enough. He would sit with his list and try to transmit each image (represented by a digit) to Shackleton. Shackleton's reply was given orally and written down before witnesses.

Professor G. E. Hutchinson of Yale declared the system "the most carefully conducted investigations of the kind ever to have been made." Professor R. A. McConnell of the University of Pittsburgh said of one of Soal's published works, "As a report to scientists, this is the most important book on parapsychology since . . . 1940. . . . If scientists will read it carefully, the 'ESP controversy' will be ended." C. D. Broad, the philosopher, said that the work was "outstanding. . . . The precautions taken to prevent deliberate fraud [were] absolutely watertight." Even parapsychologist J. B. Rhine gave glowing approval of Soal's design and results. These results *were* truly fantastic—on the order of billions to one against mere chance. . . .

Problems Appear

Not long after all this acclaim, it began to appear that there might have been some hanky-panky at work. An observer reported that she had seen Soal altering some 1's into 4's and 5's—his 1's were written very short and therefore were easily altered to produce the desired figures. When notified, Soal decided it was not "important enough" to report officially. But in 1973, when Christopher Scott and P. Haskell investigated, the case for Soal's deception was very strong. There were too few 1's and too many 4's and 5's in the target numbers. Many of the 4's and 5's in the list turned out to be "hits" in Shackleton's tests. Apparently, when the target was a 1, and the subject called out "four," it was simple and tempting for Soal to "correct" the 1 to a 4. But—and it is a huge "but"—even with these digits accounted for, the results of the tests were far better than mere chance would have them, and so the tests, though shadowed, stood as the best example ever of ESP proof.

ESP Will Never Be Demonstrated

Up until now statistical analyses have been used because investigators have been testing for ESP *ability*, a term that implies a disposition to get results above chance expectations. But a decisive experiment would provide confirmation that a person has had an ESP experience regardless of whether he is able to repeat his performance. When certain phenomena are genuinely established, then talk of "odds against chance" is downright silly. What, for example, is the probability that Woodrow Wilson was once President of the United States?

The kinds of experiments that would be impressive have never been done, and I fear the reason is obvious—there is not the slightest chance that any subject would have an ESP experience. When I say the reason is obvious, I mean it quite literally. It is obvious to ESP investigators, too. However, they would say that perhaps ESP doesn't occur under such unfavorable conditions. Perhaps indeed.

Sidney Gendin, *The Skeptical Inquirer,* Summer 1981.

In *Proceedings of the Society for Psychical Research,* Betty Markwick, a statistician, revealed early in 1979 the damning facts about Soal that had not been suspected. Aside from changing a few digits when the opportunity arose, it seems he also cleverly managed another simple ruse. Markwick found—after much labor—the places in the logarithm tables where Soal had chosen his digits. Not only had he gotten unforgivably lazy and repeated some series on the lists without properly arriving at them; he also had left *spaces* in his target list every few digits, into which he inserted "winning" target digits as the tests were conducted. No one had thought to observe him, and in fact they could not, since according to the rules his list was supposed to be secret until presented for checking. But the evidence was there, for the "E.D.s" (extra digits) that had been discovered were "hits" that agreed with Shackleton's guesses. Suddenly, there was no longer any mystery about where these results had come from.

Soal was down and out for good, and the last bigshot in the business was discredited. But it remained to J. G. Pratt, a parapsychologist at the University of Virginia Medical Center, to provide the most astonishing bit of rationalization in defense of Soal that has ever been heard in this field—a field long famous for its Catch-22s and superb alibis. Although Pratt admitted that he "must put all of this work aside marked to go to the dump heap," he could not refrain from the ingrained tendency to excuse the obvious peccadilloes of his former colleague. The work of Miss Markwick, said Pratt,

> does not provide an unambiguous interpretation . . . that would, for example, justify our concluding that Soal consciously cheated in his research. . . . I am the person who suggested that Soal might have become his own subject on some occasions when preparing the lists of random numbers on the record sheets before the sittings were held. This explanation would require that he used precognition when inserting digits into the columns of numbers he was copying down, unconsciously choosing numbers that would score hits on the calls the subject would make later. For me, this "experimenter psi" explanation makes more sense, psychologically, than saying that Soal consciously falsified for his own records.

What Professor Pratt is trying to tell us, folks, is that S. G. Soal had powers of precognition that allowed him to unconsciously predict the numbers that Shackleton was going to call the next day, and that he unconsciously inserted these predicted numbers into the list! Pratt adds that "we cannot sit in judgement of Soal regarding his behaviour, motives and character." Oh, yes, we can. And we did. Guilty as charged.

"[There is no other] discipline which aims at following the scientific methods whose data and theories are so widely disclaimed by orthodox scientists."

Orthodox Science Is Unfairly Biased Against ESP Research

Robert H. Ashby

The following viewpoint is taken from Robert H. Ashby's work *The Guidebook for the Study of Psychical Research*, a reference manual for those interested in investigating paranormal phenomena. Ashby argues that orthodox science is unfairly biased against ESP research, and is unwilling to make the necessary conceptual leap to accommodate the reality of paranormal phenomena.

As you read, consider the following questions:

1. Why does Ashby believe that orthodox science is unfairly biased against ESP research?
2. Why, according to Ashby, are paranormal phenomena often difficult to measure or test?
3. Why is ESP research important, according to the author?

Excerpted, with permission, from *The Guidebook for the Study of Psychical Research* by Robert H. Ashby. London: Rider and Company, 1972.

There is surely no field of study in which the concepts, beliefs, and biases of our 'common sense' world clash so violently with the data collected and analysed by scholars as psychical research or, as it is frequently termed today, parapsychology. Nor is there any discipline which aims at following the scientific methods whose data and theories are so widely disclaimed by orthodox scientists. Indeed, a sizable majority of scientists would doubtless contend that psychical researchers have not established that there is anything to investigate. In short, the scientific community at large still rejects the data that indicate that 'paranormal phenomena'—earlier called 'psychic phenomena'—i.e. occurrences which do not fit into currently known patterns, behaviour, or theories, ever occur. Dr. George R. Price may be cited as typical of this school of thought. He is quoted in *Science Digest* for November 1965 as saying:

> My opinion concerning parapsychologists is that many of them are dependent on clerical and statistical errors and unintentional use of sensory clues, and that all extra-chance results not so explicable are dependent on deliberate fraud or mildly abnormal mental conditions.

Such a situation in scientific circles, following ninety years of careful research into psychic phenomena, might be termed a paranormal phenomenon itself. It is, however, true that this attitude has gradually changed during the last twenty-five years and that an increasing number of younger scientists in many fields are open-minded about Extrasensory Perception (ESP) and feel that psychical research is an important area of study. The changing climate of opinion was indicated in a most encouraging manner in December of 1969 when the American Association for the Advancement of Science accepted the Parapsychological Association as an affiliate member.

The Scientific Method

Why has this fledgling science aroused such scientific hostility and scepticism? The scientific method utilised in scientific disciplines can be summarised as one in which the phenomenon under study must meet the following criteria:

1. isolation from other phenomena in nature
2. observation under conditions controlled by the scientist
3. repeated experimentation
4. results both statistically assessable and obtainable by any other scientist replicating the experiment and its conditions precisely.

Thus, one must have: isolation, observation, control, experimentation, measureable data, and repeatability both of experimentation and of results in order to establish the reality of the phenomenon. It is true, of course, that this method is more readily applied with some types of phenomena than others. Chemistry and astronomy cannot be approached in exactly the same manner; and behavioural sciences like psychology have had to modify the methodology somewhat. Nevertheless, these canons of evidentiality and predictability undergird the acceptance of phenomena by the scientific community.

The central problem is that paranormal phenomena have very rarely conformed to this pattern. They have most often been 'spontaneous', occurring without prior planning or preparation for observation, control, or experimentation. In such instances, researchers have had to depend upon witnesses to the phenomena to describe as carefully as possible what they believe occurred, and as soon as possible after the 'ostensibly paranormal' phenomenon occurred. The phrase 'ostensibly paranormal' is used to show that whether the experience was, in fact, paranormal is a judgement to be made only after all the evidence has been analysed and all 'normal' explanations have had to be rejected. Many critics of psychical research may not fully realise how many reports of strange happenings have been proven by parapsychologists to be explicable by perfectly normal means, or have been rejected as inadequately supported by convincing evidence. Probably few more than one out of a hundred reports received have ever been found worthy of publication.

ESP in the Laboratory

Such witnessed accounts of phenomena possibly paranormal in nature do not satisfy the scientist as meeting either his usual methods or his standards of evidence. Hence, parapsychologists set out to devise experiments which would conform to the scientific method. While there were numerous earlier attempts, it is during the last forty years, beginning in the United States with Dr. J. B. Rhine at Duke University, that researchers in many countries have conducted such controlled laboratory experiments and have garnered impressive evidence that ESP does occur under controlled conditions, that these experiments can be repeated by other researchers, and can sometimes yield similar extra-chance results.

These experiments have centred upon using a pack of test cards consisting of twenty-five cards with five different designs. The person trying to demonstrate ESP, the 'subject', would try to guess which card was being held by the experimenter in another part of the room, another room, or another building. Since there are five cards of each of the five designs in the pack, the chance result would be one out of five, or five right in the pack of twenty-five. If a subject could obtain appreciably more than five right in each test over a considerable number of tests, this showed that something other than chance was operating; and since there was no opportunity for the subject to use his five senses to ascertain the correct card, there was sound statistical evidence to indicate that 'something' other than chance and other than the five senses was responsible for the accurate 'guessing'. That 'something' has been termed Extrasensory Perception.

"I'm still not convinced. I wanted the pepper."

Attoe. Reprinted courtesy of *Omni* Magazine © 1990.

Dr. Helmut Schmidt, formerly a physicist with the Boeing Scientific Research Laboratories and successor to Dr. J. B. Rhine as Director of the Foundation for Research into the Nature of Man, caused a sensation by publishing in 1969 and subsequently precognitive and PK [Psychokenesis] results of experiments conducted with randomness assured by using 'single quantum processes'. Subjects tried to guess which of four bulbs would next light and indicated their choice by pressing the appropriate button. Three subjects performed a total of over

63,000 trials with precognitive success at odds of two billion to one against chance. In a second test of 20,000 trials subjects could choose either to press the button of a lamp that would light or one that would not, and the results were equally impressive. The scientific community seems to have been more impressed by Dr. Schmidt's work than that of any other parapsychologist of recent years, and his sophisticated use of highly complex technology to guarantee both randomness and accuracy of recording results is an important development. . . .

Continued Skepticism

Yet, despite this statistical evidence, many scientists still reject the reality of ESP. Why? First, because, as Dr. Price said, there *could* be errors made by the researchers in recording the results of the tests, and, because of the researchers' bias in favour of ESP, such errors would tend to support rather than to deny it. Second, where the researcher and the subject were close, it *might* be possible that the subject had 'sensory clues', i.e. heard the researcher inadvertently mumble the name of the design on the card, or saw through a badly printed card and so learned which design was being held, or noticed that the researcher tended to act in a particular way when a certain design came up in the pack. Third, since we do not know a great deal about how we learn, there *may* be a perfectly physical explanation which is possibly 'mildly abnormal' or unusual, but still within the sensory system. Last, there *might* be 'deliberate fraud' either by the subject or the researcher or both. Obviously one cannot absolutely refute such an allegation unless one were present during all the experiments and observed very carefully both parties involved; even then, of course one could be suspected by another scientist of fraudulent conspiracy with the original two, and so on *ad infinitum*. In short, the accusation of fraud is impossible to disprove completely, however honest and meticulous a researcher has been. But one may fairly ask what would either the researcher or the subject gain by such fraud? Certainly not financial rewards: there is very little money available for research, and most subjects have been volunteers; possibly fame either as a scholar or as a gifted psychic, but such reputations have more generally been viewed as notoriety than renown in the scientific community; possibly self-esteem, but this would be absurd, since the fraudulent person would know better than anyone that he was a fraud. It is most difficult to see what end would be served by such alleged collusion. It assumes either dishonesty or naïveté to an extraordinary degree over decades by hundreds of intelligent and responsible people who had no reason to cheat, but it remains the final, unanswerable criticism which has been faced by psychical researchers for ninety years.

The scientists have issued these criticisms partly because they found that the experiments described above did not prove so repeatable or so conclusive in terms of results as Dr. Rhine and his associates claimed. Why? The enormous amount of research during the last twenty-five years into the psychological states conducive to the operation of ESP has established firmly that this faculty (generally termed *'psi'* and covering all aspects of the paranormal ability) is elusive, unpredictable, emotionally triggered and repressed, sensitive to surroundings, conditions, and, especially, to attitudes towards psi itself. Psi is much more likely to operate if the subject and the researcher are predisposed to believe that psi does or may exist, and if both the conditions and the experimenters are relaxed, comfortable, and cheerful. Parapsychologists have found that some subjects perform better with certain researchers than with others; that results depend upon the subject's health and mental state; that subjects tend to lose interest in the numerous repeats of the test and boredom suppresses psi; and that many other generally uncontrollable variables can affect the performance of psi.

Psi Research

Now for a scientist to achieve the kinds of results which seem to demonstrate statistically that psi does exist, it is clear that he would need something other than the detached, sceptical frame of mind with which he prides himself as he approaches his experiments. He might need different surroundings from the sterile, utilitarian, stark laboratory; he must hope that he could establish a warm rapport with the subject; he must realise that if the subject was distraught in some way, psi might well not evidence itself; and he must recognise that most of these variables he could not control. In short, it appears that to establish for himself psi as a reality, the scientist must already believe, partially at least, that it *could* exist. This has proven too much of a departure for most scientists, and it is not surprising that their attempts to repeat Rhine's experiments have not been generally successful. And so they have gathered far less evidence of psi than psychical researchers when, for conviction, they have needed far more. Psychologist Ernest R. Hilgard explains why in *Science Digest*, November 1965:

> To demonstrate something highly implausible requires better evidence than to demonstrate something plausible. The reason is that supporting evidence for the plausible finding comes from many directions, while the implausible one must hang from the slender thread of nonrandomness until certain systematic relationships are found that tie it firmly to what is known.

Despite the widespread denial of the reality of psi by the scientific community, psychical research continues amidst rapidly growing interest in its findings and its significance among the general public. This is because if psi and its manifestations do exist a revolution in general scientific and 'common sense' thinking will be necessary. Psychical researchers ask whether some people can:

• exchange ideas or impressions via some extrasensory means termed 'telepathy'? If so, does this indicate anything about the extent of the mind's powers and range?

• perceive objects, persons, or happenings without the use of the five senses, sometimes at great distances? If so, does 'clairvoyance' demonstrate anything about the nature of man's perceptions?

• foresee events in detail without any inferential or logical reasons? If so, does this 'precognition' signify anything about man's free will?

• apparently 'step back in time'? If so, does this 'retrocognition' indicate anything about the quality, or even the existence, of time itself?

• perceive accurate visions of persons known and unknown, alive and dead? If so, do these veridical 'apparitions' mean anything in terms of man's dramatic faculties, or possibly of his basic essence, the so-called 'soul'?

• cause objects to move without touching, pushing, or throwing them in any normal manner which science considers necessary by the laws of motion? If so, does this 'telekinesis', 'psychokinesis' or 'PK' demonstrate anything about the power of thought or human will?

• perceive detailed data about an unknown person by touching objects once in that person's possession? If so, does this 'psychometry' show anything about the tactile faculty and about any normally imperceptible residue of an intimate and unique character upon an object which the sensitive's fingers seem to detect?

• communicate with 'personalities' which claim to be, and sometimes seem to be, the spirits of deceased persons? If so, does this 'discarnate communication' indicate anything about death and the possible survival of human personality?

Other Paranormal Phenomena

Do a whole range of other ostensibly paranormal phenomena occur, including 'poltergeists', dream phenomena, animal phenomena, 'apports', 'materialisations' by means of a strange substance termed 'ectoplasm', 'table tipping', wherein the table seems to move of itself and to tap out meaningful messages, 'levitation', wherein an object or a person seems to rise without any known means of doing so, 'astral projection' or 'out-of-the-body experiences' wherein the percipient claims to have left his physical body and while in his 'astral body' to have perceived persons, places, and events which he could not have perceived normally from the location of his physical body, and 'spiritual healing'? If so, do such phenomena shed any light upon the scientific framework within which we usually move and think?

A Scandal

I say it is a scandal that the dispute as to the reality of these phenomena should still be going on—that so many competent witnesses should have declared their belief in them, that so many others should be profoundly interested in having the question determined, and yet the educated world as a body should still be simply in the attitude of incredulity.

Henry Sidgwick, Presidential Address to the Society for Psychical Research, 1882.

In view of such questions and the documentation gathered since the close of the last century which suggests that some of these things do happen on occasion, it is hardly surprising that the scientific establishment has not reacted kindly to psychical research. Yet, as Dr. Rhine has pointed out, it is surely unscientific to term something 'impossible' especially in the face of the extant evidence available for careful and critical scrutiny. Unfortunately, far too few scientists have examined the evidence in such a manner. The prevalent attitude has very often been that of the Cambridge don of chemistry who, in debating the reality of psychic phenomena with Sir Arthur Conan Doyle, based his rejection of their actuality upon the fact that 'I once attended a séance'. Doyle retorted that were he to debate a topic in chemistry, how absurd his position would be were he to base his conclusions on the statement 'I once visited a chemistry laboratory'.

"Today ESP is no nearer to being established than it was a hundred years ago."

Orthodox Science Is Not Unfairly Biased Against ESP Research

C.E.M. Hansel

C.E.M. Hansel, an emeritus professor of psychology at the University College of Swansea, in Swansea, Wales, is the author of ESP and Parapsychology: A Critical Re-evaluation. *In the following viewpoint, Hansel argues that in one hundred years of ESP research, no reliable evidence has emerged to support the existence of the phenomenon.*

As you read, consider the following questions:

1. What are the two main types of ESP investigations, according to the author?
2. What kinds of methods, according to the author, have psychical researchers used to test subjects for ESP?
3. What kinds of evidence does Hansel provide to refute the findings of ESP research?

C.E.M. Hansel, "The Search for a Demonstration of ESP," in *A Skeptic's Handbook of Parapsychology*, Paul Kurtz, editor. Buffalo, NY: Prometheus Books, 1985. Reprinted with permission.

Any act is conditional on underlying processes. Visual identification of an object requires both the use of the eyes and that light is reflected from the object. Parapsychologists claim that some people have the ability to perform such acts as identifying objects when the conditions normally assumed to be necessary for their execution are absent. Such behavior they call extrasensory perception, or ESP.

If people can act in this way new processes have to be admitted as underlying brain activity and the manner in which organisms interact with the environment. The existence of ESP would thus be of profound significance not only to the understanding of human behavior but also to science in general. It would signify that there are underlying processes in nature so far undiscovered that permit ESP to occur. ESP is possible or impossible depending on whether or not such processes exist. . . .

ESP Experiments

ESP investigations have been of two main types. In the first type, the performance of a particular individual is studied. Here the subject has developed a procedure with which he claims to be able to demonstrate his psychic ability. He may not agree to modifications or alternative procedures required by the investigators. Any experimentation is then dependent on the extent to which the subject will do as he is asked by the experimenters. . . .

The second type of investigation takes the form of an experiment in which the design, method, and procedure are decided by the experimenters while the subject does as he is told to do and takes no other part in the experiment. The experiment may eventually lead to a set of conditions and a procedure with which a particular result is demonstrable. One fact evident in ESP experiments is that subjects are only successful in a fraction of their attempts. A satisfactory demonstration therefore requires a sufficient number of observations to ensure that failure is extremely rare.

For demonstrations of this nature, in the words of R. A. Fisher. ". . . We may say that a phenomenon is experimentally demonstrable when we know how to conduct an experiment which will rarely fail to give us a statistically significant result."

Such a demonstration has not been forthcoming. Rather, a large number of experiments have been reported that fail to be confirmed at the first attempt or as soon as obvious weaknesses are removed from them. . . .

A major investigation in which the investigators have made a large number of observations with a large sample of subjects and achieved a result that has astronomical anti-chance odds should be repeatable if the result has not been due to experimental error or trickery. If such an experiment fails to repeat, the cause of the original high scores must be sought. . . .

Clairvoyance is the simplest form of ESP, in that only a single individual is involved. It may be defined as the acquiring of information about some object or event without the mediation of the senses. . . .

Clairvoyance Experiments

In 1929 an experiment was reported by Ina Jephson, a Council member of the Society for Psychical Research. Jephson used 240 subjects who tested themselves in their own homes. Instructions were sent by post asking each subject to complete 25 trials guessing the identities of playing cards, but making only five attempts on any one day. The subject was instructed to take a pack of playing cards, shuffle it, and draw out a card at random keeping it face down. He had to guess the card, record his guess, and then write against it the actual value of the card followed by the suit. He replaced the card in the pack and repeated the whole operation until he had recorded 5 trials. In this manner he completed five attempts on each of five days. The 240 subjects thus completed a total of 1,200 sets of 5 trials, giving 6,000 trials in all.

The results were assessed in terms of the chances of the card (1/52), its number (1/13), suit (1/4) and color (1/2) being correct. The 6,000 guesses produced 245 complete identifications as against the chance number of 115, giving enormous anti-chance odds. High above-chance scores were also obtained for number, suit, and color.

It was suggested by Dr. S. G. Soal, a lecturer in mathematics at London University and a member of the Society for Psychical Research, that three sources of error might have been present in Jephson's experiment: (1) the use by some subjects of old packs of playing cards, some of which the subject by constant use might have learned to recognize through markings on the backs; (2) careless manipulation of the cards, which may have resulted in the subject getting information on color or suit, possibly via reflections from a polished table; (3) the carrying out by some subjects of more than five sets of guesses on a particular day and then sending in the results of the best set.

Precautions were taken to exclude these forms of error in a further experiment . . . carried out by Jephson, Soal, and Theodore Besterman, the research officer of the Society for Psychical Research. A large number of playing cards with plain backs were placed in blue envelopes that exactly fitted the cards. The envelopes were of such a nature that they could not be rendered transparent by strong light, X-rays, or solvents, such as alcohol, nor could they be opened without leaving traces. They bore on both sides the impress of the Society for Psychical Research's stamp. As an added precaution the whole operation of preparing targets and checking results was supervised by a fourth experimenter—Colonel Dick. The envelopes were sealed and sent to 559 percipients in batches of five in five successive weeks.

A total of 9,469 guesses showed no trace of any extra-chance factor. It was then clear that the original result obtained by Miss Jephson was not repeatable even though more than twice the number of subjects were tested in the repeat experiment. . . .

Telepathy

Telepathy may be defined as a hypothetical process whereby one person receives information about another person's thoughts or experiences without the mediation of the senses. Thus in telepathy experiments a second person acts as agent or sender.

The first experimental investigation of telepathy using a group of subjects and playing cards for targets was reported by John E. Coover, professor of psychology at Stanford University, in 1917. He used 105 guessers and 97 senders in a series of 10,000 trials. Coover sat with the sender in one room, and the guesser was situated in an adjoining room. The door between the two rooms was kept open. The targets consisted of playing cards 1 (ace) through 10 after the face cards had been removed. Before each guess was made Coover threw a die to decide whether the sender should see the card or not. The trials on which the card was not seen by the sender constituted a control series, in which telepathy was not possible. The remaining trials formed the experimental series, where telepathy was theoretically possible because a second person saw the cards. Sources of experimental error due to the manner in which targets were selected would be present equally in the experimental and the control series.

Coover had stated that he would require odds against chance of at least 50,000 to 1 to convince him that telepathy was possible. In the event, the difference in scores between the two groups was not significant at even the 0.05 level. From this it was concluded that no support was forthcoming for the hypothesis of telepathy.

A further experiment using playing cards was reported in 1927 by G. H. Estabrooks, a graduate student in the Department of Psychology at Harvard. He used Harvard students as subjects, selecting those who were "positively interested." Estabrooks acted as experimenter and sender, with the guesser in an adjoining room. A total of 2,300 trials was conducted. In the initial three series, subjects were highly successful in terms of the suit of the card, but when they were sent to a more distant room with better insulation for a fourth series scores dropped to chance level.

Estabrooks stated at the end of his report that further tests were being made by his assistant at Springfield College, Springfield, Massachusetts. According to J. B. Rhine, who was in the Psychology Department at Harvard at that time, "Estabrooks' 'telepathy' experiment succeeded for him but was said to have failed the next year when repeated by an assistant."

No Scientific Evidence

The total accumulation of 130 years' worth of psychical investigation has not produced any consistent evidence for paranormality that can withstand acceptable scientific scrutiny. What should be interesting for the scientific establishment is not that there is a case to be made for psychic phenomena, but, rather, that the majority of scientists who decided to seriously investigate *believed* that they had made such a case. How can it be that so many scientists, including several Nobel Prize winners, have convinced themselves that they have obtained solid evidence for pararnormal phenomena?

R. Hyman, *A Skeptic's Handbook of Parapsychology,* 1985.

Estabrooks made an observation regarding subjects that is of interest in relation to the experiments that Rhine started the following year. He wrote: "Another point is the very interesting fact that with practice a certain type of man can be weeded out beforehand. The very worst type of man for an experiment of this kind is the instructor in psychology; second only to him is the graduate student in the same subject. They simply cannot attack the problem in the proper spirit but insist on criticising the experiment and, much worse, reacting to it as they think it should be reacted to, and not as they are told to react."

The following year, Rhine accompanied William McDougall when he moved from Harvard to set up a department of psychology at Duke University. Rhine's first ESP experiment was concerned with a telepathic horse called Lady Wonder. . . . He then carried out tests on telepathy and clairvoyance using cards with symbols depicted on them. The experimenter acted as sender in telepathy experiments or merely held the cards face downward in clairvoyance experiments. Rhine tested children using numbers 0 to 9 as targets without discovering a single child whose performance warranted further investigation.

After that, in the fall of 1930, an experiment was conducted in collaboration with K. E. Zener, of the Department of Psychology. Three types of symbols were employed: numbers (0-9), letters of the alphabet, and cards containing five different symbols (star, square, circle, plus sign, and wavy lines) that had been suggested by Zener. A total of 1,600 trials was conducted with scores at chance level with each type of symbol. . . .

It is remarkable that after this, when Zener dropped out of the research leaving Rhine to his own devices, results came in thick and fast. By 1934, Rhine had found that among the 14 graduate students in the Psychology Department, 6 had ESP ability to a marked extent, one had been reported to have the ability; and the remaining 7 had not been tested. The 6 high-scoring subjects achieved results indicating, without need for statistical analysis, that something other than guesswork was involved. These graduate psychology students at Duke were obviously quite different from those at Harvard.

Rhine found that in clairvoyance conditions it was unnecessary to isolate the target card from the pack. A pack of 25 Zener cards was shuffled, cut, and placed face down in front of the subject, who then recorded his guesses for the cards starting with the top card and proceeding down through the pack. After he had recorded his guesses they were checked against the targets and produced high above-chance scores.

It was discovered that a modification could be made when using the down-through technique. If the cards were shuffled after the subject had recorded his guesses, scores were still above-chance. This resulted in the discovery of "precognition". . . .

Clairvoyance and Telepathy

Rhine came to the conclusion that subjects did equally well under clairvoyance and telepathy conditions. R. H. Thouless, noting this conclusion, suggested that a small overall above-chance score when combining the control and experimental series in Coover's experiment was due to clairvoyance operating in the control series. Since that time it has been supposed by many parapsychologists that Rhine's conclusion was correct. If the agent or sender is redundant and is omitted from ESP experiments it is far easier to arrange foolproof conditions owing to the ease with which targets can be kept secret.

In his first book, *Extra-Sensory Perception*, published in 1934, Rhine produced what he claimed to be overwhelming evidence for ESP. In the following years, a number of psychology departments repeated his experiments in the attempt to confirm his results.

The first experiment of this nature was reported by W. S. Cox (1936) of Princeton University. His 132 subjects produced 25,064 trials when attempting to guess the suits of playing cards. Cox's conclusion was: "It is evident from the above results and computations that there is no evidence of extrasensory perception either in the 'average man' of the group investigated or in any particular individual of that group. The discrepancy between these results and those obtained by Rhine is due either to uncontrollable factors in experimental procedure or to the difference in the subjects."

Pseudo-Science

Parapsychology is indistinguishable from pseudo-science, and its ideas are essentially those of magic. This does not of course mean that psi does not exist, for one cannot demonstrate the non-existence of psi any more than one can prove the non-existence of Santa Claus. But let there be no mistake about the empirical evidence: There is *no* evidence that would lead the cautious observer to believe that parapsychologists and paraphysicists are on the track of a real phenomenon, a real energy or power that has so far escaped the attention of those people engaged in "normal" science. There is considerable reason, on the other hand, to believe that human desire and self-delusion are responsible for the durability of parapsychology as a formal endeavor.

J.E. Alcock, *Parapsychology: Science or Magic?* 1981.

Failure to confirm Rhine's findings was also reported from four other psychology departments in the United States. . . . In Britain, S. G. Soal reported a similar failure to confirm the findings. Since Rhine had had little difficulty finding subjects and had voiced the opinion that about one in five of the population had ESP ability, the contrary findings using large groups of subjects were difficult to account for. Rhine came to the conclusion that the presence of critics affected the subjects and removed their ESP ability. . . .

Summary

In a hundred years of ESP research, a number of facts emerge: (1) In a small number of reported experiments, above-chance scores have been reported that are due either to ESP or to experimental error or trickery. (2) There has been a high incidence of trickery in parapsychology and a long history of inept experimentation. (3) A repeatable demonstration has not been forthcoming. . . .

Today ESP is no nearer to being established than it was a hundred years ago. The long history of trickery and inept experimentation, and the inability to confirm ambitious claims, serves to confirm the view held at the start by the majority of scientists that perception is mediated by the senses—that without sensory processes, perception is not possible.

A Test for ESP

This activity is designed to test your powers of ESP. The activity includes four experiments, each of which deals with a different aspect of ESP. The four aspects are:

Telepathy: mind-to-mind communication or thought transference

Clairvoyance: perception of objects or events outside the range of normal vision

Precognition: knowledge or perception of future events

Psychokinesis (PK): mind over matter, or the ability to affect external objects (moving them or altering their appearance, for example), using only the powers of the mind

While the experiments for telepathy and clairvoyance require at least two participants, the tests for precognition and psychokinesis can be performed alone.

To get the most out of this activity, you must approach these experiments with an open mind. For instance, if you firmly believe that ESP does not exist, do not ridicule the experiments or fake the results. Remember, no one has absolutely demonstrated that ESP does not exist. Similarly, if you really do believe in the existence of ESP, remember that the results of the experiments may not support your beliefs. After all, it has proven very difficult to replicate the results of even the most celebrated psychic researchers. While absolute honesty and objectivity are required of all participants, the experiments are also a chance to have some fun!

Telepathy

Take twenty-five blank index cards and draw one of the following symbols on each card: a cross, a square, a circle, a star, and wavy lines. Each symbol should be on five cards. Now you have your own Zener deck. Shuffle the cards. Have your partner hold the cards and concentrate on mentally sending the symbols to you, one at a time. As you indicate which symbol you believe is being sent, your partner should write down each try as a hit or a miss. Repeat the experiment until you have completed a hundred tries. If you hit more than twenty out of a hundred

142

cards, chances are that your guesses are not mere coincidence. Let your partner try the experiment, too.

Clairvoyance

Obtain twenty different picture postcards, each with a different scene on it. Have your partner place each postcard in a separate envelope and number the envelopes from 1 to 20, then seal and shuffle the envelopes. Now have your partner hand you an envelope. Try to describe the scene on the postcard sealed inside the envelope. Your partner records which envelope (1 to 20) is being described along with the description you give. Open the envelopes. See how closely the descriptions match the pictures on the postcards. The closer the descriptions, the more impressive your powers of clairvoyance.

Precognition

The simplest way to perform this experiment is to write down your dreams as soon as you wake up in the morning. Or try to wake yourself up from your dreams and write them down immediately. The important thing is to record your dreams right after waking, as our recollections of our dreams fade rapidly with time. Notice times when your dreams seem more intense than usual (they could be ESP dreams strongly announcing themselves). Review your journal from time to time to see if any dreams came true.

Psychokinesis

This test is an adaptation from one devised by authors Hans J. Eysenck and Carl Sargent. It requires a single six-sided die, a glass or cup to shake it in, and a pen and paper to record your score. When you toss the die, try to make each face of the die come up six times after you toss it. In other words, try to make the side with one dot come up six times, the side with two dots six times, and so on. Attempt to make the die land with the number you want by concentrating your mind on it. It is best to toss the die against a hard surface such as a door or a box. Since there are six faces on the die, you will toss it thirty-six times. Record each result. If you hit eleven to twelve times, that indicates some positive PK effect. Thirteen times is good, and more than fourteen hits is excellent.

If you are performing these experiments in a class or group, compare your results with those of other class or group members. Have any class members demonstrated powers of ESP? Have the results changed the opinion of any class members about the existence of ESP? You may wish to enliven your discussions by sharing with the class your recollections of any past psychic experiences.

Periodical Bibliography

The following articles have been selected to supplement the diverse views presented in this chapter.

Jennifer Boeth Donovan "Psychic Powers: Fact? Fantasy? Fraud?" *Woman's Day*, November 24, 1987.

Steve Fishman "Questions for the Cosmos," *The New York Times Magazine*, November 26, 1989.

Sidney Gendin "ESP: A Conceptual Analysis," *The Skeptical Inquirer*, Summer 1981. Available from *The Skeptical Inquirer*, Box 229, Buffalo, NY 14215-0229.

Roberta Grant "Psych Out! The Woman Who Catches Killers with Her Mind," *Redbook*, May 1989.

C.E.M. Hansel "The Evidence for ESP: A Critique," *The Skeptical Inquirer*, Summer 1984.

Terence M. Hines and Todd Dennison "A Reaction-Time Test of ESP and Precognition, *The Skeptical Inquirer*, Winter 1989.

Andrew MacKenzie "How Common Are Psychic Experiences?" *Fate*, November 1987. Available from PO Box 64383, St. Paul, MN 55164-0383.

David F. Marks "Explaining the Paranormal," *World Press Review*, May 1986.

David G. Myers "ESP and the Paranormal: Supernatural or Super-Fraud?" *Christianity Today*, July 15, 1983.

Dean I. Radin "Parapsychology Bushwhacked," *Fate*, February 1989.

D. Scott Rogo "The Sender's Role in Telepathy," *Fate*, December 1990.

Michael Ventura "Looking Quickly to the Side: The Other World of Phenomena," *Utne Reader*, September/October 1989.

Can the Future Be Predicted?

PARANORMAL PHENOMENA

Chapter Preface

While astrology is most widely known from the brief horoscope columns in newspapers and magazines, true adherents follow a much more sophisticated system. Astrologers draw up detailed charts of the skies, showing the exact locations of specific celestial bodies at specific moments, such as the moment of a person's birth or the anticipated time of the closing of an important business deal. These charts are ardently studied and interpreted by tens of thousands of amateur and professional astrologers around the world. Adherents say that astrology is an art and a science that allows people to better take charge of their lives. Agreeing, journalist Dennis Elwell writes that astrology enables people to "achieve a 'cosmic vision,' move out from our blinkered human viewpoint and . . . grasp the universal processes in a more immediate and comprehensive way."

However, few scientists believe there is any valid basis for a belief in astrology. For example, astronomer Richard Berendzen, president of American University in Washington, D.C., calls astrology "pure hokum" and adds, "It sounds a lot like science. It's got technical terms. . . . It's got jargon. . . . [But] the fact is, there's no theory for it, there are no observational data for it. . . . Nobody's ever found any validity to it at all."

The authors in this chapter debate the merits of the ancient field of astrology.

"Astrology . . . [is] one more valuable tool in the search for self-knowledge. "

Astrology Can Guide People's Lives

Frederick G. Levine

Frederick G. Levine is the author of *The Psychic Sourcebook*, a "consumer's guide" to the world of psychics. In the following excerpt, Levine discusses the basic workings of astrology. He believes that astrologers can offer definite guidance to enable people to know themselves better.

As you read, consider the following questions:

1. How does Levine say modern astrologers differ from ancient ones in their beliefs about the interaction of earth and the cosmos?
2. According to the author, how do the movements of stars and planets affect people's lives?
3. What part does psychology play in the role of the astrologer, according to Levine?

The word "psychic" is actually a misnomer when it comes to astrology, numerology, and palmistry. These systems of divination can, in some ways, actually be considered "sciences," since they represent well-ordered systems of calculation that can be learned by anyone and then applied using objective criteria, requiring no psychic ability. They are based on the idea of "correspondences"—that all phenomena in the universe, whether physical or spiritual, are interrelated on some fundamental level, and that the patterns found in the physical universe—for instance, the movement of the planets—are reflected in the realm of human endeavor. By first taking a close look at astrology we will get a better understanding of the mechanism by which these practices work.

Astrology dates back about 4,000 years to the Chaldean and Babylonian civilizations. We can be sure that human beings were observing the motions of the heavens from the time they first gazed upward, but the actual mapping of the movements of planets and stars evolved along with civilization as a way of charting the change of the seasons to facilitate agriculture. Very early on, however, stargazers also began to use the planetary cycles to mark human and cultural events—what later became known as "mundane astrology." We can speculate that at this early point in human history the connection between humanity and nature was still strong, and that on some level people were still very much aware of the intertwining of the cycles of the natural world and the human organism. . . .

Direct Effect of the Planets

The ancient astrologers believed that the planets actually had a direct influence on human events, and although modern astronomers dismiss this idea, there is at least some evidence that a connection exists. Take, for example, the fact that the length of a woman's menstrual cycle corresponds to the phases of the moon, or that the gravitational fields of the sun and moon are strong enough to cause the rising and falling of tides on the Earth (and that the human body is 70 percent water!). Current theories of cosmology posit that at the moment before the "big bang" that created the visible universe, all matter and energy existed at a single point in space and time. This means that on a profoundly real level, everything that exists in the universe is fundamentally related. Physicists now also tell us that all matter is bound up in fields of energy, so much so that the explosion of a supernova in a distant galaxy impacts on our solar system in some way.

In spite of all these indicators that there might be some grain of truth in the ancient view of astrology, most modern astrologers believe that the mechanism by which astrology works is much more subtle. They reject the idea that celestial events assert a direct physical force on earthly occurrences and instead take a more holistic view of the process. This thinking is based upon the metaphysical axiom, "As above, so below." This means that there are larger patterns of energy that govern all interactions in the universe and that these patterns or cycles are reflected in the movements of stars and planets in the same way they are reflected in the movements of people and cultures. Thus it is not that planetary motions *cause* events on earth, but simply that those motions are *indicators* of universal patterns. Linda Hill, a New York astrological consultant of 14 years' experience, explains this relationship:

> I don't think anyone knows exactly why it works; it just works. Carl Jung used the term synchronicity. It's simply a synchronization. Ecologically, why does every microscopic protozoa affect everything else? Well, there's a chain that links it back—some kind of a relationship between the microcosm and the macrocosm. We are a part of everything *and* we are individuals. We are part of this whole solar system, and somehow we are uniquely imprinted at birth. We are somehow synchronized to the celestial patterns that were present at our birth. It's not that the planets are doing it *to* us, it's that we're synchronized *with* them. It's not a causal relationship. . . .

The holistic patterns that astrology deals with are chiefly manifested in the dynamics of relationships. The relationships between planets reflect the relationship of the individual to the world at large. Although this relationship takes many forms, it essentially involves the ways in which a person sees the events that take place in his life. The point of astrology is not so much to try to alter or avoid those events as to put them into a context that enables an individual to use them as opportunities for growth. The astrologer does this by preparing a horoscope.

A Map of the Planets

A horoscope is basically a map of where all the planets and zodiac constellations are at a specific time. A natal horoscope charts the positions of the planets at the time of your birth. Mundane horoscopes chart the planetary positions at the time of particular world events, such as the establishment of nations or of political groups. A business or financial horoscope would fix the positions of the planets at the time a new business is launched or contract is signed. A horary ("of the hour") horoscope is designed to answer a specific question a person might have—the chart is drawn up for the moment at which the astrologer is asked the question. Synastry is the process of comparing two individual natal charts to determine the compatibility of two people. Sometimes a third chart will also be drawn up for the relationship itself, which is considered an entity in its own right.

The astrologer begins preparing your horoscope from the moment you call for your appointment. You will be asked for the *exact* time and place of your birth. (For myself, it wasn't enough to say that I was born in New York City; the astrologer wanted to know what borough the hospital was in!) Your time of birth should be given down to the minute since the positions of the planets are constantly changing and the entire chart changes every four minutes. (An astrologer can determine, for instance, that the sun entered the zodiac sign of Aquarius on January 20, 1959, at precisely 7:19 P.M.) Your birth time is first converted into Greenwich mean time and then into sidereal time, which is a universal time measurement based upon the stars rather than the rotation of the earth.

Blueprint of the Universe

At this point the astrologer will look up your sidereal birth time in a book called an ephemeris, to determine what the exact positions of the sun, moon, and planets were then. Your sun sign, which is the one used in magazine and daily newspaper horoscopes, is determined by the position of the sun at your time of birth. In the same way the 12 signs of the zodiac mark the path of the sun during the course of a year, they are said to embody the evolution of the individual throughout the course of his life. . . .

Astrology Aids Understanding

Astrology isn't voodoo, but rather a system of world outlooks, which enables people to know themselves and their place in life, and provides them with a key to spiritual development. . . .

Astrologers can help resolve problems of human relationships and make recommendations for finding a compatible mate. Astrologers can help parents understand their children by defining their personality traits.

Pavel Globa, *Soviet Life*, December 1989.

The planets, which move through the signs, represent distinct archetypal energies or functions in relation to the whole person. A planet manifests its function within the context of the sign that it is in, much in the way that a person's wishes and desires are expressed through the mediation of his personality and psychological makeup. Thus planets in Aries express their energy assertively and forcefully, for example, while planets in Gemini are manifested logically and verbally.

In addition to the zodiac signs, the astrologer also charts the planets with regard to the 12 houses, which, unlike the signs and planets, are purely artificial divisions. There are different ways of dividing up a horoscope into houses, and each astrologer has his own preferred method. The houses indicate the area of your life in which a planet will manifest its energy, whereas the sign is the "style" in which that energy is asserted. The second house, for example, is the house of personal values and money; the seventh house is the house of one-on-one relationships, such as professional partnerships, marriage, or even patient-therapist.

To understand how all this comes together, take the example of someone with Venus in Aries in the second house: such a person would have a great love of personal values and money, which would be expressed forcefully and with great impulsiveness, and he would tend to attract money, since Venus is the planet of attraction. Similarly, a person with Venus in Gemini in the seventh house would have a strong desire for marriage or partnership, especially with someone who is logical and intellectual, but would find it difficult to remain with just one partner.

Ascendants, Aspects, and Transits

In addition to these elements of your chart, an astrologer will also determine your ascendant, or rising sign, the transits of the planets (their movement through the zodiac), and the aspects of the planets (the angles formed by their relationship to each other). There are also a number of other celestial movements and astronomical relationships that can be factored into the horoscope for a more precise reading.

The degree of research and calculation necessary just to prepare a horoscope is extensive, which is one of the reasons why astrologers are generally more expensive than other types of psychic readers. (It is also the reason why magazine and newspaper horoscopes, based purely upon the 12 sun signs, are at best hopelessly general and at worst, outright frauds.) The advent of personal computers, however, has enabled the skilled astrologer to cut her calculation time drastically. . . .

When all the research and calculations are done, it is still the ability of the astrologer to synthesize all the information in a coherent manner that finally determines the accuracy of the reading. . . .

Most astrological work involves psychological analysis—using the natal horoscope to help a person understand who he is, what his inner composition is made up of, and what patterns of behavior tend to manifest themselves most strongly, so he can work with them in dealing with life's twists and turns. Pinpointing those twists and turns is the job of predictive astrology, which relies heavily upon the transits and aspects of planets. The transits don't necessarily predict that a specific event will occur as much as they indicate a tendency for something to happen at that point in time. In this way they trigger the potentialities that are present in the natal chart. As Linda Hill explains:

> Transits are like cosmic weather conditions: which forces are impacting us at any given time; why sometimes we feel terrible and sometimes we feel great and sometimes we feel powerful and sometimes like we want a change. They begin at certain times, they end at certain times. We tend to remember, when bad things are happening, that they're going to pass, but we forget that when good things are happening, they're also going to pass. So you have to maximize the good times by knowing how long you have to get things handled before they pass and you have to know, if you're in a difficult period, when there's going to be a letup and how it can be used positively, as opposed to just sort of caving in and going to bed with it. Because it can always be transmuted and transformed into something useful for your own growth. . . .

Although these readings sound very cut-and-dried, a skilled astrologer relies as much upon his intuitive skills as upon his objective knowledge. So although we might not consider astrology a function of psychic ability, neither is it a pure science. . . . In a way, we've come full circle: although there are astrologers who approach their work in a purely scientific way, at some point, every skilled reader is going to have to rely upon less tangible methods of interpretation. Whether those intuitions are purely the product of extensive study and experience or the manifestation of psychic ability depends upon the astrologer and upon how you view psychic ability as a whole. But like other methods of divination, astrology clearly integrates us with a level of knowing that lies deeper than the rational mind. Perhaps if we concern ourselves less with the mechanics of that insight and more with its content, we will come to appreciate astrology as yet one more valuable tool in the search for self-knowledge.

"Astrology . . . has no discernible basis in fact. "

Astrology Cannot Guide People's Lives

Paul Kurtz

Paul Kurtz is a noted philosopher and founder of the Committee for the Scientific Investigation of Claims of the Paranormal (CSICOP). He has written more than two dozen books, many of them on paranormal topics, and is the editor of the humanist magazine *Free Inquiry*. In the following viewpoint, he discusses some of the weaknesses he sees in astrology and some of the reasons belief in it persists.

As you read, consider the following questions:

1. Why does Kurtz believe that astrology is sometimes dangerous?
2. Kurtz describes experiments by Paul Couderc and Michel Gauquelin in which hundreds of people were sent the same horoscope. What does Kurtz believe the results prove?
3. Why does the author think people cling to astrological beliefs?

Excerpted, with permission, from *The Transcendental Temptation: A Critique of Religion and the Paranormal* by Paul Kurtz. Buffalo, NY: Prometheus Books, 1986.

Astrology is a cumbersome though enormously fascinating system of belief, and it continues to captivate the human imagination. With the advent of modern astronomy . . . astrology was given a rude shock, and during the eighteenth and nineteenth centuries it seems to have been thoroughly discredited, at least among the educated classes. Yet it never disappeared entirely, and it has been revived in the twentieth century, with great popularity in even the most advanced, affluent, and highly educated societies of the Western world. Today, horoscopes appear in large-circulation newspapers and magazines, and professional astrologers outnumber professional astronomers. Why is this so? Is it because astrology is true? Are its empirical claims valid? Does it work?

Sun-Sign Astrology

We may evaluate astrology . . . by examining the concrete empirical descriptions and prognostications of astrologers in order to ascertain whether or not they are accurate. We will do this, first, by evaluating the accuracy of sun-sign descriptions and, second, by analyzing horoscopes. Most people are familiar with sun-sign astrology, for this is what appears in popular newspaper columns. No idea is more influential in astrology than the notion that a person's traits are determined by the position of the sun in his or her chart. Linda Goodman summarizes the effect of sun signs as follows:

> The sun is the most powerful of all the stellar bodies. It colors the personality so strongly that an amazingly accurate picture can be given of the individual who was born when it was exercising its power through the known and predictable influences of a certain astrological sign.

Following is a list of these signs and a brief description of their meanings:

The Constellations of the Zodiac, Namesakes and Selected Sun-Sign Characteristics

Constellation and symbol	Animal namesake	Selected characteristics
Aries	ram	headstrong, impulsive, quick-tempered
Taurus	bull	plodding, patient, stubborn
Gemini	twins	vacillating, split personality
Cancer	crab	clinging, protective exterior shell
Leo	lion	proud, forceful, born leader
Virgo	virgin	reticent, modest
Libra	scales	just, harmonious, balanced
Scorpius	scorpion	secretive, troublesome, aggressive

Sagittarius	archer/horse	active, aims for target
Capricornus	goat/fish	tenacious
Aquarius	water carrier	humanitarian, serving mankind
Pisces	fish	attracted to sea and alcohol

Exhaustive scientific testing of sun-sign astrology has been done. The results are invariably negative. R. B. Culver and P. A. Ianna, in *The Gemini Syndrome: A Scientific Evaluation of Astrology*, examined the claims in detail. For example, people born under the sign of Aries are supposed to have the following physical characteristics, according to one astrologer: "A longish stringy neck like a sheep; a look of the symbol in the formation of eyebrows and nose; well-marked eyebrows; ruddy complexion; red hair, active walk." Focusing on red hair, Culver and Ianna point out that this would exclude blacks and Orientals, and most Hispanics, who have black or dark brown hair. They conducted a survey of 300 redheads to find out the sign under which they were born, and found (1) that only 27 of them were born under Aries, and (2) that no one sign showed a predominance of red hair. Natural red hair, which is a genetic trait, is not determined at the moment of birth.

No Pattern of Physical Characteristics

The Astrologer's Handbook describes many physical characteristics. Scorpios are depicted as follows: "In appearance, they are generally of robust and strong build. They often possess keenly penetrating eyes and a strong aura of personal mystique and magnetism." Culver and Ianna provide an evaluation of other physical characteristics, such as neck size, skin complexion, body build, height, weight. Again they find there is no correlation with any of the signs, so that one characteristic or type predominates over the others.

An important and often dangerous element in astrology is its diagnosis of medical conditions and diseases. Yet Culver and Ianna find that there is no correlation between the sun signs and illnesses, such as diabetes, heart disease, rheumatism, or even acne. They find these distributed equally across the signs.

Much less is said today about the physical aspects of astrology because of the patent quackery associated with it, yet that is an essential part of its tradition. Most emphasis now is on personality traits, occupations, and compatibility between people. Concerning personality traits, we find the following account of those born under Capricorn:

> Because Saturn rules Capricorn, the natives have a tendency to [be] melancholic and, at times, lonely. . . . They have sensitive personalities and want very much to be appreciated. . . .

They are neat and methodical in their work and tend to be slave drivers at home. . . . Capricorns are excellent executives and remain in subordinate roles for a short time only.

Those born under Libra "are intellectual, and actively seek knowledge, new ideas, and mental stimulation. . . . they frequently play the role of peacemaker. . . . Libras are ruled by the planet Venus which gives them charm and grace . . . with a desire for popularity."

The problem with these descriptions of traits is that they are so general they can be applied to almost anyone, especially since they tend to focus on positive qualities. Of Sagittareans we read the following: They are "naturally serious thinkers, concerned with the well-being of society as a whole as well as with their own lives. . . . they are honest, just, and generous . . . they are energetic and naturally outgoing."

It is difficult to measure abstract traits; they tend to be elusive. In any case, tests have shown no correlation between the predicted personality traits and the signs under which a person is born. Culver and Ianna examined traits from aggression and ambition to understanding and wisdom and found no apparent correlation.

One way to measure the accuracy of astrology is by correlating occupations and careers with sun signs. Studies have been made of sports champions, actors, army officers, men of science, politicians, artists, etc. by consulting various reference works that list occupation. Thus John D. McGervey examined the birthdays of 16,634 scientists in *American Men of Science* and 6,475 entries in *Who's Who in American Politics* and found no basis for the assertion that occupations tend to predominate under certain signs. Other thorough statistical studies done by E. Van Deusen and Culver and Ianna likewise show no correlations. . . .

Horoscopes

So much for sun-sign astrology, which has no discernible basis in fact and yet enjoys tremendous popularity with a vast public. Most professional astrologers will admit, however, that sun-sign astrology is only part of their diagnosis, and hence unreliable by itself. They maintain that although the sun is the strongest influence on a person, the positions of the planets must be charted for a completely accurate account. Here it is not simply the monthly range, but, as we have discovered, the exact time and place of birth that must be recorded. Each horoscope is like a personal fingerprint or signature. Only a trained, professional astrologer can give a precise diagnosis. So the question can be raised: Are detailed horoscopes accurate? I am afraid that the same criticisms we made of sun-sign astrology can be raised against the more elaborate horoscopes and that they also fail the test of adequacy—but for a variety of subtle reasons.

How accurately do horoscopes analyze personality? A number of researchers have randomly distributed horoscopes in order to test their fit. The French astronomer Paul Couderc advertised in a French newspaper that free horoscopes were available for those who wished them. Every respondent was sent the same bogus horoscope. It included such phrases as "You have inner conflicts . . . Life has many problems . . . you sometimes upset people," etc. He asked for comments and received them from 200 persons. A large number of people claimed that the account fit their personalities perfectly.

Dangers of Astrology

Commenting on astrology and similar pseudosciences, a university professor of astronomy remarked, "It's dangerous to cling to this superstition because it abdicates responsibilities for your actions and your own destiny. That's a very dangerous illusion to live by."

Bob Larson, *Straight Answers on the New Age*, 1989.

The next case concerns the horoscope of a person born on January 17, 1898, at 3:00 A.M. in Auxerre, France. It reads in part:

As he is a Virgo-Jovian, instinctive warmth of power is allied with the resources of the intellect, lucidity, wit. . . . He may appear as someone who submits himself to social norms, fond of property, and endowed with a moral sense which is comforting—that of a worthy, right-thinking, middle-class citizen . . . The subject tends to belong wholeheartedly to the Venusian side. His emotional life is in the forefront—his affection towards others, his family ties, his home, his intimate circle . . . sentiments . . . which usually find their expression in total devotion to others, redeeming love or altruistic sacrifices . . . a tendency to be more pleasant in one's own home, to love one's house, to enjoy having a charming home.

An advertisement was placed in a French newspaper by Michel Gauquelin inviting people to send in their name, address, birthday, and birthplace. About 150 replied; each person was sent a full, ten-page horoscope, from which the quotation above is taken, a return envelope, and a questionnaire. Of those who answered the questionnaire, 94 percent said they were accurately portrayed in the horoscope and 90 percent said that this judgment was shared by friends and relatives. It was the horoscope of Dr. Marcel Petoit, a mass murderer. Dr. Petoit posed as an underground agent who would help refugees fleeing from the Nazis. Instead, he lured them to his home, robbed them, and dissolved their bodies in quicklime. Indicted for twenty-seven murders, he cynically boasted of sixty-three. So much for the accuracy of horoscopes! . . .

Why Does Astrology Persist?

The question that can be raised is why, in spite of a lack of evidence for its claims, and considerable negative evidence to the contrary, does astrology persist as a belief-system? . . .

One explanation is that the general public has not been exposed to the benefits of scientific criticism. Generally, proastrology propaganda is far greater than any negative criticism. If many were given scientific studies, they might be persuaded to reject the claims. There is no guarantee, however, that even if many people were aware of the negative arguments, they would reject astrology.

A second explanation is that gullibility is often very strong in the human breast, and that many people tend to accept claims that appear authoritative. They are often deceived by con men and women. Here, the guru is the astrologer, who is speaking mumbo-jumbo but is quite persuasive. There is still another element that enters in, however, and that is self-deception; this applies to both the client and the practitioner.

Astrology, like religion, is a faith; it is based upon, and reinforced by, subjective validation. In other words, the prognostications and evaluations of the astrologers appeal to a kind of inner intuition. The readings are so general that they can be applied to almost anyone. The truth is in the eye of the beholder, who stretches the diagnosis to meet his own case. "You are outgoing, yet often want to be alone," or "you are sympathetic, but often not appreciated by others." Where a horoscope is cast and the astrologer meets the client on a one-to-one basis, the former is often able to adapt the reading to the context of psychological interaction, and the reading may be facilitated by what the reader observes about the person. The reading depends upon common sense and shrewd intuition.

Astrology Speaks to Human Aspirations

There is a deeper and more profound lesson from our study of astrology, and that is that the transcendental temptation is probably influencing a person's attitude toward what he is being told. In his conscious or unconscious is something like the following: The universe has a plan, and this includes the heavens. The plan encompasses each and every individual, including myself. Thus, my personal character and destiny is tied up with the stars. There is something beyond, and what I am or will become is synchronized with that.

Astrology thus speaks to a person's desires and aspirations and gives a cosmic explanation for even the most trivial, inconsequential or idiosyncratic happening in the lives of individuals. The temptation to believe in a transcendental force tends to reinforce people's hopes and wishes, and allows for subjective validation. Whether astrology is empirically true or false is not the central issue. Whether it works—or is made to work—by fulfilling a hunger for meaning is of vital significance. And that, I submit, is its psychological function, and the key to its continuing hold on the human imagination through the centuries.

159

"[Astrology] is the most ancient, most validated,
most followed tool of self-awareness yet devised
by humanity."

Astrology Is a Science

Grant Lewi

Grant Lewi (1902-1951) was a prominent astrologer whose work
helped to popularize this field. His publisher, Llewellyn Publications, continues to update his popular books. In the following
excerpt, Lewi describes some of the reasoning behind astrology
as well as how the position of specific cosmic bodies can influence people's lives. Lewi believed knowledge of astrology could
help individuals control their destinies.

As you read, consider the following questions:

1. According to Lewi, what kinds of self-knowledge can people
   obtain from their horoscopes?
2. Summarize the influences the author says the sun, moon, and
   planets have on people's lives.
3. Does Lewi believe astrology is based on predetermination,
   that is, the belief that everything that will happen in life is
   determined before we are born?

From *Astrology for the Millions* by Grant Lewi. St. Paul, MN: Llewellyn Publications, 1990.
Reprinted with permission.

You are born under certain conditions about which (except perhaps on a most esoteric level) you have absolutely no say. From your parents and ancestors you inherit physical and mental characteristics. You come into a pre-existing environment, that came of age before you were born. At the moment of birth, you arrive with inherited equipment into the world and were denied tangible choice in the matter. . . .

Astrology's value to self-understanding begins and in the long run rests securely on the fact that it *provides you with a permanent record of what surrounded your life at its beginning.* The record of that moment when you were thrust into the world, stating the conditions that surrounded your birth, can provide you with a clear statement of those things for which analysts and individuals working along other lines of research probe laboriously only to emerge at the end with less-than-certain results.

Horoscope, or Vitasphere

The picture of what surrounded your life at its beginning is called the *horoscope,* or more appropriately the *Vitasphere* (from *vita,* life; and *sphere,* globe). The Vitasphere is generally represented as a flat surface, though it is in reality the representation of a globe, with the earth at the center and the Planets and stars above, below, all around, just as they were situated at the moment of your birth. The Vitasphere—your horoscope—is, in effect, your Universe of life. At the center is you. Around you, symbolized by the Planets and the starry constellations, are the forces of heredity and environment impinging upon you from all directions, as they were at the moment you emerged into human existence.

The Vitasphere is a blueprint of your personality and character as indicated by the position of the Sun, Moon and the Planets on the date and exact time of your birth. From your Vitasphere you can determine just exactly (1) the mental, physical and psychic hereditary equipment with which you were born, (2) the environmental pattern into which you were born and (3) how (1) and (2) interact to produce the unique person that is you.

The following chart is the Vitasphere of a famous person, the late President John F. Kennedy. You can see that it contains all of the major bodies of the solar system: the Sun (☉), the Moon (☽), and the Planets Mercury (☿), Venus (♀), Mars (♂), Jupiter (♃), Saturn (♄), Uranus (♅), Neptune (♆) and Pluto (♇). The Vitasphere shows the relationship of the Planets to the Earth and to each other and their relationship to that which came into existence at the specific point of time for which it is made. All the attributes that made up John F. Kennedy are coded in this horoscope. A trained astrologer could take that horoscope and trace the ebb and flow of Kennedy's life. In your own Vitasphere are contained the attributes that your life expresses and all the forces that operate upon you.

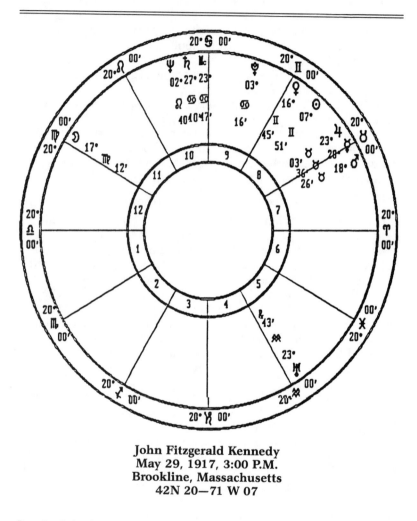

John Fitzgerald Kennedy
May 29, 1917, 3:00 P.M.
Brookline, Massachusetts
42N 20—71 W 07

Grant Lewi, *Astrology for the Millions*, 1990.

The horoscope, properly understood, is far from vague. First, and foremost, it provides an index to the inheritance of the person for whom it is done. On your horoscope you would see an indication of your physical body, your mental qualifications, your psychic and psychological biases. Given these fundamentals, it records the channels along which sensory and emotional impressions will be transmitted from the outer world to your inner nature, and it shows how your nature will respond to and make use of these impressions. It provides an index to the flow of your energies and the directions they are likely to take. It warns how you will react to experience as it flies headlong into your face, and how you will set up and use defenses which, in our complex lives, so greatly complicate nature's first law of self-preservation. Beyond all these, it indicates the deep psychic bias which is our collective ancestral inheritance, and how this will express itself, creatively or destructively, as we seek to become fully human and fully ourselves. . . .

The Sun and the Moon

The two most important heavenly bodies in the Vitasphere are the Sun and the Moon. Together they express what might be termed the masculine and feminine natures. In this day of depth psychology, feminism and New Age discoveries, the old truth of astrology has found increased substantiation in the broadening perspectives of the Self. Each of us has a Sun and a Moon in our Vitasphere; each of us has a masculine and feminine side, or *animus* and *anima*. Each of us has a more-or-less developed assertive aspect, a mode of living. We also have intuitive aspects, ability to assimilate and digest the data that floods into us from the environment.

Vital energy pours over us from the *Sun* daily and makes life possible and energizes us for the pursuit of our myriad activities. It also inspires us to the consciousness of a destiny toward which we can and should aspire. The Sun represents our ego, our individuality, or, to use the insight of modern science, all those things generally categorized as left-side brain activity. This would include, astrologically speaking, the external nature of the individual, the physical attributes superficially considered, the expressiveness, the extroverted qualities, and the manner in which *you* will assert, or fail to assert, yourself in contact with life.

The Sun also represents the brain, as a physical organ, and the Sun's relationships to the other Planets indicates brain soundness and brain strength. The Sun does not suggest intelligence so much as it hints at the physical soundness of the brain as an organ. It is possible to have a brain in perfectly good working condition but of little intelligence, imagination, adaptability or wisdom. In like measure it is possible to have a weak, unstable brain, distorted by chemicals and unbalanced forces, which nevertheless possesses considerable intelligence and wisdom.

Where the Sun occurs in the Vitasphere will highlight specific characteristics. For example, Kennedy's Sun was in Gemini. This accounts for his outgoing nature, his ability as a conversationalist and a politician, not to mention his famous wit. Geminis (people are usually labeled by the sign of the Sun in their

Vitasphere) tend to be rational, idealistic and given to humanitarian causes.

The location of the Sun in your Vitasphere will indicate how you assert your individuality in everything from your career to your friendships. It will indicate whether you tend to be straightforward with people or subtly seek to get your way by manipulation or deceit. It will suggest your basic approach to people as either a sensuous, emotional or mental being.

The Moon takes in the light from the Sun and reflects it upon the world. To the individual, the Moon represents the inner realm. As the Sun traces the individuality, so the Moon defines the personality. It is a general indicator of the inner nature, pointing to the use you will make of the physical attributes indicated by the Sun. It provides an index to psychic and mental qualities, particularly those that arise from the functioning of those physical capacities most related to the Sun. Under the Moon's rulership are such abilities as intuition, sensitivity, understanding and initiative. The Moon controls the extent to which data is assimilated into the intelligence, the mode of impressions as they are absorbed by the intelligence and their nature when they emerge from the intelligence.

When you look at the Moon in your own chart, you will begin to understand the subtle (and not-so-subtle) forces that come into play as you interact with others. You will gain some idea of why and how you balance the search for higher values (love, peace, faith) with the desire to acquire material possessions. You may have any one or several of hundreds of personality "quirks" which stand out like a sore thumb (or a diamond ring!) when you are with people. For example, Kennedy's Moon can be found in Virgo (♍). Such positioning tends to give a person an acute sense of self-worth, an essential quality for anyone who would aspire to the most powerful office in the world. It also indicates a person who gives great attention to detail, an attribute Kennedy was famous for possessing.

Other Planets

Where the Sun and the Moon in the Vitasphere represent the two essential characteristics of the individual, Mercury and Venus represent the channels by which the individual—the personality—receives and processes data. Mercury controls the perception of sense data, while Venus controls the emotive life. . . .

Mars, Jupiter and Saturn represent the relation between the individual and the outer world. The Sun and Moon represent the Self and Mercury and Venus the tools of perception with which the Self is equipped. Mars, Jupiter and Saturn take all the assets of the Self for interaction with the outside world: production and consumption, career, luck and fate, and finally destiny.

The last three, very slow-moving Planets (Uranus, Neptune

and Pluto) define specific characteristics that are shared by large numbers of people born in specific time periods. [For instance] . . . Pluto, which stays in a single sign for 12-30 years, will denote characteristics of a generation. . . .

The Sun, the Moon and the Planets move through the heavens against the backdrop of the Stars. As astrology developed, this backdrop was mapped by dividing the sky into twelve segments, each of which was designated by a particular constellation. Thus the signs developed. Each sign, it was discovered, represented a different mode or nature through which the Sun, Moon and the Planets would manifest. Thus the personality, represented by the Sun, will tend to manifest in one of the twelve modes, depending upon which sign of the zodiac it is found. In like measure the Moon and the Planets will vary. We have already illustrated this principle in the chart of Kennedy.

Many words have been written trying to summarize and delineate the meaning of a particular Planet's expression in particular signs. In the end one must get the feel for what it means to have, for example, Mars manifesting through Gemini or Venus located in Aries. The Vitasphere indicates tendencies in the individual life, not the exact content life will take; given a few facts and all the Vitasphere's data, however, some amazingly precise predictions can often be made. . . .

[By now] . . . you should have some idea of what astrology is and how it works. You should know that astrology is the science of observing the movements of the Planets and discerning the relationships between those movements and the course of human lives. You should be aware that astrology can tell you a great deal about yourself with a great deal of precision. It cannot tell you how to run your life or what decisions to make (though many astrologers-turned-busybodies may like to try), and astrology most certainly does not lay before you a predetermined future.

Astrology does offer vital information about the Self—you as an individual—and the forces that are currently influencing your life. It discloses hidden potential, untapped resources and talents, and possible areas of deficiency. It is the most ancient, most validated, most followed tool of self-awareness yet devised by humanity.

"In every test, the astrologers' claims have been refuted."

Astrology Is Without Scientific Basis

Shawn Carlson

When he wrote the following viewpoint, Shawn Carlson was a visiting scholar at Berkeley Labs in California. In the following viewpoint, Carlson asserts that although astrology is interesting, it certainly is not science. He points out inconsistencies in astrological belief, describes scientific experiments that do not support astrology, and argues that the public should be protected from astrological charlatans who take advantage of people's gullibility by claiming to be able to guide their lives.

As you read, consider the following questions:

1. List two of the inconsistencies in astrological belief that Carlson finds troubling.
2. Carlson says that although astrology has no scientific basis, many people still believe in it. What factors does he say account for that belief?
3. What dangers does the author believe astrologers pose for gullible clients?

From "Astrology," by Shawn Carlson, *Experientia*, vol. 44, 1988. Reprinted with permission of the publisher, Birkhauser Verlag, Basel, Switzerland.

Astrology, the oldest and most entrenched of all the 'occult arts', has been a source of entertainment, controversy and livelihoods for nearly four thousand years. It is not just an idle pastime, taken seriously by only a few. Astrology pervades our popular culture. It has captivated the imaginations of tens of millions and influenced decisions of great import. Great battles have been waged, empires have fallen, and fortunes made and lost on the advice of astrologers. Although harassed by the Church and attacked by skeptics throughout history, astrology has risen in modern times to become a world industry, affecting the lives of millions every day. . . .

Astrological Theories and Beliefs

All astrologers are united in the belief that knowing the positions of the 'planets', (all planets, plus the Sun, Moon, and other objects that astrologers define) enables them to make accurate statements about life on Earth. They believe that ancient peoples discovered subtle connections between the planets and all life on Earth, and passed this knowledge down. The mechanism of these relationships is left unspecified. Although some astrologers do try to invoke gravity, electromagnetism, 'planetary vibrations' etc., to explain how astrology functions, most admit ignorance. They simply know, they say, that astrology works. . . .

Astrologers divide the Sun's path into twelve 30° sectors, called the 'signs of the zodiac': Aries, Taurus, Gemini, Cancer, Leo, Virgo, Libra, Scorpio, Sagittarius, Capricorn, Aquarius, and Pisces. The signs are so named because, when Ptolemy first established the Western system of astrology in 140 A.D., they corresponded roughly to the twelve constellations that happened to reside in the Sun's annual path.

The first sign, Aries, begins at the position of the Sun on the first day of spring. This 'vernal equinox' is located by considering the Earth at the center of the celestial sphere. The axis of the Earth's rotation is tilted so the ecliptic plane does not cut the Earth straight through its equator. If we project the Earth's equator out to the celestial sphere it forms a ring called the 'celestial equator.' The celestial equator crosses the ecliptic plane in two places, the autumnal and vernal equinoxes. The sign of Aries begins at the spring crossing.

Defining the signs with respect to the vernal equinox has lead astrology into some difficulty. The Earth can be thought of as a large spinning top. If the Earth traveled alone in space, its axis would stay forever fixed in one direction. However, the constant tug from the Sun and Moon causes the Earth's axis to slowly drift, or 'precess.' As the axis shifts, so does the celestial equator. Thus, the position of the vernal equinox slowly moves with respect to the background stars. Although this precession is very slow, only 1/72° per year, the vernal equinox has shifted over the centuries so much that the signs of the zodiac no longer correspond to the background constellations for which they were named. Most of the sign of Aries now overlaps the constellation of Pisces, for example. Thus, if the newspaper horoscopes tell you that your Sun sign is Aries, odds are that the Sun was really in the constellation of Pisces when you were born.

This presents modern astrologers with the problem of which zodiac they should use: the Sidereal zodiac which references the planets to the background stars, or the Tropical zodiac which references the planets to the vernal equinox. The choice is fundamental and there is no agreement. Two astrologers using different zodiacs will generally come up with contradictory conclusions about the same client. In fact, neighboring signs carry many nearly opposite character associations. Thus, the precession has caused two nearly opposite meanings to be applied to the same sections of sky. Clearly, both systems cannot be correct.

Disagreement Among Astrologers

But this is only one of many fundamental disagreements between astrologers. To keep track of the planets' locations as the Earth rotates, astrologers divide the sky into 12 'houses' which rotate with the Earth. Astrologers believe that the effect a planet has on a person strongly depends on which house it resided in when that person was born. For instance, it is believed that Mars, if on the horizon when a person is born, affects that person differently than it would have had it been at its highest point in the sky. The rules astrologers use to divide up the sky constitute a 'house system.' There are at least three fundamentally different house systems being widely used today, all of which lead to different interpretations of a person's personality. Two of these, the Placidean and Koch systems, fail to define houses for the 12.5 million people born above a latitude of 66.5°. Thus, although astrologers believe they can describe all people's characters, the house systems most preferred cannot be used to construct natal charts for all people. . . .

Worst of all, there is no agreement as to how the whole chart should be interpreted. There is no agreement even on a basic philosophy of interpretation. Some astrologers believe that every factor in a chart has its own meaning and makes its own contribution which can be included by rigorously following a set of rules. Others teach that chart interpretation is a gestalt process and emphasize the importance of intuition in deciding what factors are dominant in a given chart. Still others use the chart in conjunction with 'psychic' impressions. Such interpretations range from mostly astrological interpretations with only a little bit of 'psychic' information, to mostly 'psychic' use of the chart for inspiration.

168

As a field of knowledge, astrology is a quagmire of contradictions. The many different schools of interpretation use many different methods of chart construction and offer many mutually inconsistent conclusions about a given person's character. The different schools disagree violently on most of the fundamental issues involved in chart interpretation, each believing itself to be the school closest to the ultimate astrological truth. Since at most one school could be correct, the majority of astrologers must be fooling themselves and their clients.

Astrology for the Frail

Astrologers sense the deep insecurity of people who would trust them rather than themselves. That the astrologically inclined are likely to be dependent is an old observation. They seek certainty in the stars—powerful, mysterious, remote, and seemingly eternal. The paradoxical notion that these distant entities are somehow concerned with the destiny of each individual restores order to what might otherwise seem to be an utterly capricious existence. At the same time it lifts the weight of responsibility from the shoulders of the frail.

Murray L. Bob, *The Skeptical Inquirer*, Fall 1988.

Many modern authors dress astrology up as a worthy scientific discipline. Some claim the basic astrological thesis has been confirmed in the laboratory by numerous scientists who were initially critical of astrology. However, astrologers only cite that literature they interpret as supportive, and ignore the vast literature that contradicts them. Other astrologers believe they have 'scientifically' demonstrated astrology's veracity because they have directly observed astrological influences acting in their clients' lives. Unfortunately, these astrologers have only observed that, under very poorly controlled conditions, they can convince themselves that they are able to give their clients accurate astrologically derived information. What astrologers don't seem to realize is, if the game is played in their way, they can't possibly lose!

There are numerous ways of satisfying clients. A common sense knowledge of psychology, knowing what people generally like to believe about themselves, and being sensitive to body language are all that is necessary for a very impressive 'cold reading' of a client. In the many astrological readings that I have observed the astrologers back-peddled when they erred, then reinterpreted the chart until they ultimately said something with which the client agreed. On summing up the reading, they only emphasized the points of agreement.

These tactics, and the fact that most people willing to spend their money on such counseling believe in astrology already, make it easy to see why astrologers are so successful. That people recognize general personality descriptions as accurate for themselves, and can be satisfied even when astrologers use a wrong chart to describe their personality, is well established. . . .

Experiment Failed to Support Astrology

In 1985, I published the results of a carefully controlled experiment. Its purpose was to give outstanding astrologers the best possible chance to apply their craft in a controlled setting to see if they could get accurate information about people they had never met.

Three recognized expert astrologers consented to act as advisors on the experiment's design. They also selected those of their peers they considered sufficiently competent to participate, made 'worst case' predictions for how well their colleagues would do, and approved the design as a 'fair test' of astrology. Twenty-eight of the ninety astrologers who had been recommended by the advisors agreed to participate.

Volunteer test subjects took a widely used and generally accepted personality test, the California Personality Inventory (CPI), to provide an objective measure of their character traits. The astrologers chose the CPI as the personality test which came closest to describing those character attributes accessible to astrology. A computer constructed a natal chart for each subject.

Natal Charts

The experiment consisted of two parts. In the first, the natal charts were divided up amongst the astrologers. For each natal chart, the astrologers wrote personality descriptions covering material that they felt sure the subjects would be able to recognize as accurate. The subjects received their own astrologically derived personality description and two others chosen at random, and were asked to select the description that they felt best fit them. Extensive controls were established to eliminate self-attribution and other possible biases. If astrology does not work, one would expect only one third of the subjects to select the correct personality descriptions. The astrologers' own 'worst case' prediction was that the subjects would score at least 50% correct.

In the second test, the natal charts were again divided up amongst the astrologers. For each natal chart, the astrologers were given three CPI test results, one of which correctly corresponded to the given natal chart. They were asked to make a first and second place choice as to which CPI came closest to matching each natal chart, and rate how well each fit the natal chart on a one to ten scale. If the natal chart contains no information about the subject, the astrologers had a one in three chance of making a given selection correctly. Their worst case prediction here, too, was a score of at least 50% correct.

The subjects failed to select the correct personality description more than one third of the time. However, if people tend not to know themselves very well they would be unable to select the correct descriptions no matter how well astrology worked. Since the CPI descriptions are known to be accurate, each subject was also asked to select his or her own CPI from a group of three. Since the subjects were also unable to do this, their failure to select the correct astrological description could not be held against astrology.

However, astrologers' confidence in their abilities comes from their clients' ability to recognize astrologically derived personality descriptions as accurate. The subjects' failure here means either astrology does not work, or people do not know themselves well enough to recognize the astrologers' descriptions as accurate when reviewed in a controlled setting in which two alternative descriptions are also presented. Either way, these results show that astrologers' faith in their abilities is unfounded.

The astrologers failed to match the correct CPI's to the natal charts. They scored exactly chance and were very far (3.3 standard deviations) from their 'worst case' prediction of 50% correct. Even worse, the astrologers did no better when they rated a CPI as being a perfect fit to a natal chart. None of the astrologers scored well enough to warrant being retested. Thus, even though the astrologers started off very confident that they would pass this test, they failed. . . .

Safeguard Society from Fraud

In summary, astrology is an ancient form of divination that has changed little since its founding on superstition and ignorance nearly four thousand years ago. Astrologers' many anecdotal success stories are unconvincing because anecdotal evidence is easily altered by poor observation, faulty memory, ignoring failures, and deliberate distortion. Careful investigation into astrology's tenets gives no comfort to its practitioners and followers. In every test, the astrologers' claims have been refuted. Even when astrologers themselves define their abilities, select which of their peers are competent to participate in the test, predict how well they will do and sanction the test as 'fair', they fail to perform better than if astrology did not work at all.

If an astrologer is a skilled counselor and a caring person, he/she may be of benefit to his/her clientele. However, most astrologers have no training in counseling. Many studied astrology because its unconventionality appealed to their own unconven-

171

tional natures. A few are outright charlatans who use astrology as a scam to bilk the gullible. A person with a real problem, is, in my opinion, courting disaster in seeking astrological counseling. One would be much safer in the hands of a trained, licensed, respected and reputable counselor.

Hoodwinking the Gullible

Astrology seems to work when the astrologer reading the chart is a skillful observer of human nature. The astrologer picks up quickly on what the client would like to hear and tells him whatever will make him happy.

Astrologers also throw around a lot of technical terms like ascendents, trines, aspects, and so on. Many even use a computer. The jargon and paraphernalia help convince the client that the astrologer really knows the subject inside out. The fact that the mumbo-jumbo is used to make the reading sound convincing passes unnoticed by the client, who usually brings to the encounter a willingness to believe.

John Mosley, *Astronomy*, February 1990.

Society requires safeguards to protect the public against charlatanism, fraud, and quackery. Our standards rightly require one to demonstrate, before impartial observers, that one can perform the service for which one charges. Considering the effect they have on peoples' lives, it is clear that astrologers should be held to the same standards as auto mechanics, plumbers, hairdressers, and other accredited professionals. This means two things. First, astrologers should be certified as counselors before they be permitted to perform their counseling service. Second, they should stop advertising abilities they can not demonstrate. Astrologers may reasonably claim that they have a language for the psyche that some people find insightful, but they must stop claiming that they can get accurate information about a person from a natal chart unless they can prove it in a double-blind examination.

Certainly, astrologers should support testing by an impartial accrediting body to weed out all practitioners who cannot perform successfully. In addition to resolving the age-old schisms between various astrological schools, this would go a long way towards protecting the public against fraud and incompetence. Until this is done, astrology must be perceived as a threat to the public health and, as such, struggled against.

"Nostradamus is almost unique in the scope of his foresight. Hence his title 'The King Among Prophets.'"

Nostradamus Made Accurate Predictions

Erika Cheetham

Erika Cheetham is best known for her books on the sixteenth-century French astrologer and prophet Nostradamus. She is fully convinced of his prophetic powers and believes that his centuries-old words hold significant warnings for civilization today. In the following viewpoint, Cheetham comments on the prophet's role and analyzes several examples from Nostradamus's work.

As you read, consider the following questions:

1. What does Cheetham say makes Nostradamus unique among prophets?
2. Cheetham gives several examples of Nostradamus's predictions of modern technology. Do her interpretations seem sound?
3. What amazing success rate does the author cite for Nostradamus?

Condensation reprinted by permission of The Putnam Publishing Group from *The Further Prophecies of Nostradamus* by Erika Cheetham. Copyright © 1985 by St. Lucia Foundation.

Editor's note: Nostradamus is perhaps best known for his series of prophecies called Centuries. *He set out to compose ten groups of prophetic quatrains (four-lined verses), each group containing one hundred verses (thus the name* Centuries). *Nostradamus actually completed more than seven hundred of his proposed one thousand quatrains.*

In the following viewpoint, the author identifies the quatrains she refers to by a Roman numeral representing the book, or Century, it comes from, and by an Arabic numeral representing the number of the poem in that book, i.e., V.8 is verse number eight from century five.

I suppose that in trying to decide whether valid prediction is possible, one has to attempt to define one's terms. Is a prediction valid if a sufficiently large number of people believe that it is? Does one need some more objective, less involved test of accuracy? If so, in what manner and by whom shall the tests of accuracy be carried out? These questions are easy to ask and hard to answer. . . .

I obviously accept that some valid predictions are possible, or I should not be writing this. . . . I hope . . . to convince the skeptical reader that prediction can be possible and is surprisingly frequent and successful for all its expected uncertainties. . . . I believe that prediction is valid and should be taken and used much more seriously than it is.

People Want Predictions

Prediction exists in the first place because there is a demand for it; "demand creates its own supply," which every modern consumer knows, and indeed, can scarcely avoid. The simplest form of prediction can hardly be distinguished from advice, requiring a yes or no, an answer to a simple question, such as "Should I marry such and such a man?" or "Should I make a journey to such a place in such a month?" and often enough, "Will this business venture be successful?" Many of the questions put to oracles in ancient Greece were of this type, but the positive and negative answers were provided in several different ways. The petitioner basically believed in the benevolence of the oracle, and that better results would flow from following the advice given than from not following it. In one sense, if the oracle's statement was definitely followed, benefits might follow — they were never guaranteed. But by negatively ignoring the oracle the questioner was placing himself in a position of considerable danger. Oracles were often double-tongued; misinterpretation could be fatal. A good example is the experience of Philip of Macedon, father of Alexander the Great, when consulting the Delphic Oracle. The Oracle uttered the cryptic words: "Wreathed is the bull for the war and the end fulfilled. And the slayer too is ready." The king misread the statement as meaning he would be victorious but the ensuing battle led to his death. . . .

Some theorists, among them J. W. Dunne, believed that a faculty of precognition was not at all unusual and might even be normal. Whatever truth that has for small-scale personal events, I do not believe it to be true for the larger-scale public domain of events. The ability to make inspired predictions on the grand scale for centuries ahead is very rare indeed. Nostradamus is almost unique in the scope of his foresight. Hence his title "The King Among Prophets.". . .

A Remarkable Prophet

"Celestial Scientist," prophet, doctor of medicine, herbalist and creator of cosmetics and fruit preservatives, this 16th century "Renaissance man" has remained until this century a most extraordinary and unique character. His ten volume work "The Centuries," containing the greater part of his one thousand prophecies is constantly in print and still defies explanation. We do not know how a single man could have "seen" into his future with such accuracy. . . .

The prophecies fulfilled during his own lifetime made him the rage of European courts. . . . But *Nostradamus and the Millennium* is much more about our own time and our own future. Nostradamus occupied a great deal of his energy with this era, predicting a time of great strife, disease, war, natural disaster and change—change that would herald the end of the millennium.

John Hogue, *Nostradamus and the Millennium,* 1987.

If any credence is to be given to a particular prophet and his predictions, they must be clearly proven to be genuine and preferably to have appeared in print during his lifetime, and be seen to be fulfilled since the prophet's death. Oral legend is too vague and subject to too many distortions. But it is also essential that the reader understand the "philosophy of prediction" if one may term it that. The function of a prophet is to give warning of possible future disaster. It does not preclude the option of free will, and its message is: do what is necessary, in time, or this particular situation may happen. Man is a free agent; he must therefore sum up each individual set of circumstances and use his option to act. Since prophets are, almost without exception, excellent purveyors of doom and gloom, man must always be aware that a prediction records only one possible side of the coin. Man can change the future should he so wish. When this happens the prophet may well appear to be proven wrong. All, including Nostradamus, have obviously written erroneous predictions, but it is impossible to know whether these are genuine mistakes in the interpretation of astrological data or whatever, or the result of a man's deliberate action, choosing to alter the possible future. . . .

It may well be possible for an intelligent person to divine what might happen in the near future. In fact, in the short term, I think it certainly is possible. But when people such as Nostradamus, who is exceptional at this, provide us with a wealth of proper names, dates, places and events ranging over four centuries, usually specifically interlinked, it takes more than the average skepticism to deny that he certainly had some sort of prophetic gift.

Like all prophets, Nostradamus has his limitations. He cannot always understand the content of the vision he sees, or finds it almost impossible to explain in his sixteenth-century vocabulary. The necessary words just did not exist. Thus, in V.8 he attempts to describe bombs in the following terms:

Sera laissé le feu vif, mort caché
Dedans les globes horrible espouvantable . . .

There will be let loose living fire and hidden death, fearful inside dreadful globes . . .

V.8

Rockets seem to be described as machines of flying fire.
Du feu volant la machination . . .

VI.34

Submarines become iron fish enclosing men, usually traveling with a warlike intent.

Qu'en dans poisson fer et lettres enfermée
Hors sortira qui puis fera la guerre.

II.5

When documents are enclosed in the iron fish, out of it will come a man who will then make war. In IV.43 he envisages weapons heard fighting in the skies.

Seront ouis au ciel les armes battre . . .

IV.43

All these ideas are reasonably clear to twentieth-century interpreters, but they were not so to Nostradamus' contemporaries. His grasp of the concept of flying machines, airplanes, is particularly vivid, as is, also, their possible use in a warlike situation.

Nostradamus Foretold Air Travel

Les fleurs* passés diminue le monde,
Long temps la paix terres inhabitées;
*Fleurs—read fléaux; plague, pestilence.

176

Seul marchera par ciel, terre, mer et onde,
Puis de nouveau les guerres suscitées.

I.63

Pestilences extinguished, the world becomes smaller, for a long time the lands will be peacefully inhabited. People will travel safely through the sky, [over] land and sea; then wars will start up again.

The most interesting aspect of this quatrain is the manner in which Nostradamus grasps the very twentieth-century concept that air travel makes the whole world accessible—it "becomes smaller." It is worth noting that the so-called era of world peace since 1945 is the longest unbroken one this century. But it is soon to be broken if we are to believe Nostradamus. The extinguished pestilence may refer to disease or the after-effects of the Second World War. Nostradamus also has an uncanny comprehension of pilots needing oxygen when flying and their use of radio to communicate. If one bears these two facts in mind, plus the limitations imposed by his vocabulary and chosen verse form, the next quatrain, I.64, becomes readily intelligible.

Centuries Ahead of His Time

The writings of Nostradamus are virtually unique, because several of his quatrains indisputably relate to events many decades ahead of his own time. In this respect, he differs from the great majority of 'fortune-tellers', who may be able to predict events that are a few years ahead of their predictions but would never pretend to know of events centuries into the future. Most make their predictions about individuals or governments. They must be fulfilled in a single lifetime, and the great majority of personal predictions, from simple premonitions to horoscope readings (using successful data), are fulfilled within an average period of less than thirty years from the time when they are delivered. . . .

Nostradamus is the great exception to the principle that fulfillment-spans are usually short. No other famous non-biblical prophet produced nearly four thousand lines of closely packed detail about events centuries beyond his own lifetime.

David Pitt Francis, *Nostradamus: Prophecies of Present Times?*, 1985.

De nuict soleil penseront avoir veu
Quant le pourceau demi-homme on verra;
Bruict, chant, bataille au ciel battre aperceu;
Et bestes brutes a parler lon orra.

I.64

At night they will think they have seen the sun, when they see the man who is half-pig. Noise, screams, battles seen fought in the skies. The brute beasts will be heard to speak.

Nostradamus describes a vivid picture of a battle in the air—the sun being exploding bombs or perhaps a searchlight piercing the sky. The piglike man, which no commentator had deciphered before my book of 1973, *The Prophecies of Nostradamus,* seems a clear picture of a pilot in silhouette wearing an oxygen mask, helmet and goggles. The oxygen breathing apparatus does look remarkably like a pig's snout. The battle is clearly described as being fought in the air; the screams may be the sound of dropping bombs as they whine to earth. The battle is clearly watched, "aperçu," by people on the ground. It is important to understand the wording of the last line. The aeroplanes, "bestes brutes," are heard talking to others. Could this be a forecast of radio communication? Certainly this quatrain helps to convince me that Nostradamus' visions were of two dimensions, both visual and aural. . . .

The Great Fire of London

A more spectacular prediction was that of the Great Fire of London of 1666. It is to be remembered that during the sixteenth and seventeenth centuries it was common to write dates without the thousand prefix, i.e., 666 instead of 1666. This can still be seen on tombstones of the period. This device is used in II.51.

Le sang de juste à Londres sera faulte
Brulés par fouldres de vingt trois les six;
La dame antique cherra de place haute
Des mesme secte plusieurs seront occis.

II.51

> *The blood of the just will be demanded of London, burned by fire in three times twenty plus six. The ancient lady will fall from her high position and many of the same denomination will be killed.*

One of the certain factors is that the only fire occurring in London in a year '66 is the Great Fire of 1666. The "dame antique" who falls is usually interpreted as the Cathedral of St. Paul's which was destroyed as were many other churches of the Catholic faith. People fled from their wooden houses seeking shelter from the flames in the stone-built churches, but due to the intense heat even these buildings did not escape. The "blood of the just" probably refers to the fact that the victims of the fire were undeserving of their fate. This phrase is also used, when Nostradamus talks of a great plague in a maritime city "which will not stop until death is avenged by the blood of the just . . . the great lady is outraged by the pretense." This last line is almost certainly St. Paul's, the "dame antique" of II.51, outraged because Protestantism was soon afterward reintroduced to England under William III. . . .

Nostradamus regarded Hitler as the second antichrist, Napoleon being the first. . . . Those Hitler quatrains which write of him by name use the orthography Hifter—the long *l* or *f* being very ambiguous in the sixteenth century. Visually Hitler may with reason be written into this word—the letters are so alike.

The other descriptions of this man seem even more accurate. The reader must decide. I personally accept them, as much for the surrounding evidence, when I find he is termed "The Captain of Greater Germany," the Third Reich, and the "man of the croix gammé," the swastika, "the offspring of Germany who observes no law."

> *Bestes farouches de faim fleuves tranner*
> *Plus part du champ encore Hister sera*
> *En caige de fer le grand sera traisner*
> *Quand rien enfant de Germain observera.*

II.24

> *Beasts wild with hunger will cross the rivers, the greater part of the battle will be against Hitler. He will cause great men to be dragged in a cage of iron, when the son of Germany obeys no law.*

Even if one ignores the word Hister/Hitler, the last line seems to describe the Führer very clearly. Born in Austria, he was certainly an offspring of Germany proper. It is interesting that before the early 1930s most commentators believed Hister to mean the river Danube from its old Latin name of Ister. But many of these named quatrains certainly do not refer to a river, rather to a man who is a world force. Several quatrains link Hitler with England, which is geographically impossible if it is understood as the river.

Undeniable Prophetic Gift

When people such as Nostradamus . . . provide us with a wealth of proper names, dates, places and events ranging over four centuries, usually specifically interlinked, it takes more than the average skepticism to deny that he certainly had some sort of prophetic gift.

Erika Cheetham, *The Further Prophecies of Nostradamus*, 1985.

What is so very important, and an example of the dangerous self-fulfilling aspect of prophecy, is that Hitler recognized himself in these quatrains very early on and Paul Joseph Goebbels, his later Minister of Propaganda, was using them definitely by 1936. However, Goebbels was a fanatic believer in astrology through the influence of his wife, and it may be that he introduced his Führer to them indirectly. In 1939 an obscure book, *Mysterien von Sonne und Seele*, by Professor Hans-Herman Kritzinger, included a chapter on Nostradamus, which indicated that in 1939 a major crisis in Great Britain would coincide with a Polish one. Frau Dr. Goebbels drew her husband's attention to it and this fanned the flame of fervor in the Nazi believers. This incident, what led up to it and the tragic results to Ernst Krafft, Hitler's main astrologer, are vividly described by Ellic Howe in his book, *Nostradamus and the Nazis*. . . .

End of Civilization

I have begun to perceive in the Prophecies an inexorable link which appears to lead toward the end of civilization as we know it, unless some great power (Nostradamus' Allies?) stands up not only against its force but against its propaganda. I personally believe in free will but unless it is exercised by those in a position of influence, soon, calmly and deliberately I cannot but foresee the imminent doom of mankind, a wasteland where we shall find no salvation, for there will be none. I have often been accused of being a pessimist; perhaps people who interest themselves in prophets, in men of "doom and gloom," usually are.

It is important to remember that I, as a translator and tentative interpreter of the *Prophecies* cannot possibly *know* if Nostradamus will be proved correct or not in the future. What he has written that has been accurate in the past is astounding, but he has made mistakes as well. After all, he did write over four hundred years ago. Technically he should score about five "bull's eyes" out of 4000. His average, according to the "credibility reading" of various computers I have used, varies between 50 and 70 percent. They can offer no explanation for this, any more than I can. . . .

At their best prophecies provide an inspired guide to rational calculation, but they should always be interpreted cautiously. The philosopher George Santayana expressed the belief that those who would not learn from history were condemned to repeat it. Can I suggest that those who will not heed prophecy may be condemned to suffer from it?

"We need not go further than Nostradamus' early local activities . . . to see just how bad a prognosticator he was. "

Interpretations of Nostradamus's Predictions Are Biased

James Randi

James Randi is a well-known magician, founder of the Committee for the Scientific Investigation of Claims of the Paranormal (CSICOP), and popular debunker of paranormal phenomena. Randi has found no evidence that convinces him that such phenomena exist. The popularity of Nostradamus led Randi to write a "biography" in which he examines Nostradamus's life and his prophecies. In the following viewpoint, Randi points out the many ways Nostradamus's faithful interpreters may have skewed their interpretations to fit their own beliefs. Note that Randi identifies Nostradamus's quatrains with a combination of two arabic numerals, i.e., 2-24 is the twenty-fourth quatrain in the second Century.

As you read, consider the following questions:

1. List several of the ways Randi says Nostradamus's followers misinterpret the prophet's words to suit their own purposes.
2. Both Randi and Cheetham comment on Nostradamus's predictions of the London fire and the rise of Hitler. Who sounds more believable to you? Why?

There are a great number of very specialized "rules" applied to handling interpretations of the Nostradamus writings, rules developed by the Nostradamians to allow great latitude in assigning—and creating—correlations between historical fact and prophecy. Probably some of these usages and devices were actually used, but others seem unlikely in the extreme. It is particularly important to note that these gimmicks are invoked when needed, but ignored when not called for. For example, when Nostradamus names the city of Narbonne, a center well known to him and mentioned twelve times in his writings, the interpreters have accepted that he is actually referring to the city in some instances, but they assign another function to the name (proper personal name or rank) when necessary to wring meaning from the verse in which it appears. The French word "noir," meaning "black" in English, is most often presumed to be an almost-anagram (see the rule for creating anagrams up ahead) for the French word "roi" (in English, "king"); in some instances it is simply accepted as "black" because it fits better. The Provençal spelling would have been "roy."

Once they establish—to their satisfaction—that a certain usage or rule makes the prophecy work, the Nostradamians invoke it again and again for any subsequent situation that even remotely resembles the one in which the artifice was established. J.C. De Fontbrune clearly expressed the way he did his own research:

> The reader will discover, through the translation of each quatrain, how I have proceeded in order to squeeze the text to the maximum, considering that the only 'key' possible is philological.

The aim is to discover some supposed clever, obscure clue or hint that Nostradamus placed in his verses for future generations of scholars to discover. The fact that the quatrains may have expressed notions about quite ordinary matters in a quite ordinary fashion seems repugnant to these learned folks.

They use the theory they are trying to prove, to prove the theory they are trying to prove. They accept modern usage and spellings ("Nostradamus could see the future, couldn't he?") when those serve the need, but fall back on Latin, Old French, Provençal and Greek when they are needed. *I* cannot accept that Nostradamus knew modern English or French.

Arbitrary Rules

Nostradamian Stewart Robb came upon a quatrain which he believes predicts a specific event. The verse says, "Near Saint Memire," but the event he wishes to connect with it didn't happen there. Robb is so convinced his hero has prophetic powers that he actually states:

> The rebellion that overthrew him was centered around the

Cloister of St. Meri, so Nostradamus either heard the name imperfectly or was anagrammatizing it.

Here are a few of the arbitrary but very useful rules we must be aware of:

(1) Anagrams may be used. An anagram, according to the Oxford English Dictionary, is "A transposition of the letters of a word, name or phrase, whereby a new word or phrase is formed." The Nostradamians, however, allow one, two or more letters to be added, changed, or dropped. Thus, Hadrie can become Henrie, Henry, Harry or a number of other words or names.

(2) Punctuation, we are told, may be inserted where absent, or changed when present, since Nostradamus often failed to use it or to use it correctly.

(3) Symbolic references, using animals, mythical creatures or other words to represent the "intended" thing are said to be quite common in Nostradamus' work.

Vague Predictions

Nostradamus composed four-line verses (quatrains), which are arranged in groups of one hundred, appropriately known as centuries. His quatrains were supposed to be used to predict the future, but they are so vague and general that they do not clearly say what is to occur. Indeed, they could not be understood until they were interpreted retrospectively after an event had happened. Thus the latter-day interpreter is left to his own devices to fit the facts to the prediction. But which facts apply to what period? The game is open to ad hoc prophecy and a wide range of permissive interpretations, so that virtually anything can be made to fit.

Paul Kurtz, *The Transcendental Temptation*, 1986.

---

(4) Quatrains may be used as self-contained units, in sets of two lines, as single lines, in pairs, or any way needed. Parts of quatrains may also be combined.

(5) Names of persons or places, we are told, can be "hidden" in common words. As an example, the French word "Pasteur" ("pastor," in English) can actually mean Louis Pasteur.

(6) Foreign derivations—from *any* language—are embraced. We can easily accept Latin sources, since Nostradamus and other writers of his day used the language. They also delighted in demonstrating their erudition by dropping in classical names and allegorical references as well as obscure foreign words.

(7) Validations for "discoveries" are obtained through *other* "discoveries." This is, quite simply, circular reasoning. . . .

Here, then, are examinations of two pieces of the evidence

most used to prove that Nostradamus had prophetic ability. These quatrains are constantly dragged out before us as indisputable proof of his powers, so we will explore them in some detail. . . .

> *Le sang du iuste à Londres fera faulte,*
> *Bruslés par fouldres de vint trois les six:*
> *La dame antique cherra de place haute,*
> *De mesme secte plusieurs seront occis.*

2-51

> *The blood of the just shall be wanting in London,*
> *Burnt by thunderbolts of twenty three the Six[es],*
> *The ancient dame shall fall from [her] high place,*
> *Of the same sect many shall be killed.*

Death, foreign intrigue, wonders of Nature, a mystery woman and suspicious religious overtones are all here in this quatrain, with its vivid imagery which has titillated generations of Nostradamians. It does tell of an historic event, but the verse itself is a Q3K. [Randi's designation for a "prophecy" written *after* an event took place.]

In the spurious edition of *Centuries* that Garenciéres used, the word "Feu" in place of "fouldres" in the second line is wrong. It has been used almost universally by the Nostradamians because it suits their Great Fire of London interpretation better; the original, correct word as shown above, means "thunderbolts." Also, the Rigaud edition of the quatrains says, "de vint [vingt] trois les six," not "vingt & trois," as many other editions do, thus showing an appreciable variation introduced into the text.

The Great Fire of London

Here, the Nostradamians would ask us to believe that their hero was writing about an event that was 111 years in his future: In 1666, London was devastated by a fire that destroyed four-fifths of that city. Garenciéres, for whom the Great Fire was a very recent event (it occurred only six years before his book was published) was an ardent Monarchist. Ever intent upon adding his own charming mysteries to the muddy brew, he postulated that this fiery disaster was a divinely administered expiation for the 1649 execution of Charles I; the unexplained seventeen years of delay in the retribution seems of no importance to his analysis. He also explained that the last half of line two means, "the number of Houses and Buildings that were burnt," rather than the more popular interpretation by almost everyone else that it means 66, therefore somehow giving them 1666. How that date was obtained by him—or by others, for that matter—is difficult to see. Nonetheless, several of the Nostradamians go on to explain that "La dame antique" refers to St. Paul's Cathedral, which was consumed in the fire, along with many other churches, thus the claimed validation of the line, "Of the same sect many shall be killed."

Problems with History

I consulted many references here and in England, and so far as I have been able to determine, St. Paul's Cathedral was never called "The Old Lady," as many Nostradamians claim. The word "antique" in Old French meant "old" *or* "eccentric." The latter derivation is similar to that of the English word "antic." Usually, in French, "old lady" would be expressed by, "vieille dame." Though the old pre-fire St. Paul's Cathedral was the highest church then known, there is no "high place" from which it could have fallen. Some fans, recognizing this discrepancy, claim that a statue of the Virgin Mary stood atop St. Paul's, and that it was that figure that Nostradamus was referring to as the Old Lady. Not so. My early edition of the *Encyclopaedia Britannica* provides a clear, detailed line illustration of the old pre-fire cathedral that shows it was severe Gothic in style, with a squared roof area and no external statues at all. Another contrived notion falls from its high place. We are left with only the reference to London to tie this quatrain to the Great Fire in that city.

An Ingenious System

Undoubtedly the unrivalled success of Nostradamus' oracles is due to the fact that, avoiding all orderly arrangement, either chronological or topographical, and refraining almost entirely from categorical statements, it is impossible ever to say that a particular prognostic has missed the mark. . . . Nostradamus provided an ingenious sytem of divination in which the misses can never be recorded and only the hits come to the surface. For the reputation of the would-be prophet, such conditions are naturally ideal.

Herbert Thurston, in *The Mask of Nostradamus*, 1990.

This quatrain is a Q3K. It refers to an actual event which was taking place as Nostradamus was penning his opus, but a very different event, and certainly *not* the Great Fire of London. Here are the historical facts:

(1) In 1554, the ferociously Catholic queen Bloody Mary (I) of England announced a wholesale cleansing of her kingdom, and in January of 1555, she began executing Protestant heretics in London. Their only crime was the variety of their Christianity and their stubborn refusal to abjure it. Many were prominent churchmen, intellectuals and statesmen.

(2) They were burned at the stake with the "merciful" addition

of having bags of gunpowder tied between their legs or around their necks to quicken their passage. When they eventually expired, it was with a spectacular explosion. The trial, sentencing and burning of these unfortunates began January 22, 1555, in neat groups of six.

(3) Queen Mary, haggard, totally obsessed with religion, disappointed in love, ill with dropsy and other assorted diseases repeatedly imagined that she was pregnant by her Spanish husband Philip. The consort was seldom at home and in 1555 left England and Mary for good. She wandered about her palace half-naked while these atrocities were being committed in her name. She died three years later, incoherent and considered quite insane. It was strongly suspected that her exit was hastened.

(4) Over 300 Protestants died this way at that time.

"Prophecy" After the Fact

Consider these facts, and compare them line-for-line with Quatrain 2-51 as seen in this much better translation:

(1) The blood of the innocent will be an error at London,
(2) Burned by thunderbolts, of twenty-three, the six(es),
(3) The senile lady will lose her high position,
(4) Many more of the same sect will be slain.

I think my point is plain. Will and Ariel Durant's *Story of Civilization,* from which some of this information was drawn, adds this comment:

> . . . nowhere in contemporary Christendom—not even Spain— were so many men and women burned for their opinions as during [Mary I's reign].

And Nostradamus? The first edition of the *Centuries,* in which this quatrain is printed, is dated May 4, 1555—more than three months *after* the first set of heretics mounted the faggots in London. I believe that the seer was writing of an event which certainly would have made news in France, and—in view of what we now know about his true religious beliefs—about which he was thus expressing his righteous horror. . . .

Adolf Hitler

Bestes farouches de faim fleuues tranner,
Plus part du champ encontre Hister sera.
En caige de fer le grand fera treisner,
Quand rien enfant de Germain obseruera.

2-24

Beasts mad with hunger will swim across rivers,
Most of the army will be against the Lower Danube.
The great one shall be dragged in an iron cage
When the child brother will observe nothing.

186

In prophecy, it seems that the Antichrist is always imminent. There are different demons for different ages, with Napoleon being replaced by Hitler who in turn is squeezed out by Khomeni, a Khadafy, and so on. To discover a currently prominent devil in Nostradamus is the dearest wish of each devotee of the prophet.

On Roman maps of the area, the lower portion of the Danube River is known as either "Ister" or "Hister." Nostradamus, as we have seen, often used Latin words and names. [In [another] quatrain "Hister" is joined with the Rhine River, strengthening our right to believe it to refer, certainly in that verse and very likely in this one, too, to the Lower Danube.]

The Nostradamians sorely need to find an important figure like Adolf Hitler in the prophecies; he just could not have been missed by their hero. Though Nostradamian Stewart Robb recognizes the real meaning of "Hister," he admits the fact then rationalizes it by saying:

> Hister is an old, old name for the Danube, old even when Nostradamus resuscitated it for some good reason of his own. But the passage of the centuries has brought it up to date. It was the obvious word for the prophet to use. It meant the Danube: it also served as an anagram for Hitler. . . . The change of one letter was permissible in anagram writing (see Dictionnaire de Trevoux). What other word could serve better than *Hister* to specify both the name, and the place of origin of [Hitler]?

I have searched diligently to discover the source of this "change of one letter" rule, and cannot locate the "Dictionnaire de Trevoux," either. *All* of the definitions and discussions of the word "anagram" that I have found omit any mention of this practice. I leave it to my readers to answer Mr. Robb's question as posed above.

More Convoluted Reasoning

The most astonishing fact about Mr. Robb's discussion on what he calls the "Three Hister Quatrains" is that he admits "Hister" refers to the Lower Danube, but claims it is used here to represent Adolf Hitler, then he proceeds to point out the relationship of the Lower Danube to the Hitler story. He is using "Hister" *both* ways!

As for "de Germain," it is easy to interpret that as meaning "of Germany." Such a usage is reasonable enough, given the strong influence on modern France of English vocabulary, and it can be found in modern French dictionaries. But from the 12th to the 16th century, "de germain" meant "brother" or "near relative" and nothing else. The word "German" came to be used in France only after World War II, to mean an inhabitant of Germany.

Everett Bleiler, as Liberté E. LeVert, suggests that though the

Nostradamians have chosen to associate Hitler with this quatrain, it was evident to those of the 1550s that something else was being hinted at. His printing of line four uses "Rin" in place of "rien," thus giving the meaning "child of the Rhine." I believe a better translation of his printing would be "When the child brother will observe the Rhine." However, Mr. Bleiler says:

> For Nostradamus's contemporaries . . . [the verse] embodied clear references to recent advances by the Turks, in which much of the Hungarian plain was lost and Austria was gravely threatened.

Mr. Bleiler goes on to say that

> The 'child of the Rhine' was Charles V, in Flanders, and his brother was Ferdinand, titular King of Hungary.

His analysis is based upon what I believe (because of the Rigaud version which I have consulted) to be a faulted printing of line four, which he translates as, "When a child of the Rhine shall keep watch over his brother."

Bleiler's idea of the Turkish action is quite interesting, though, since in 1529 the Turks had encamped along the Lower Danube and threatened the city of Vienna. Emperor Charles V, the largely absentee ruler of Germany, stopped the Turks at that point. Later, seeing that Henry II, Nostradamus' monarch, had invaded Germany from the west, he tried to regain that territory and failed. His brother, Ferdinand, arranged the Peace of Augsburg in 1555, the year that the *Centuries* (containing this quatrain) was published.

Mr. Bleiler's suggestion, that Quatrain 2-24 is a Q3K, may quite possibly be valid. But where is the Man in the Iron Cage?. . .

We need not go further than Nostradamus' early local activities at home in Salon to see just how bad a prognosticator he was. Unfortunately for his reputation, we have a detailed account of a horoscope he drew up for a High Justice in Salon de Provence, and the statement of that man's son that shows *not one* correct astrological prediction by Nostradamus. He was strikingly wrong in every respect, especially in missing the subject's death date by twenty-one years.

Recognizing Statements That Are Provable

We are constantly confronted with statements and generalizations about social and moral problems. In order to think clearly about these problems, it is useful if one can make a basic distinction between provable statements for which evidence can be found and unprovable statements which cannot be verified because evidence is not available, or the issue is so controversial that it cannot be definitely proved.

Readers should be aware that magazines, newspapers, and other sources often contain statements of a controversial nature. The following activity is designed to improve your skill at distinguishing between statements that are provable and those that are not.

The following statements are taken from the viewpoints in this chapter. Consider each statement carefully. *Mark P for any statement you believe is provable. Mark U for any statement you feel is unprovable because of the lack of evidence. Mark C for any statement you think is too controversial to be proved to everyone's satisfaction.*

If you are doing this activity as a member of a class or group, compare your answers with those of other class or group members. Be able to defend your answers. You may discover that others come to different conclusions than you. Listening to the reasons others present for their answers may give you valuable insights in recognizing statements that are provable.

P = *provable*
U = *unprovable*
C = *too controversial*

189

1. Astrology dates back about four thousand years to the Chaldean and Babylonian civilizations.

2. Natal horoscopes, which are used to help people understand who they are and what patterns of behavior they follow, can help people deal with life's twists and turns.

3. Astrology integrates us with a level of knowledge that lies deeper than the rational mind.

4. Today, horoscopes appear in large-circulation newspapers and magazines, and professional astrologers outnumber professional astronomers.

5. Researchers Culver and Ianna find that there is no correlation between the sun signs and illnesses.

6. Sun-sign astrology has no discernible basis in fact.

7. The universe has a plan, and this includes the heavens; the plan encompasses each and every individual, including myself; thus, my personal character and destiny are tied up with the stars.

8. From your horoscope, you can determine the exact mental, physical, and psychic heredity you were born with.

9. The location of the sun in your horoscope indicates how you assert your individuality in everything from your career to your friendships.

10. The sun, the moon, and the planets move through the heavens against the backdrop of the stars.

11. Astrology has influenced decisions of great import: great battles have been waged, empires have fallen, and fortunes made and lost on the advice of astrologers.

12. Astrologers should be held to the same standards as auto mechanics, plumbers, hairdressers, and other accredited professionals.

13. Astrologers divide the sun's path into twelve sectors, called the "signs of the Zodiac."

14. Sixteenth-century astrologer and prophet Nostradamus regarded Hitler as the second anti-Christ.

15. Nostradamus's accuracy, according to the "credibility reading" of various computers, varies between 50 and 70 percent.

16. In 1554, the ferociously Catholic Queen Mary I of England began executing Protestant heretics in London.

17. The legend of Nostradamus, faulty as it is, will survive us all.

Periodical Bibliography

The following articles have been selected to supplement the diverse views presented in this chapter.

Geoffrey Dean
"Does Astrology Need to Be True? Part 1: A Look at the Real Thing; Part 2: The Answer Is No," *The Skeptical Inquirer*, Winter 1986-87, Spring 1987.

D.C. Doane
"The Great Astrology Test," *Ladies' Home Journal*, January 1990.

Christopher C. French, Mandy Fowler, Katy McCarthy, and Debbie Peers
"Belief in Astrology: A Test of the Barnum Effect," *The Skeptical Inquirer,* Winter 1991.

Peter Glick
"Stars in Our Eyes," *Psychology Today*, August 1987.

Donald Michael Kraig
"I See by the Papers," *Fate*, July 1990. Available from PO Box 64383, St. Paul, MN, 55164-0383.

Robert Morey
"When Christians Meet Astrology," *Christian Herald*, December 1988. Available from 40 Overlook Dr., Chappaqua, NY, 10514.

Martin Perlman
"Written in the Stars," *The Skeptical Inquirer*, Summer 1990.

Galina Ryzhova
"It's All in the Stars," *Soviet Life*, December 1989. Available from 1706 18th St. NW, Washington, DC, 20009.

Dava Sobel
"Dr. Zodiac," *Omni*, December 1989.

Can Humans Interact with the Spirit World?

PARANORMAL
PHENOMENA

Chapter Preface

Human beings have always attempted to communicate with spirits, gods, and worlds beyond their own mundane existence. For example, paleontologists believe that even the earliest human tribes had shamans, holy people who intervened with the spirits for their community. Cave paintings and artifacts found in graves more than fifty thousand years old also attest to early humanity's belief in the supernatural. Today, many people continue to attempt communication with the spirit world.

But, just as in the days of the ancients, no one really knows whether communication with a supernatural world is possible. For example, does someone who receives a message from a long-dead relative through a spiritual medium really communicate with the dead? Does a near-death experience prove a hereafter?

The authors of the following viewpoints continue the debate over whether a spiritual dimension exists.

"I believe in reincarnation. I always have. "

Memories of Past Lives Prove Reincarnation

Michael Talbot

Author Michael Talbot has written five books: two novels, two books discussing the relationship between science and the paranormal, and a book on reincarnation. He claims that he recalls having lived at least twenty different lives. In the following viewpoint, he discusses evidence from his own life and from the research of noted psychologist and past life researcher Helen Wambach that seems to prove that people do reincarnate. In addition, he asserts that knowledge of one's past lives can provide insight into problems in one's present life.

As you read, consider the following questions:

1. What personal experiences convinced the author that he has lived past lives?
2. State two of the results of Helen Wambach's studies that the author says favor reincarnation.
3. In what ways does Talbot say knowledge of past lives can help people in this one?

I believe in reincarnation. I always have.

The reasons for my conviction are simple. For as long as I can remember I have always had memories of former existences. When I was a small child, this resulted in my refusing to call my parents "mother" and "father" until I was five years old, when they gently persuaded me to stop calling them by their first names because I was embarrassing them in front of their friends. My refusal was not due to any absence of affection on my part. I did not have a mature intellectual understanding of what the tracts of strange memories inside my head meant, but I was vividly aware that I possessed a continuity, a history beyond the child's body in which I found myself. So it did not make sense to me to call the two kind people who were taking care of me my parents.

This was not the only precocity that my parents were forced to contend with. They rapidly discovered that they had a child on their hands who insisted upon drinking several cups of strong black tea every day, who preferred sitting cross-legged on the floor to sitting in chairs, and who was fanatically drawn to things Asian. I also recall asking my mother about several ways that I remembered having died before. Fortunately, there was no longer any trauma attached to these memories, and my mother was able to dismiss them.

Spontaneous Memories

It wasn't until I grew older that I began to understand the import of this strange farrago of memories. By the time I was an adolescent, I realized that I had clear but fragmented recollections of what appeared to be over a dozen different past lives. In a few instances I even remembered names and other obscure but specific details about certain geographic locations. Although it is difficult for me to prove that these spontaneous recollections are actual evidence of past lives, in a few instances the information that came bubbling out of me seemed otherwise of inexplicable origin. As a very small child, after I finished the traditional "Now I lay me down to sleep" prayer taught to me by my parents, I automatically followed it with a request to God "to release the suffering of all conscious beings . . ." It was only later that I discovered that the ending I had given the prayer was of Buddhist origin. Similarly, as a young adult, although I had had only two months of piano lessons as a child, I discovered that with just a few months of practice I was able to play difficult pieces by Chopin and Rachmaninoff.

But to me the most persuasive evidence that my fragmented memories are actual remnants of past-life experience comes not from the place names, the historical facts, or mysterious pieces of information that I remember, but from the fact that when I look back on this succession of memories, I seem to see the germs of many of the elements that make up my current personality. Sketchy though it is, I see an epic story that tells me where many of my faults and positive attributes, my habits, belief systems, and my various strengths and weaknesses began. Just as most people can look back on their childhoods and see events that helped sculpt their current identity, I see a similar progression of self-development over the lifetimes I remember.

I would like to say at this point that I do not have any memories of having been a famous historical personage, nor do I have any tales to relate about having been a pharaoh or even a lesser pope. Indeed, most of the past lives that I remember are relatively undistinguished and have little about them of interest save for the personal significance they hold for me. . . .

Wambach's Work

Some of the most persuasive evidence in favor of reincarnation was offered by the late psychologist Dr. Helen Wambach. Throughout her twenty-nine year investigation of the past-life phenomenon, Dr. Wambach amassed compelling evidence that she reported in her two books, *Reliving Past Lives* and *Life Before Life.*

Reincarnation Is Proven

What I am talking about here is not belief, but established, proven fact: these [reincarnation] cases have met the extremely tight guidelines for "reincarnation only" evidence, and any reasonable person, scientist or not, will have to ponder them. To reject the evidence is a display of that other scientifically useless attitude, *disbelief*. Neither believer nor doubter be, but a seeker for facts on which to form an opinion. That opinion eventually leads to a conviction, and it is that strong conviction, based on demonstrated fact, which has made it possible for me to view reincarnation in general as a natural part of human existence, common to all.

Hans Holzer, *Fate*, April 1990.

One of the methods Dr. Wambach most frequently employed was to hypnotize a group of adults and then ask them standardized questions about their past lives. After hundreds of such group sessions she would compile the data and examine it statistically to see if the responses corresponded more with historical fact, or more with what one would expect if the past-life memories that were surfacing were merely the result of unconscious fantasy.

For example, she would ask all of the adults in her sessions where they had been in A.D. 25. She reasoned that if the responses were only fantasy, most American adults would associate such a time period with Israel or Rome. Similarly, she figured that most Americans would associate the year 1700 with pilgrims and early America, and the early 1860s with stories about the Civil War.

To her surprise, in a statistical sampling of 1,050 regressions most of the responses she got for A.D. 25 involved past lives in Turkey, Pakistan, and around the Indus River. In the 1700s, 63 percent were in Mediterranean Europe and northern Europe, and in the early 1850s, although half of her subjects reported living in various areas in the United States, only three of her subjects mentioned any involvement with the Civil War!

Hypnotic Evidence

Geographic distribution was not the only topic Wambach asked her subjects about. Surveys have shown that given the choice, a majority of Americans would prefer to live life as a male. However, it is a biological fact that at any given point in history roughly half of the human population was male and half female. If the information she was calling forth was the result of fantasy, Wambach reasoned that her survey should show more memories of male past lives than female, but this was not the case. As she discovered, "regardless of the sex they had in their current lifetime, when regressed to the past, my subjects split neatly and evenly into 50.3 percent male and 49.7 percent female lives."

One criticism that has been leveled against reincarnation is that too many individuals claim to remember lives as rulers and other historical personages, and Wambach investigated this facet of the past-life phenomenon as well. However, far from finding a preponderance of lives lived in fantasized splendor, she found that most of her subjects remembered humble and peasantlike previous existences. Indeed, more than 90 percent of the past lives her subjects recalled were lived as primitive food gatherers, nomadic hunters, or farmers, and less than 10 percent recalled aristocratic former lives.

In short, the more Wambach looked, the more evidence she found that the past lives her subjects reported under hypnosis were not the product of fantasy. The circumstances of the incarnations they recalled followed too closely the ebb and flow of history. Not only did they report accurately about the footwear used, the types of foods eaten, and the population densities of the various areas in which they had lived, but Wambach found that even when she regressed groups of people from completely different cultural backgrounds, her statistical data did not vary appreciably.

Evidence such as Dr. Wambach's is persuasive. But as I continued my research of the past-life phenomenon, what impressed me even more than historical correlations was the fact that past-life information has many practical applications. For several decades increasing numbers of psychologists and psychotherapists have found that a host of human ills are treatable through past-life regression.

Exploring the Past to Help the Present

Exploring past lives can lead to the release of guilt, bitterness, and self-pity. You can see the parts of the puzzle come together. You can experience yourself as whole and perfect. You learn that each relationship, each experience in your life, has meaning and purpose. As you work with the process, you find mental blocks to your success and happiness removed. You learn to look at your life as an opportunity to be tender and caring, to be your very best. You can gain insight into how to manage your life, to explore your subconscious, and to become aligned with your purpose. To explore your past lives is to be like an embryo, to be involved in your own birth, to be a central figure in the plan for the new being. This is not a psychological process, it is a journey. It is a beginning.

Elaine Stephens, *Whispers of the Mind*, 1979.

For example, clinical psychologist and noted past-life therapist Edith Fiore has found that many eating disorders appear to be connected to past-life causes. In one instance Fiore regressed a woman whose craving for salty foods had left her with dangerously high blood pressure and discovered that in a previous life the woman had been a native American boy who had starved to death when his tribe ran out of salt to cure their meat. Another man who had an uncontrollable craving for chocolate whenever the weather got cold discovered that he had been given a cup of hot chocolate in a past life after he had nearly frozen to death. Fiore states: "I now find that almost all patients with chronic weight excess of ten pounds or more have had a lifetime in which they either starved to death or suffered food deprivation for long periods. I've met 'aborigines,' 'American Indians,' 'natives' of deep Africa and people from many countries who found themselves without food and often water. Starvation in past lives continues to affect the person in the present one, resulting in a compulsion to overeat. One woman patient who had a persistent fluid-retention problem—found herself, several lifetimes ago, dying from dehydration and starvation, as well as smallpox."

Eating disorders are not the only problems researchers have connected to past-life causes. Other ills that various past-life therapists have reported include alcoholism, cigarette smoking, and other drug addictions, allergies, arthritis, asthma, cancer, depression, diabetes, epilepsy, eye problems, fears, phobias, and obsessions, headaches and other body pains, hyperactivity and childhood autism, insomnia, multiple personalities, relationship problems and child abuse, sexual dysfunctions, stress, and nervousness.

Most exciting of all, past-life therapists from around the world report that in many cases the unearthing of the memories responsible for these disorders alleviates them. An incident encountered by Dr. Stanislav Grof, chief of psychiatric research at the Maryland Psychiatric Research Center and assistant professor of psychiatry at Johns Hopkins University School of Medicine, provides a typical example. For years a patient Dr. Grof calls Norbert suffered from severe pains in his shoulder and pectoral muscles. Norbert, a psychologist and minister by profession, sought all manner of professional help, but after repeated medical examinations no source for his problem could be discovered. Finally, in desperation Norbert sought Dr. Grof's help.

Dr. Grof, a longtime researcher in the past-life phenomenon, decided to place Norbert in a state of past-life awareness. After being regressed, Norbert suddenly found himself in the midst of a military battle. From the uniforms the soldiers were wearing, Norbert was even able to identify the melee as one of the battles in Cromwell's England. Suddenly, as Norbert watched the flurry of soldiers around him, he felt a sharp pain and realized that his chest had been pierced by a lance. At last he had found the cause of his mysterious affliction and after regaining consciousness he discovered that his chronic shoulder pains had vanished.

"Past-life reports obtained from hypnotically regressed subjects are the fantasy constructions of imaginative subjects. "

Memories of Past Lives Do Not Prove Reincarnation

Nicholas P. Spanos

A Canadian professor of psychology, Nicholas P. Spanos has written extensively on hypnosis and reincarnation. In the following viewpoint, he points out that most "knowledge" of past lives comes during hypnotic regression, and, he states, hypnosis is not a neutral science. In fact, the very nature of hypnosis is to suggest ideas and actions to the subject. He believes that memories of past lives do not prove reincarnation; they are merely fantasies encouraged by the conditions of hypnosis.

As you read, consider the following questions:

1. Spanos says that while people are under hypnosis, they are passively instructed to do something, to "remember," for example. What does he mean?
2. What explanation does Spanos give for the past lives and hidden selves people reveal while under hypnosis?
3. How did the results of Spanos's experiments compare to those of Helen Wambach?
4. Which author do you find more convincing—Talbot or Spanos? Why?

Nicholas P. Spanos, "Past-Life Hypnotic Regression: A Critical View," *The Skeptical Inquirer*, Winter 1987-1988. Reprinted with permission.

Some people who have been administered hypnotic-induction procedures followed by suggestions to regress back past their birth times report that they experienced past lives. For instance, a 22-year-old Caucasian woman, while recently "regressed" in our laboratory, claimed that the year was 1940 and that "he" (her past-life identity involved a change of sex) was a Japanese fighter pilot. How are reports of this type to be explained? The parsimonious answer is that they are suggestion-induced fantasy creations of imaginative subjects. If the subjects hold prior beliefs about the validity of reincarnation and/or if they are given encouragement to do so by the hypnotists, they may come to interpret their fantasies as evidence for the existence of actual past-life personalities.

For some (e.g., [reincarnation researcher Helen] Wambach), the parsimonious answer will not do. Instead, hypnotically engendered past-life reports are taken as evidence for the validity of reincarnation. Certainly this is the interpretation most commonly conveyed in popular books and articles on the topic. A few mental-health professionals also accept the reincarnation interpretation and even offer past-life therapy to alleviate problems in a client's present life that purportedly stem from unresolved difficulties in some previous incarnation.

The Nature of Hypnosis

Although "hypnosis" has gained a good deal of contemporary scientific legitimation, it continues to be uncritically conceptualized by many as involving profound alterations in consciousness (i.e., the "hypnotic trance state") that produce fundamental changes in perceptual and cognitive functioning. For instance, hypnotic procedures are sometimes seen as enabling subjects to transcend normal volitional capacities (e.g., to eliminate pain, to retrieve "repressed" memories) or as causing subjects to lose voluntary control over mental and behavioral functions (e.g., hypnotically amnesic subjects are supposedly *unable* rather than unwilling to remember). If hypnosis can do all of these remarkable things, then perhaps regression to past lives isn't so farfetched after all. Thus my first concern is to examine what the available experimental data really tell us about the nature of hypnotic phenomena.

After more than a century of research, there is no agreement concerning the fundamental characteristics of the supposed "hypnotic trance state" and there are no physiological or psychological indicators that reliably differentiate between people who are supposedly "hypnotized" and those who are not. Despite widespread belief to the contrary, hypnotic procedures do *not* greatly augment responsiveness to suggestions. Nonhypnotic control subjects who have been encouraged to do their best respond just as well as hypnotic subjects to suggestions for pain reduction, amnesia, age-regression, hallucination, limb rigidity, and so on. Hypnotic procedures are no more effective than non-hypnotic relaxation procedures at lowering blood pressure and muscle tension or effecting other behavioral, physiological, or verbal-report indicators of relaxation. Hypnotic procedures are no more effective than various nonhypnotic procedures at enhancing imagery vividness or at facilitating therapeutic change for such problems as chronic pain, phobic response, cigarette smoking, and so on. In short, the available scientific evidence fails to support the notion that hypnotic procedures bring about unique or highly unusual states of consciousness or that these procedures facilitate responsiveness to suggestions to any greater extent than do nonhypnotic procedures that enhance positive motivation and expectation.

Hypnosis Offers Suggestions

It is important to understand that hypnotic suggestions do not directly instruct subjects to do anything. Instead, suggestions are phrased in the passive voice and imply that something is happening to the subject (e.g., "Your arm is rising," instead of "Raise your arm"). This passive phrasing communicates to subjects the idea that they are supposed to act *as if* the effects suggested are happening automatically. In other words, hypnotic suggestions are tacit requests to become involved in make-believe or *as if* situations. A subject is tacitly instructed to behave as if he is unable to remember, as if his arm is rising, as if he is five years old, and so on. Good hypnotic subjects (a) understand the implications of these tacit requests, and (b) use their imaginative abilities and their acting skills to become absorbed in the make-believe scenarios contained in suggestions. Thus, by actively using their imaginative abilities, good hypnotic subjects can create and convey the impression that they are unable to remember, unable to lift their "heavy" arms, and so on. The method actor who throws himself into the role of Richard III causes himself to experience the thoughts and emotions that are relevant to his character. Good hypnotic subjects throw themselves into generating the experiences and enactments that are relevant to their roles as hypnotized and as responsive to suggestion.

Age-regression suggestions inform a subject that he is growing younger and younger and returning to an earlier time in his life. Thus a responsive hypnotic subject who is "regressed" to age five states that he is five years old, prints in block letters, and so on. Despite such performances, a good deal of research now indicates that these subjects do *not* in any real sense take on the cognitive, perceptual, or emotional characteristics of actual children. Instead of behaving like real children, age-regressed subjects behave the way they *believe* children behave. To the extent that their expectations about how children behave are inaccurate, their age-regression performances are off the mark. For example, adults commonly overestimate the performance of young children on cognitive and intellectual tasks. Hypnotically age-regressed subjects who are given such tasks usually outperform real children whose ages match those to which the subjects have been regressed.

Unreliable Basis for Belief in Reincarnation

Hypnosis has been used by psychologists to elicit strange reports. . . . In any case, the material generated by the hypnotized person in a past-life regression seems, on analysis, to contain a blend of fictional tales and information that had once been learned and apparently forgotten. C.S. Zolick reports on a study that shows that subjects reconstructed a past life (or lives) by combining events from their own lives with stories taken from books and plays they had read or seen. It is difficult to use these so-called reports as evidence for past-life existence, for hypnosis is an unreliable basis for such an inference.

Paul Kurtz, *The Transcendental Temptation, 1987.*

In short, age-regression suggestions are invitations to become involved in the make-believe game of being a child once again. People who accept this invitation do not, in any literal sense, revert psychologically to childhood. Instead, they use whatever they know about real children, whatever they remember from their own childhood, and whatever they can glean from the experimental test situation to create and become temporarily absorbed in the fantasy situation of being a child. To the extent that their information about childhood is incorrect, their regressed behavior deviates from the behavior of real children.

Hidden Selves

Just as subjects can be given suggestions for age regression, amnesia, or pain reduction, they can also be led to develop the idea that they possess "hidden selves" that they didn't earlier know about. For example, in a number of studies good hypnotic subjects were informed that they possessed "hidden selves" that they were normally unaware of, but who the experimenter could talk to by giving the appropriate signals. When they received these signals, many of these subjects behaved as if they possessed secondary selves that had experiences that differed from those of their "normal selves." When the signals were withdrawn, these subjects often behaved as if they were unable to remember their "hidden self" experiences.

Some investigators interpret such findings to mean that good hypnotic subjects really do carry around unconscious hidden selves with certain intrinsic and unsuggested characteristics. However, a good deal of evidence indicates instead that so-called hidden selves are neither intrinsic to hypnotic procedures nor unsuggested. Quite the contrary, hidden-self performances, like other suggested responses, appear to reflect attempts by motivated and imaginative subjects to create the experiences and role behaviors called for by the instructions they are given. By varying such instructions subjects can be easily led to develop "hidden selves" with whatever characteristics the experimenters wish. Thus, depending upon the instructions they are given, good hypnotic subjects will enact "hidden selves" that report very high levels of pain, very low levels of pain, or both high and low levels of pain in succession. Subjects can also be led to act as if they possess hidden selves that can remember concrete words but not abstract words; or the opposite, hidden selves that see stimuli accurately, see stimuli in reverse, or don't see stimuli at all, and so on.

In short, a subject who behaves as though he possesses a "hidden self," like one who behaves as if he has regressed to age five, is acting out a fantasy. The fantasy performance is usually initiated by the suggestions of the hypnotist, it is imaginatively elaborated upon and sustained by the subject, and (frequently) it earns validating feedback from the experimenter/hypnotist who interacts with the subject as if he or she really did possess a hidden self with particular characteristics.

Past-Life Hypnotic Regression

The few experimental studies that have examined past-life regression have yielded findings that are consistent with the picture of hypnotic responding described above. For example, we completed two experiments on this topic. In the first, 110 subjects were tested for responsiveness to hypnotic suggestions (i.e., hypnotizability). In separate sessions, all of these subjects were individually administered a hypnotic procedure and suggestions to regress to times before their births and then to describe where and who they were. During their individual sessions, 35 subjects enacted past lives. Each subject told the experimenter that he or she was a different person and was living in a different time. Most went on to provide numerous details about where they lived, their past-life occupations, their families, interests, and so on. Subjects who reported past lives scored higher on hypnotizability than those who did not, and were more likely than those who did not to believe that they had experienced some earlier portents of past lives (e.g., déjà vu experiences, dreams).

Among the 35 subjects who reported past lives, there were wide individual differences both in the vividness of the experiences and in the credibility that subjects assigned to them (i.e., the extent to which they believed them to be real past lives as opposed to fantasies). The vividness of past-life experiences was predicted by the subjects' propensity to be imaginative. Thus the frequency with which subjects reported vivid daydreaming and the frequency with which they reported becoming absorbed in everyday imaginative activities (e.g., reading novels) correlated positively with the vividness of their past-life experiences. The best predictor of how much credibility subjects assigned to their past-life experiences was a composite index of their attitudes and beliefs about reincarnation. People who believed in reincarnation, who thought the idea plausible, and who expected to experience past lives assigned higher credibility to their past-life experiences than did those who scored low on this index.

Explanations of Past-Life Regressions

Professionals are skeptical about past-life regression because they know that people are capable of creating realistic, consistent, and vivid personalities that have no basis in fact—e.g., in dissociative disorders like fugue and multiple personality. Also, novelists, dramatists, and thespians have been entertaining us for thousands of years with their ability to create believable, fictional characters. People who are credulous about past-life regression show the same naiveté about hypnosis that has appeared in criminal cases like *State v. Mack*, in which "hypnotically refreshed" testimony contained obvious absurdities and was thrown out of court. Controlled research indicates that people are likely to fabricate under hypnosis, and they are likely to come out of hypnosis believing their fictions are real. A modern theory of hypnosis would explain past-life regression as the product of normal factors like suggestion, role-playing, loss of inhibition, a desire to please the hypnotist, and source amnesia.

Jonathan Venn, *The Skeptical Inquirer,* Summer 1988.

The past-life reporters in our first experiment almost always indicated that their past-life personalities were the same age and race as themselves and usually reported that the past-life personalities lived in Westernized societies. In our second experiment, all subjects were given general information about reincarnation. However, those in one group were further informed that it was not uncommon for people to have been of different sexes or races in past lives and to have lived in exotic cultures. Control-group subjects were given no specific information concerning the characteristics they might expect in their past-life personalities. Among subjects who gave past-life reports, those given the specific information were significantly more likely than controls to incorporate one or more of the suggested characteristics into their past-life descriptions.

Wambach's Work

Wambach contended that the historical information obtained from hypnotically regressed past-life responders was almost always accurate. To test this idea in both of our experiments we asked subjects questions that were likely to have historically checkable answers (e.g., Was the responder's community/country at peace or war?). Contrary to Wambach, subjects who gave information specific enough to be checked were much more often incorrect than correct, and the errors were often the type that actual persons from the relevant historical epochs would have been unlikely to make. For example, the "Japanese fighter pilot" described at the beginning of this article was unable to name the emperor of Japan and stated incorrectly that Japan was at peace in 1940. A different subject stated that the year was A.D. 50 and that he was Julius Caesar, emperor of Rome. However, Caesar was never crowned emperor, and died in 44 B.C. Moreover, the custom of dating events in terms of B.C. or A.D. did not develop until centuries after A.D. 50.

[Researchers] R. Kampman and R. Hirvonoja also obtained support for the fantasy-construction hypothesis. After obtaining past-life reports from hypnotic subjects these investigators encouraged subjects to connect various elements of their past-life descriptions with events in their current lives. In this way they often uncovered the sources of information used by subjects to construct their fantasies. We obtained similar findings. For instance, during a post-hypnotic interview, the subject who reported having been Julius Caesar indicated that he was taking a history course and found the section on ancient Rome particularly interesting. Other subjects reported post-hypnotically that, during the previous summer, they had visited the countries where their past-life personalities resided, or suddenly remembered that their past-life wives resembled and had the same names as old girlfriends from their current lives, and so on.

In summary, the available data strongly indicate that past-life reports obtained from hypnotically regressed subjects are the fantasy constructions of imaginative subjects who are willing to become absorbed in the make-believe situation implied by the regression suggestions.

"Many people I know spend time each day tuning in to their inner wisdom and guidance. . . . Channelling has become a part of their everyday existence."

Spirits Speak Through Human Mediums

Zöe Hagon

Trained as a physiotherapist, Zöe Hagon is a well-known healer and therapist who combines holistic and spiritual methods. Hagon conducts international workshops focusing on spiritual wholeness. In the following viewpoint, she discusses the nature of spirits contacting the human world, claiming that every individual has the capability of contacting spirits for guidance in this life.

As you read, consider the following questions:

1. How does the author define *channeling*?
2. What does Hagon say is necessary for people to channel?
3. How does Hagon explain the current interest in channeling?

From *Channeling: The Spiritual Connection* by Zöe Hagon. Dorset, England: Prism Press, 1989. Reprinted with permission.

In physical terms, a channel is a route through which anything passes or progresses; to channel something is to direct it towards a particular course. Similarly, in the psychic or spiritual sense, a channel is someone who is able to transmit psychic or spiritual energy into our physical reality. It is someone who is sufficiently able to bypass their intellect and/or ego, in order to allow this energy through. In other words, channels are people who have learnt to get themselves—their conscious minds—out of the way in order to bring through information, healing and so on from another dimension or reality into our physical world.

This channelling comes from a variety of sources and may be available for many different reasons. Often it is intended for the individual alone, but information may also come through specifically to be communicated to the world at large. . . .

Channelling usually takes place while the receiver is in either a meditative or a trance (unconscious) state; in other words, while the conscious mind is relaxed. It is as simple as 'the still, small, voice within', and many people, often unknowingly, tune into this on a regular basis. They listen to their intuition, their inner feelings, their gut reaction, and act accordingly.

Channeling Sources

To me, channelling seems to come from four main sources: the Higher Self, or the superconscious within; the God Energy; the universal or collective unconscious; or spirit beings from another plane of consciousness, sometimes known as guides, masters and so on.

The purpose of channelling may be purely for the benefit of the person concerned: a way of that person tuning in to his or her own inner guidance, which is strictly for him or her at that time. It may also come through in order to help others in the form of information, as spiritual healing (as in the laying on of hands), or for the release of earthbound spirits. It may be wide-scale information that is to be printed in the form of a book, for example *The Course in Miracles* or *Seth Speaks*, or it may come through as a teaching, such as the information transmitted by well-known spirit entities such as White Eagle, Silver Birch, or currently Ramtha and Lazaris. Some channelling may come through in the form of a message from Great Uncle Fred who died last year and wants to communicate with those he left behind, and some may be in the form of music, poetry or art, such as in paintings of dead relatives, spirit guides or message paintings.

However, what is really important, regardless of the source, is that ANYONE can be a channel for their own inner wisdom: anyone can go within and tune in to their own inner wisdom. Ken Carey, author of the channelled *Starseed Transmissions*, in a talk to the Findhorn Foundation in 1986, said that 'everyone of us is capable of blending our individual consciousness with the universal consciousness of the Creator'; and certainly, over the past few years, more and more people have begun to accept responsibility for their own lives, and to understand the process of tuning in to themselves on a deeper level. . . .

The Desire to Go Within

The most important aspect of this whole subject of channelling is the desire and the ability to go within—to know who we really are, not to think of ourselves in a particular role (usually associated with job or family) but to find that 'still, small voice' within ourselves where we can actually begin to get a sense of who we are and why we're here and where we belong in the pattern of life. It is a matter of finding the silence within which we can listen and begin to hear and see what really is.

The question now arises as to why channelling has suddenly become fashionable. What is it about channelled messages that have such a popular appeal and why is the word 'spiritual' coming out of organised religion and into everyday life and living?

Channeling and Trances

The flexibility to channel comes from a desire to broaden our perspective and our perception. It comes from the realization that our conscious personality is comprised of an extended system of habits and responses that we have adopted in order to survive in the world. We begin to realize that we have locked ourselves in, repeating patterns of intellectual, emotional, and behavioral response. The desire to break out of these patterns and to perceive life in a new, fresh way provides the flexibility necessary to channel.

If desire for expansion creates the emotional motivation to channel, trance or deep meditative states provide the proper atmosphere for channeling. Trance and channeling go hand in hand. Trance allows an individual to disconnect from the conscious personality—with all of its habitual responses, reactions, and interpretations. Trance allows us to create the state of openness and receptivity we need to resonate with and channel another being.

Kathryn Ridall, *Channeling*, 1988.

One explanation may be the democratic nature of the *phenomenon*—the fact that anyone can channel messages from another level. Many people who have recently achieved fame and fortune started out as housewives, businessmen and so on; they didn't spend years of training and deprivation in order to unveil their gift, as would have been the case in the past. Another reason for the recent popularity of channelling could well be the fact that many channels tell people what their egos want to hear. For example, 'You're perfect just as you are' or 'You can achieve whatever you want' and so on.

Some people seem to find it easier to accept advice from a nonphysical entity who doesn't instill the fear associated with most authority figures; and still others may be lured by the fact that the rich and famous have made much of channelling. For example, Shirley MacLaine and other movie stars have written about their experiences, and have been seen on television listening to the words of wisdom from their particular disembodied guru, and now run workshops to do with the teachings from these various channels. . . .

However this doesn't really answer the question as to why channelling has emerged so strongly at this time. . . .

As the world has seen an increase in both violence and disease, it is as if we are witnessing the symptoms of a fatal disease in modern Western society. Many people are finding they just cannot cope with life, and yet many others are beginning to seek understanding of themselves and their purpose in society. In recent years more and more people have begun to recognise and to use more than just their five physical senses. They are becoming aware of levels of existence beyond themselves, beyond their physical selves. To many it's as if a veil has been lifted and they can become aware of a source of knowledge and wisdom which can best be described as universal or infinite consciousness. . . .

In Touch with Universal Consciousness

Today, there are people all over the world who are in touch with this universal consciousness. Many have spent years of self-development in learning how to tap in to this wisdom and knowledge; for some it has been a swift process. Some individuals believe that they have incarnated at this time specifically to act as channels for the release and dissemination of this information, and many are strongly aware of the guiding force from within their being.

Like attracts like, and these channels seem to draw to them people of similar natures—people who intuitively feel the truth of the messages coming through, and so they form groups and/or communities to put into practice the wisdom and lifestyle advocated, that which is totally reflecting the universal consciousness. Although the inspiration received may seem different in each instant, and often reflects the personality of the group, the fundamental message is the same. . . .

In the closing chapter of *Opening to Channel*, the two authors, Sanaya Roman and Duane Packer, write: 'We have watched hundreds of people gain mastery over their lives as they connected with their guides or source selves, awakening to their inner teachers and discovering their abilities to transform themselves and others. We have watched people succeed with their lives, become happier, more prosperous, and discover their life purpose through channelling'.

Spirit Guides

Once you bring through a high-level guide, or connect with your soul self, you will be on an accelerated growth path. Opening to channel creates a greater link between the superconscious self and the ordinary self. This opening creates or accelerates a spiritual awakening. Your guides will be able to assist you with this awakening. They will help you experience more joy, more confidence, and more awareness of who you are. When you work with guides you will notice shifts and changes in your life. The changes may not be drastic, but over a period of months or years you will know yourself in entirely new ways.

Orin and DaBen in *Opening to Channel* by Sanaya Roman and Duane Packer, 1987.

Many people I know spend time each day tuning in to their inner wisdom and guidance in order that their lives can become more fulfilling and productive. Channelling has become a part of their everyday existence, an integral part without which they would feel empty, incomplete or alone. This tuning in brings wisdom and understanding, calmness and joy, and is a continuous process that, if the person so wishes, remains with that person throughout the whole of his or her life. It is similar to having a constant friend with whom to discuss everything, but without any of the usual demands of friendship; there is a closeness hard to find in a physical relationship, but with none of the battles that often take place.

There is often information coming through that can be totally practical, or words that seem to bring new concepts and understanding into the lives of those who hear it. Whatever form it takes, there is no doubt that channelling can be a strong force for good in one's life, and one that can allow intense opening up to occur on all levels.

4

"If one has real problems and real distress, the pastiche of pop psychology and metaphysics offered up by the channelers may prove to be as deleterious . . . as the fake treatments proffered by medical quacks."

Spirits Cannot Speak Through Human Mediums

James E. Alcock

A professor of psychology at York University in Toronto, Canada, James E. Alcock is a well-known skeptic and lecturer on the paranormal. In the following viewpoint, he points out that what we call channeling today is a form of spiritism that has been around for centuries. However, he says, there is no sound, objective evidence to support the validity of channeling. He concludes that channeling can be as dangerous as quack medicine.

As you read, consider the following questions:

1. According to the author, what message do the supposed eternal entities have for humankind?
2. What are some of the reasons Alcock thinks channeling is fake?
3. What does Alcock say are the dangers of channeling?

James E. Alcock, "Channeling: Brief History and Contemporary Context," *The Skeptical Inquirer*, Summer 1989. Reprinted with permission.

"Channeling" describes what supposedly occurs when an individual serves as a conduit for some otherwordly entity to communicate with people of this world. It can take many forms: The channeler might be wide awake, in a trance, or even asleep ("dream channeling"). The channeler may speak or produce automatic writing, or even operate through a Ouija board. . . .

The immortal entities who take advantage of the sudden abundance of channelers to speak to the people of this world most often bear names of a biblical or a mythic quality: Archangel Michael, Moses, the Invisibles, Ramtha, and even Jesus, are examples. Despite the erstwhile obscurity of many of the entities, they have been able to propel the people who channel them into some fame and often considerable fortune. For example, Penny Torres, a California housewife, was rocketed into prominence by channeling a 2,000-year-old man called Mafu, who teaches that humanoid colonies live under the earth and that extraterrestrials live among us.

Famous Entities

J.Z. Knight, who channels Ramtha, is the best-known and most financially successful of the channelers. Ramtha supposedly was born on Atlantis and conquered the entire world 35,000 years ago. Knight gives us some insight into the process of channeling: She claims that in order to channel Ramtha, her soul first must leave her body. To do this, she raises the vibrations of her soul so she can meet Ramtha at his vibratory level; then she experiences the sensation of moving down a tunnel and traveling toward a light that becomes larger and larger. Once she enters that light, she knows that her soul has left her body and been replaced by Ramtha; her own essence has transcended to another time and space.

Not all entities have such arcane origins as Ramtha and Mafu. Elwood Babbitt, another leading channeler, channels Einstein, among others, and at least two channelers serve as mouthpieces for John Lennon.

Although the term is new, channeling has been around for a long time. It is sometimes claimed that all shamans and prophets, including the Oracle of Delphi, Moses, and even Jesus Christ, were channelers, but a less heady view places the origin of channeling with the renowned mystic Emanuel Swedenborg (1688-1772), who was the first Western medium in that he conversed with the souls of departed men and women rather than just with spirits. An accomplished and prolific scientist, at age 55 he resigned his university appointment and became dedicated to the study of the spiritual and occult. He would lay in trances for days on end, conversing not only with the souls of the recently departed but with Moses, Abraham, and Jesus Christ as well.

The next major milestone in the history of channeling occurred in 1848, when Mr. and Mrs. John Fox of Hydesville, New York, heard a number of mysterious rappings in their home, rappings that seemed always to occur in the presence of two of their children, Kate (1841-1892) and Margaret (1838-1893). By assigning a different number of raps to each letter of the alphabet, the rappings were deciphered as being messages from the world beyond. The Fox sisters subsequently enjoyed a worldwide reputation as mediums, starting an interest in mediumship that was to endure well into the twentieth century. Although they confessed in later years that they had created the rappings themselves by using their toes, ankles, and knees, even today there are some who disbelieve their confessions.

An important figure in the history of channeling is Helene Petrovna Blavatsky (1831-1891). In 1875, Blavatsky founded the Theosophical Society, an organization dedicated to study of the occult. She traveled the world in search of manifestations of the supernatural. She claimed to have direct astral access to two Tibetan mahatmas, and in 1888 she "channeled" on their behalf a book entitled *The Secret Doctrine*, which became an occult tour de force. . . .

A Recent Wave of Channeling

The most recent wave of channeling began with the 1972 publication of *Seth Speaks* by Prentice-Hall. The book was prepared by Jane Roberts (1929-1984) and her husband, Robert Butts, and supposedly presents the communications of Seth, the first "unseen entity" that came to be accepted by large numbers of people. The interest produced by Seth developed to the level of frenzy when [actress] Shirley MacLaine began her New Age writings about entities, channeling, and related themes. Like a latter-day Madame Blavatsky, MacLaine has ranged the world in search of spiritual understanding. In 1983, her book *Out on a Limb* became a best-seller, with more than four million copies being sold. Because of her fame, this book brought many people to the occult bookshelf who otherwise might have stayed away. Three years later, her ABC-TV miniseries introduced millions of others to the notion of unseen entities.

What do these eternal entities have to tell us now that they can so readily communicate with this world? Their basic message, which reflects well-established themes found in occult literature, is that we are spiritual and immortal beings in a universe that is essentially spiritual. We move through a series of embodied and disembodied lives until we eventually unite with God, and indeed, within each of us is some form of projection of God. By learning to contact that part of God within us, we can harness a force that will allow us to surmount our problems and find happiness and success. We create our own realities;

and so if we want to be happy, we simply need to create a happy reality. There is no need for us to follow a guru, for we are as gods, each one of us.

Relinquishing Control

It's impossible to disprove the existence of invisible beings and very difficult to prove the existence of fraud in the realm of the paranormal. What *is* verifiable is that a great many people do believe in channeling and have committed themselves, spiritually and psychologically, to it.

While they are determined to make some sense of life, it is ironic that they have gone to the opposite extreme of embracing what appears to be nonsense. But a heads-and-hearts-in-the-sand attitude isn't likely to create the better world they imagine when they're curled in a fetal position, letting entities tell them fairy tales. It's not so much the advice, much of it cockeyed, that is harmful as it is the fact that most of these seekers are implicitly being encouraged to relinquish control of their lives. Even as these beings purport to be saying we should look inward for answers, they offer false hopes and false visions, solidifying the dependency that brought them followers in the first place.

These beloved entities insist there's no downside to life: that, flawed as we are, be we selfish and slothful, we can still find happiness—not only now but eternally—with a little help from the other side. Unwittingly or not, channelers prey on our credulity and fear, making comfortable ignorance the only prerequisite for bliss.

Katherine Lowry, *Omni*, October 1987.

This message is presented in different ways by different channelers. Often it is hard to discern it from the noisy claptrap in which it is packaged. Indeed, modern channelers are responsible for some of the most outrageous rubbish imaginable, often delivered in almost childishly silly accents and peppered with repetitive clichés. Consider, for example, some of Ramtha's pseudoarchaic prose:

> I be that which is termed indeed, servant unto God Almighty, that which is called the Principal Cause, the Light Force, the Element, that which is termed the Spirit, that which is conclusive all of Itself, that which is termed the All in All, that which is called life indeed.

Ramtha might be well-advised to contact Moses or Joshua for some advice on style.

We now know that the trance mediums of the late nineteenth and early twentieth centuries were almost certainly fraudulent, the whole lot of them. Even Madame Blavatsky was condemned as a fraud by some who investigated her. Are today's channelers simply cheating?. . . Such charges no doubt are fitting in many cases. However, the channelers present a product conveniently resistant to verification or falsification. Most of the information they provide is difficult to assess because of its quasi-philosophical nature. And because the communicating entities usually claim to be exalted beings who left their incarnations a very long time ago or were never incarnated physically in the first place, there is no record to be found of their earthly existence, and no questions to be asked to check the accuracy of their recall.

Why would channelers bother to channel if they were not honest? For one thing, it brings them considerable attention, and for another, it brings them money. The Seth books sold by the hundreds of thousands. People pay up to $1,500 for a seminar with J.Z. Knight's Ramtha, and she has been able to gross between $100,000 and $200,000 for an evening's work! Knight admits that she earns millions of dollars a year from her appearances and the sale of Ramtha materials.

The Seth Books

What about the Seth books? Since they seem, for many people, to stand a league above the other channeled texts in terms of quality and metaphysical surface appeal, they merit some additional discussion. The Seth materials were dictated over hundreds of sessions but *almost always without witnesses;* Seth apparently spoke at a slow enough pace for Jane Roberts's husband to write down the utterings verbatim using a *personal* shorthand. He did not even use a tape recorder, saying that he found it more personal to write out Seth's comments. Roberts was conscious during the Seth sessions. Indeed, she reported that it was often difficult for her to know where she stopped and Seth began.

Jane Roberts was an author and poet who as such must surely have worked to develop her literary and creative skills. Indeed, long before Seth, she was producing poetry that in her husband's words "clearly reflected her intuitive understanding of some of the concepts Seth came to elaborate upon much later." She was also an avid reader. She and her husband freely admitted to having studied Buddhism, Zen, Taoism, shamanism, voodooism, and the like, and they admitted that there is a similarity between Seth's pronouncements and the contents of some of those belief systems.

In light of all this, the Seth materials must surely be viewed as less than extraordinary. There certainly was the time and the talent for fraud to play a role, but we cannot discriminate between that possibility and the possibility of unconscious production. Indeed, at one time Roberts herself considered that maybe all the Seth material emerged from her own subconscious. At any rate, given these circumstances, there seems little need to consider the involvement of any supernatural agency. . . .

Simplistic, Vague Messages

Much has been made of the sagacity and profound insights communicated by [channelers'] messages. These alleged qualities have been regarded as clear proof of the messages' supernatural origins because, it is argued, the channelers themselves have neither the erudition nor the intellectual power to produce such material without help. But in actual fact, if the messages are examined objectively, ignoring their assumed origins, they prove to be simplistic, repetitive, and extremely vague. They quite lack the clarity, the tightness of argument, and the succinctness of expression that characterize productive thinking. On the contrary, they seem to consist solely of strings of loosely associated gobbets of naive ideas and verbal formulae. They are well within the intellectual capacity of channelers of even moderate education.

Graham Reed, *The Skeptical Inquirer*, Summer 1989.

It should not be too surprising that many people from all backgrounds and professions have embraced channeling, for its essence is hassle-free religion. One gains meaning in life and escape from existential anxiety without the commitment and the conformity that cults and sects demand. There is no proscription of the pleasures of the flesh as there is in mainstream religions; there are no temptations to avoid, no sins to eschew. The entities' hedonistic and narcissistic wisdom is also predigested and therefore brings no need to wrestle with philosophical enigmas and no lifelong quest for truth.

[However] . . . there is a clear danger in seeking advice from channelers, or at least in following it: People are diverted from trying to grapple in a rational and realistic way with the difficulties of living. For most people, probably all that is lost is a bit of money for whatever comfort was gained. But if one has real problems and real distress, the pastiche of pop psychology and metaphysics offered up by the channelers may prove to be as deleterious for the psyche as the fake treatments proffered by medical quacks can be for the body.

"For years I have been trying to discover a physiological explanation for NDEs. And for years I have come up empty-handed. . . . [They are], pure and simple, an experience of light."

Near-Death Experiences Prove Life After Death

Raymond A. Moody Jr.

Raymond A. Moody Jr., rose to prominence with the 1975 publication of his book *Life After Life*. In it he described the mystical experiences of hundreds of people who clinically "died" and then came back to life. Moody called these incidents *near-death experiences* (NDEs). In the following viewpoint, Moody explains why he considers NDEs spiritual events.

As you read, consider the following questions:

1. What are the nine components that Moody says make up the typical NDE?
2. What aspects of the NDE does the author find particularly difficult to explain by conventional scientific means?
3. What does Moody mean when he calls NDEs "experiences of light"?

What happens when people die? That is probably mankind's most often asked and perplexing question. Do we simply cease to live, with nothing but our mortal remains to mark our time on earth? Are we resurrected later by a Supreme Being only if we have good marks in the Book of Life? Do we come back as animals, as the Hindus believe, or perhaps as different people generations later?. . .

Many ordinary people . . . have been to the brink of death and reported miraculous glimpses of a world beyond, a world that glows with love and understanding that can be reached only by an exciting trip through a tunnel or passageway.

The NDE

This world is attended by deceased relatives bathed in glorious light and ruled by a Supreme Being who guides the new arrival through a review of his life before sending him back to live longer on earth.

Upon return, the persons who "died" are never the same. They embrace life to its fullest and express the belief that love and knowledge are the most important of all things because they are the only things you can take with you.

For want of a better phrase to describe these incidents, we can say these people have had near-death experiences (NDEs). . . .

NDEers experience some or all of the following events: a sense of being dead, peace and painlessness even during a "painful" experience, bodily separation, entering a dark region or tunnel, rising rapidly into the heavens, meeting deceased friends and relatives who are bathed in light, encountering a Supreme Being, reviewing one's life, and feeling reluctance to return to the world of the living. . . .

Spiritual Experiences

There are several theories—theological, medical, and psychological—that try to explain the near-death experience as physical or mental phenomena that have more to do with brain dysfunction than with an adventure of the spirit.

But there are a couple of things that present enormous difficulty to these researchers: How is it that the patients can give such elaborate and detailed accounts of resuscitations, explaining in their entirety what the doctors were doing to bring them back to life? How can so many people explain what was going on in other rooms of a hospital while their bodies were in the operating room being resuscitated?

To me, these are the most difficult points for the NDE researchers to answer. In fact, so far they have been impossible to explain except with one answer: they really occurred. . . .

Let's look at some examples of these unexplainable events.

• A forty-nine-year-old man had a heart attack so severe that after thirty-five minutes of vigorous resuscitation efforts, the doctor gave up and began filling out the death certificate. Then someone noticed a flicker of life, so the doctor continued his work with the paddles and breathing equipment and was able to restart the man's heart.

"I SAID, 'YOU DON'T BELIEVE ALL THIS BALONEY ABOUT OUT-OF-BODY EXPERIENCES, 'DO YOU?'"

The next day, when he was more coherent, the patient was able to describe in great detail what went on in the emergency room. This surprised the doctor. But what astonished him even more was the patient's vivid description of the emergency room nurse who hurried into the room to assist the doctor.

He described her perfectly, right down to her wedge hairdo and her last name, Hawkes. He said that she rolled this cart down the hall with a machine that had what looked like two Ping-Pong paddles on it (an electroshocker that is basic resuscitation equipment).

When the doctor asked him how he knew the nurse's name and what she had been doing during his heart attack, he said that he had left his body and—while walking down the hall to see his wife—passed right through nurse Hawkes. He read the name tag as he went through her, and remembered it so he could thank her later.

I talked to the doctor at great length about this case. He was quite rattled by it. Being there, he said, was the only way the man could have recounted this with such complete accuracy.

A Blind Woman's Vision

• On Long Island, a seventy-year-old woman who had been blind since the age of eighteen was able to describe in vivid detail what was happening around her as doctors resuscitated her after a heart attack.

Knowledge of God

Most [NDE] survivors fall head over heels in love with God.

During their experience they were bathed in God, immersed in God, filled to overflowing with God; and they returned convinced of God. Doubt may be a tool of science but it means nothing to a survivor. They have no doubt. They have discovered God. They *know* God is.

P.M.H. Atwater, *Coming Back to Life*, 1988.

Not only could she describe what the instruments used looked like, but she could even describe their colors.

The most amazing thing about this to me was that most of these instruments weren't even thought of over fifty years ago when she could last see. On top of all this, she was even able to tell the doctor that he was wearing a blue suit when he began the resuscitation.

• Another amazing case that says NDEs are more than just tricks of the mind was relayed to me by a doctor in South Dakota.

Driving into the hospital one morning, he had rear-ended a car. It had been very upsetting to him. He was very worried that the people he had hit would claim neck injury and sue him for a large sum of money.

This accident left him distraught and was very much on his mind later that morning when he rushed to the emergency room to resuscitate a person who was having a cardiac arrest.

The next day, the man he had rescued told him a remarkable story: "While you were working on me, I left my body and watched you work."

The doctor began to ask questions about what the man had seen and was amazed at the accuracy of his description. In precise detail, he told the doctor how the instruments looked and even in what order they were used. He described the colors of the equipment, shapes, and even settings of dials on the machines.

But what finally convinced this young cardiologist that the man's experience was genuine was when he said, "Doctor, I could tell that you were worried about that accident. But there isn't any reason to be worried about things like that. You give your time to other people. Nobody is going to hurt you."

Not only had this patient picked up on the physical details of his surroundings, he had also read the doctor's mind. . . .

These are only a few of the cases that prove to me that NDEs are more than just hallucinations or "bad dreams." There is no logical explanation for the experiences of these people. Although tunnel experiences and beings of light can easily be chalked off as mere "mind play," out-of-body experiences baffle even the most skeptical in the medical profession. . . .

An Experience of Light

For years I have been trying to discover a physiological explanation for NDEs. And for years I have come up empty-handed.

It just seems to me that all the so-called explanations are incomplete or ill formed. For the most part, the people who have derived them are people who have never taken the trouble to talk with NDEers, look them in the face, and listen to their stories.

If they did, maybe they would come to the same conclusions that philosopher William James did in describing mysticism.

He said that this is an experience that is noetic. It is self-certifying because it is a form of knowledge. It is so personal as to be beyond words. And it is profoundly life-changing.

It is, pure and simple, an experience of light.

"Serotonin [a chemical within the brain] . . . somehow triggers the temporal lobes to 'release' the NDE in the face of imminent danger or death."

Near-Death Experiences Have Biological Explanations

D. Scott Rogo

A prolific author of books and articles on the paranormal, D. Scott Rogo (1950-1990) wrote several books about the possibility of life after death. In the following viewpoint, he reviews current scientific research that attempts to explain NDEs as biological rather than mystical events. Although Rogo's own views tend more to the mystical, he presents the research on its own merits.

As you read, consider the following questions:

1. According to the author, what did Daniel Carr propose as the cause of NDEs?
2. How does Rogo say Juan C. Saavedra-Aguilar and Juan S. Gómez-Jeria refined Carr's theory?
3. What does Melvin Morse think triggers the NDE, according to Rogo?

D. Scott Rogo, "On the Psychic Frontier," *Fate*, September 1990. Reprinted with permission.

When public and scientific interest in the near-death experience (NDE) surged in the 1970s, there were two rival theories for such encounters. One group of researchers felt that the experience was real. Perhaps something really did "separate" from the brain and fly to the Great Beyond. Other researchers decried this simplistic and basically metaphysical model, claiming that the experience was merely hallucinatory.

Neither side won this scientific battle. Those researchers taking a literalist view of the NDE couldn't explain the fact that cultural beliefs contaminate the experience. The debunkers and skeptics, on the other hand, couldn't cope with Dr. Michael Sabom's evidence (presented in *Recollections of Death*) that people undergoing NDEs sometimes "watch" and correctly report on their surgical operations.

This long-standing stalemate between the believers and the skeptics has recently entered into its second chapter. Some researchers interested in the NDE have begun focusing on the neurology and neurophysiology of the experience.

Encoded in the Brain?

If the experience is real, what changes in the brain result from leaving the body? If the experience is a complex hallucination, where in the brain is it encoded?

The possibility that the NDE represents a phenomenon linked specifically to events within the brain was originally suggested in the 1970s. The first researchers to suggest this model were the Czech-born psychiatrist Dr. Stanislav Grof and his (then) wife, the internationally known anthropologist Dr. Joan Halifax. They tackled the puzzle of the NDE in 1977, two years after the original publication of Dr. Raymond Moody's pioneering *Life After Life*.

In their book *The Human Encounter with Death*, Drs. Grof and Halifax suggested that NDEs were coded into the brain and "emerged" when the organ underwent life-threatening stress. The two researchers never posited where in the brain such a complex phenomenon was coded, nor by what neurobiological process it emerged.

The concept of the "encoded experience" did, however, explain the inner consistency to which NDEs conform. That the NDE could be a purely neurophysiological phenomenon was reinforced in 1980 by U.C.L.A. [University of California, Los Angeles] psychopharmacologist Dr. Ronald Siegel who showed that NDEs and hallucinations produced by psychoactive chemicals (such as LSD) share considerable ground. Dr. Siegel published his observations in a lengthy paper published in the *American Psychologist*. The article received considerable play in the popular press—much to the consternation of its writer, who received death threats, dung and

Bibles filled with bullets from people who didn't like his views!

Again, the specific neurological mechanism by which these episodes emerge was left undescribed.

The basic ingredients for a comprehensive neurophysiological explanation of the NDE dates only from 1982, when Dr. Daniel Carr—a Boston physician—drew upon the recent discovery of natural opiates in the brain in building his theory. . . . These peptides have the (purported) power to induce pleasure, elevate mood and produce anaesthesia in people. Dr. Carr suggested that these chemicals were the biological triggers for the NDE and could explain the positive emotions reported by NDE survivors.

How Do NDEs Happen?

Dr. Carr posited that endorphins released near death stimulate the hippocampus, a small organ within the brain that constitutes part of the limbic system. The limbic system is a group of organs in the "older" section of the brain, from the standpoint of evolution, and takes part in regulating our primitive emotions. The limbic system is in turn buried deep within the brain's temporal lobes, which produce sensory hallucinations when stimulated.

NDEs in the Brain

There is clear evidence that within the temporal lobe [of the brain] are neuronal connections that, when electrically stimulated, produce OBEs [Out of Body Experiences]. . . .

Our model hypothesizes that near-fatal events, psychoactive agents [drugs], or stress could trigger OBEs.

Melvin L. Morse et al., *Journal of Near-Death Studies*, Fall 1989.

Dr. Carr suggested that NDEs are deeply moving hallucinations caused by a cascade effect: Chemical stimulation within the hippocampus spreads to the limbic system, which spreads to the temporal lobe where it causes vivid hallucinations. The Boston physician supported his theory by referring to considerable biochemical findings on the endorphins and other neurohormones. . . .

While his biochemical model was ingenious, there was a critical flaw in Dr. Carr's thinking. Endorphins function in the brain similar to narcotics such as morphine, since they bind to the same neural receptors. We should expect considerable common ground between morphine hallucinations and the characteristics of the classical NDE. That's where Dr. Carr's theory falls apart, for morphine hallucinations resemble vivid nightmares completely unlike the NDE.

While the release of endorphins has been rejected by NDE researchers as the primary source of the NDE, some elements from Carr's original model have shown up in second generation neurophysiological theories for the NDE. Could the experience, for example, be "located" within the temporal lobes? (These lobes fold under the brain's frontal cortex, which constitutes the seat of mankind's executive and planning functions.) The possible role the temporal lobes play in the NDE is the controversy which I'd like to discuss.

Role of Temporal Lobes

The first comprehensive temporal lobe model for the NDE was recently presented in the Summer 1989 issue of the *Journal of Near-Death Studies* by Dr. Juan C. Saavedra-Aguilar and Dr. Juan S. Gómez-Jeria of the University of Chile. Here is their theory briefly summarized:

The two researchers begin their paper by pointing out that seizures within the temporal lobes can cause both sensory and motor disturbances, including:

1) strange physical sensations within the body
2) localized tremors and even complex movements and behavior
3) rising and sinking feelings
4) visual hallucinations
5) intense emotional changes
6) flashbacks and distortions in self-perception.

Within this range of temporal lobe symptoms lie the "building blocks of the NDE," suggest the Chilean researchers.

By what mechanism is the complex phenomenology of the NDE built?

The Chilean researchers tackle this issue by drawing upon the same neurological factors Carr used in 1982—that biological stress releases endorphins into the limbic system. This phenomenon is well known to brain experts and is not mere speculation. This chemical overload hyperstimulates the limbic system/temporal lobes, suggest the South American neurologists, a situation compounded by lack of oxygen to the brain in general.

The resulting rapid firing of neurons within the temporal lobes (technically called disinhibition) would produce a range of hallucinations that the brain could "interpret" as an NDE.

The brain performs this function, they posit, by piecing together scattered phenomenology in terms of the patient's cultural expectations. In other words, the brain—trying to make sense of their hallucinations—structures them and transfers them into a linguistic form that conforms to the subject's religio-cultural beliefs.

Dr. Bruce Greyson, editor of the *Journal of Near-Death Studies,* realized that the Chilean researchers' proposals were controversial. When he published their paper, he invited nine neurological experts to comment on it. The Summer 1989 issue of the *Journal* contained these critical commentaries.

Most of the paper's discussants offered their congratulations to the Chilean researchers.

Some researchers found the proposals of the Chilean researchers extremely flawed. Several criticisms of their conceptual model for the NDE were given by Dr. Glen O. Gabbard and Dr. Stuart W. Twemlow, two psychiatrists from Kansas interested in NDE research. They pointed out in their rebuttal that:

1) The symptomatology of temporal lobe epilepsy is so inclusive that anything, theoretically, could be linked to it.

2) The Kansas psychiatrists especially criticize their colleagues for confusing similarity with causation. Because two psychological experiences resemble each other doesn't mean they are produced by the same mechanism.

3) The model proposed by the Chilean researchers is based on chemical signals produced when the brain undergoes stress. Some people, however, experience NDE-like episodes spontaneously when they are facing neither death nor biological stress.

The debate over the neurological model proposed by Dr. Saavedra-Aguilar and Dr. Gómez-Jeria is bound to continue, but theirs is not the last word on the NDE and temporal lobe function. Hardly had the furor over their model settled than a rival neurophysiological model was presented in the subsequent issue of the *Journal of Near-Death Studies!*

NDEs and Children

For some time now, Dr. Melvin Morse and his colleagues at the University of Washington have been studying NDEs reported by children. . . . They have been impressed by the consistency of the experiences claimed by children near death. Even their drawings of their perceptions look surprisingly alike. Such findings have suggested to Dr. Morse that the NDE is probably directly encoded into the brain, not pieced together in the manner suggested by Drs. Saavedra-Aguilar and Gómez-Jeria. But where in the brain? By what neural mechanisms does it enter consciousness?

In order to explain these problems, Dr. Morse draws upon the pioneering research of the late Dr. Wilder Penfield, a Canadian neurosurgeon who experimented in the 1940s and '50s with electrically stimulating his patients' brains while they were undergoing surgery to correct intractable epilepsy. Dr. Penfield discovered that stimulation to the cortex of the temporal lobes resulted in visual hallucinations, hearing music and eerie sensations of leaving the body. These sound suspiciously like the fundamental components of the NDE. The Canadian surgeon even mapped out where in the cortex these sensations can be evoked.

Believing that he has found the location of the NDE within the brain, Dr. Morse next proposes the precise neurochemical trigger that leads to its emergence into consciousness. The brain is partly regulated by neurotransmitters, chemicals involved with everything from mood to sleep to our perception of pain.

Dreams and Hallucinations

"These people have had an intense experience, and I don't for a second think these people are lying," says Irving Biederman, a Fesler-Lampert professor of artificial intelligence and cognitive science in the University of Minnesota's psychology department. "But thinking they've experienced something and actually having had that experience are two different things."

Biederman theorizes that people who claim to have had near-death experiences may have hallucinated or experienced nothing more than intense dreams.

Paul Levy, *Minneapolis Star-Tribune Sunday Magazine*, September 2, 1990.

Serotonin is one of these primary neurotransmitters especially linked to the regulation of our sleep/wake cycles and everyday moods. Serotonin seems to be implicated in our response to threat when it is produced in high levels to relieve stress and calm our reactions. Dr. Morse and his colleagues suggest that this chemical—ubiquitous within the brain—somehow triggers the temporal lobes to "release" the NDE in the face of imminent danger or death.

Evaluating Sources of Information

When historians study and interpret past events, they use two kinds of sources: primary and secondary. Primary sources are eyewitness accounts. For example, the account of a person under hypnosis describing a previous life he or she lived is an example of a primary source. A writer's description of the hypnotized subject's experience in a book about reincarnation is an example of a secondary source.

To read and think critically, one must be able to recognize primary sources. This is not enough, however, because eyewitness accounts do not always provide accurate descriptions. For example, many people do not accept testimony under hypnosis as legitimate. Therefore, they would not consider the primary source described in the previous paragraph as a reliable source. The reader must decide the value of each account, keeping in mind the potential biases of the eyewitness.

Test your skill in evaluating sources of information by completing the following exercise. Imagine you are writing a report about the meaning of near-death experiences. Listed are a number of sources which may be useful for your research. *Place a P next to those descriptions you believe are primary sources. Place an S next to those descriptions you believe are secondary sources.* Next, based on the above criteria, *rank the primary sources, assigning the number (1) to that which appears the most valuable, (2) to the source likely to be the second-most valuable, and so on, until all the primary sources are ranked. Then rank the secondary sources, again using the above criteria.*

If you are doing this activity as a member of a class or group, discuss and compare your evaluations with other members of the group. Others may come to different conclusions than you. Listening to their reasons may give you valuable insights in evaluating sources of information.

1. A book called *Near-Death Experiences Through the Ages* that discusses NDEs reported in a variety of sources.

2. A letter in *The National Inquirer*, a supermarket tabloid, in which a man tells of his own NDE.

3. An account your neighbor tells you of her grandmother's NDE while in the hospital.

4. A book called *Halfway to Heaven*, in which each chapter is a transcript of an interview between the psychologist author and a person who experienced an NDE.

5. A group of articles in a scholarly journal in which several scientists each discuss what research has proven— and disproven—about NDEs.

6. A popular movie whose plot revolves around a character's NDE.

7. A book called *Near-Death Experiences in History* which is a collection of first-hand accounts of NDEs taken from papyrus scrolls, medieval histories, and other sources.

8. An article in *Time* magazine in which an NDE researcher describes a typical NDE.

9. The transcript of a special documentary in which the journalist interviews several people who have had NDEs and several scientists who comment on them.

Periodical Bibliography

The following articles have been selected to supplement the diverse views presented in this chapter.

Brooks Alexander	"Theology from the Twilight Zone," *Christianity Today*, September 18, 1987.
A.J. Ayer	"What I Saw When I Was Dead," *National Review*, October 14, 1988.
Arthur S. Berger	"Order Out of Chaos in Survival Research," *The Skeptical Inquirer*, Summer 1990.
Paul Berry and Paul Kurtz	"Brushes with Death: The Evidence from Near-Death Experiences Point to a Hereafter," *Psychology Today*, September 1988.
Berry L. Beyerstein	"Neuropathology and the Legacy of Spiritual Possession," *The Skeptical Inquirer*, Spring 1988.
Susan Blackmore	"Out-of-Body Psychology," *Fate*, December 1988. Available from PO Box 64383, St. Paul, MN, 55164-0383.
Amy Sunshine Genova	"The Near-Death Experience," *McCall's*, February 1988.
Esther V.M. Hamel	"Detour to Hell," *Fate*, January 1991.
Gerri Hirshey	"Reincarnation? Channeling? Hell, No, I Won't Go!" *Glamour*, December 1987.
Hans Holzer	"Channeling and Past Lives: The Real Story," *Fate*, June 1990.
Hans Holzer	"Proof of Reincarnation," *Fate*, April 1990.
Katharine Lowry	"Channelers," *Omni*, October 1987.
Graham Reed	"The Psychology of Channeling," *The Skeptical Inquirer*, Summer 1989.
Robert T. Reilly	"Heaven Can Wait: Do Near-Death Experiences Take the Fear Out of Dying?" *U.S.Catholic*, January 1988.
Marjorie Roberts	"A Linguistic 'Nay' to Channeling," *Psychology Today*, October 1989.
D. Scott Rogo	"Reincarnation Therapy: Does It Work?" *Fate*, August 1990.
Dennis Stacy	"Transcending Science," *Omni*, December 1988.
Carol Tavris	"Spiritual Possession and the Brain," *Vogue*, July 1988.

Bibliography of Books

Do Paranormal Phenomena Exist?

Maurice L. Albertson et al.
Paranormal Research. Ft. Collins, CO: Rocky Mountain Research Institute, 1989.

James E. Alcock
Science and Supernature: A Critical Appraisal of Parapsychology. Buffalo, NY: Prometheus Books, 1989.

John Beloff
The Relentless Question: Reflections on the Paranormal. Jefferson, NC: McFarland & Co., 1990.

Kenneth L. Feder
Frauds, Myths, and Mysteries. Mountain View, CA: Mayfield Publishing Company, 1990.

Patrick Grim, ed.
Philosophy of Science and the Occult. Albany, NY: State University of New York Press, 1990.

Terence Hines
Pseudoscience and the Paranormal. Buffalo, NY: Prometheus Books, 1990.

H.J. Irwin
An Introduction to Parapsychology. Jefferson, NC: McFarland & Co., 1989.

Joe Nickell with John F. Fischer
Secrets of the Supernatural: Investigating the World's Occult Mysteries. Buffalo, NY: Prometheus Books, 1988.

D. Scott Rogo
Psychic Breakthroughs Today. New York: Harper & Row, 1987.

Victor J. Stenger
Physics and Psychics: The Search for a World Beyond the Senses. Buffalo, NY: Prometheus Books, 1990.

Rhea White
Using the Library to Find Out About Parapsychology. Dix Hills, NY: Parapsychological Sources of Information Center, 1989.

Colin Wilson
Beyond the Occult: A Twenty Year Investigation into the Paranormal. New York: Carroll & Graf Publishers, 1988.

G.K. Zollchan, J.F. Schumaker, and G.F. Walsh, eds.
Exploring the Paranormal. Dorset, UK: Prism Press, 1989.

Are UFOs Real?

Edward Ashpole
The Search for Extra-Terrestrial Intelligence. London: Blandford Press, 1990.

Paul Deveraux
Earth Lights Revelations. London: Blandford Press, 1990.

Ann Druffel and D. Scott Rogo
The Tujunga Canyon Contacts. New York: Signet/New American Library, 1989.

Lawrence Fawcett
UFO Coverup: What the Government Won't Say. Englewood Cliffs, NJ: Prentice-Hall, 1990.

Raymond E. Fowler
The Watchers: The Secret Design Behind UFO Abductions. New York: Bantam Books, 1990.

Timothy Good
Above Top Secret: The Worldwide UFO Cover-Up. New York: William Morrow, 1988.

Philip J. Klass
UFO Abductions: A Dangerous Game. Buffalo, NY: Prometheus Books, 1989.

Greg Long
Examining the Earthlight Theory: The Yakima UFO Microcosm. Chicago: The J. Allen Hynek Center for UFO Studies, 1990.

Thomas R. McDonough	*The Search for Extraterrestrial Intelligence.* New York: John Wiley & Sons, Inc., 1987.
Carl Sagan and Thornton Page, eds.	*UFOs: A Scientific Debate.* New York: W.W. Norton & Co. Inc., 1974.
John Spencer and Hilary Evans, eds.	*Phenomenon: Forty Years of Flying Saucers.* New York: Avon Books, 1989.
Jacques Vallee	*Confrontations.* New York: Ballantine Books, 1990.
Frank White	*The SETI Factor: How the Search for Extraterrestrial Intelligence Is Changing Our View of the Universe and Ourselves.* New York: Walker and Company, 1990.

Abduction Accounts. The following is a brief list of some of the more recent and prominent personal accounts of alleged abductions by extraterrestrials.

Edith Fiore	*Encounters: A Psychologist Reveals Case Studies of Abductions by Aliens.* New York: Doubleday, 1989.
Budd Hopkins	*Intruders: The Incredible Visitations at Copley Woods.* New York: Random House, 1987.
Gary Kinder	*Light Years: An Investigation into the Extraterrestrial Experience of Eduard Meier.* New York: Atlantic Monthly Press, 1987.
Whitley Strieber	*Transformation: The Breakthrough.* New York: William Morrow/Beech Tree Books, 1988.
Ed Walters and Frances Walters	*The Gulf Breeze Sightings.* New York: William Morrow, 1990.

Does ESP Exist?

Milbourne Christopher	*ESP, Seers and Psychics.* New York: Thomas Y. Crowell, 1970.
Jan Ehrenwald	*The ESP Experience: A Psychiatric Validation.* New York: Basic Books, 1978.
Kendrick Frazier, ed.	*Science Confronts the Paranormal.* Buffalo, NY: Prometheus Books, 1986.
Henry Gordon	*Extrasensory Deception.* Buffalo, NY: Prometheus Books, 1987.
C.E.M. Hansel	*ESP and Parapsychology: A Critical Re-evaluation.* Buffalo, NY: Prometheus Books, 1980.
Ray Hyman	*The Elusive Quarry: A Scientific Appraisal of Psychical Research.* Buffalo, NY: Prometheus Books, 1989.
Joseph Banks Rhine	*Extrasensory Perception.* Boston, MA: Boston Society for Psychic Research, 1934.
D. Scott Rogo, ed.	*Mind Beyond the Body.* New York: Penguin Books, 1978.
Benjamin B. Wolman, ed.	*Handbook of Parapsychology.* New York: Van Nostrand Reinhold Company, 1977.

Can the Future Be Predicted?

John Andenberg and John Weldon	*Astrology: Do the Heavens Rule Our Destiny?* Eugene, OR: Harvest House, 1989.
Erika Cheetham	*The Final Prophecies of Nostradamus.* New York: Putnam, 1989.

Roger B. Culver and Philip A. Ianna	*Astrology: True or False? A Scientific Evaluation.* Buffalo, NY: Prometheus Books, 1988.
Dennis Elwell	*Cosmic Loom: The New Science of Astrology.* London: Unwin Hyman, 1987.
David Pitt Francis	*Nostradamus: Prophecies of Present Times?* Wellingborough, UK: The Aquarian Press, 1985.
Michel Gauquelin	*Written in the Stars.* Wellingborough, UK: The Aquarian Press, 1988.
Muriel Bruce Hasbrouck	*Tarot and Astrology: The Pursuit of Destiny.* Rochester, VT: Destiny Books, 1989.
Charles R. Strohmer	*What Your Horoscope Doesn't Tell You.* Wheaton, IL: Tyndale House Publishers, 1988.
Paul Wright	*Astrology in Action.* Sebastopol, CA: CRCS Publications, 1989.

Can Humans Interact with the Spirit World?

Mark Albrecht	*Reincarnation: A Christian Critique of a New Age Doctrine.* Downers Grove, IL: Inter-Varsity Press, 1987.
P.M.H. Atwater	*Coming Back to Life: The After-Effects of the Near-Death Experience.* New York: Ballantine Books, 1988.
Jean K. Foster	*Epilogue: Insights into Life Before and After Death/A Channeled Book.* Kansas City, MO: Uni*Sun Books, 1988.
Elizabeth Fuller	*Everyone Is Psychic.* New York: Crown Publishers, 1989.
Martin Gardner	*The New Age: Notes of a Fringe Watcher.* Buffalo, NY: Prometheus Books, 1988.
Henry Gordon	*Channeling into the New Age.* Buffalo, NY: Prometheus Books, 1990.
Barbara Harris and Lionel C. Bascom	*Full Cricle: The Near-Death Experience and Beyond.* New York: Pocket Books, 1990.
Mary Olson Kelly, ed.	*The Fireside Treasury of Light: An Anthology of the Best in New Age Literature.* New York: A Fireside Book/Simon & Schuster, 1990.
Hester Mundis	*101 Ways to Avoid Reincarnation.* New York: Workman Publishing Co., 1989.
Kathryn Ridall	*Channeling: How to Reach Out to Your Spirit Guides.* New York: Bantam Books, 1988.
Kevin Ryerson and Stephanie Harolde	*Spirit Communication: The Soul's Path.* New York: Bantam Books, 1989.
John S. Spong, ed.	*Consciousness and Survival: An Interdisciplinary Inquiry into the Possibility of Life Beyond Biological Death.* Sausalito, CA: Institute of Noetic Sciences, 1987.
Helen Wambach	*Reliving Past Lives.* New York: Bantam Books, 1978.
Ian Wilson	*The After Death Experience: The Physics of the Non-Physical.* New York: William Morrow, 1987.
Carol Zaleski	*Otherworld Journeys: Accounts of Near-Death Experiences in Medieval and Modern Times.* New York: Oxford University Press, 1987.

Index